Missives

Missives

D J Cusine LLB, NP
Professor, Department of Conveyancing and
Professional Practice of Law, University of Aberdeen

Robert Rennie LLB, PhD
Solicitor, Motherwell

Butterworths/Law Society of Scotland
Edinburgh
1993

United Kingdom	Butterworth & Co (Publishers) Ltd, 4 Hill Street, EDINBURGH EH2 3JZ, 88 Kingsway, LONDON WC2B 6AB
Australia	Butterworths Pty Ltd, SYDNEY, MELBOURNE, BRISBANE, ADELAIDE, PERTH, CANBERRA and HOBART
Belgium	Butterworth & Co (Publishers) Ltd, BRUSSELS
Canada	Butterworth Canada Ltd, TORONTO and VANCOUVER
Ireland	Butterworth (Ireland) Ltd, DUBLIN
Malaysia	Malayan Law Journal Sdn Bhd, KUALA LUMPUR
New Zealand	Butterworths of New Zealand Ltd, WELLINGTON and AUCKLAND
Puerto Rico	Equity de Puerto Rico, Inc, HATO REY
Singapore	Butterworth & Co (Asia) Pte Ltd, SINGAPORE
USA	Butterworth Legal Publishers, ST PAUL, Minnesota; SEATTLE, Washington; BOSTON, Massachusetts; AUSTIN, Texas and D & S Publishers, CLEARWATER, Florida

A CIP Catalogue record for this book is available from the British Library.

ISBN 0 406 00593 1

Typeset by Phoenix Photosetting, Chatham, Kent
Printed and bound in Great Britain by Mackays of Chatham PLC, Kent

Preface

The legal profession is often said to be the second oldest profession in the world. Whether this is so or not, lawyers have been around in Scotland for some centuries, and accordingly, twenty-five years is a relatively short period in the lifetime of that profession. Twenty-five years ago, when the authors were apprentices, missives were short – in most instances of about six clauses in length. Things have undoubtedly changed. In those now seemingly far-off days, missives were concluded quickly and most of the 'conveyancing' consisted of examining the title. Rarely were titles seen prior to the conclusion of a bargain, on the assumption that there were very few titles which are fundamentally bad. Even on the odd occasion when such a title was encountered, fellow solicitors usually co-operated so that the transaction proceeded as smoothly as possible.

We need not dwell here on the reasons for the change in the length of missives and conveyancing practice. There is no doubt that the process of concluding a bargain is much lengthier now and great care has to be taken in that connection.

What we have attempted to do in the following pages is to set out the law while at the same time taking account of what actually happens in practice. Although the law in some instances is not clear, conveyancers are, or ought to be, infinitely adaptable, but it is how to adapt, for example, to the ever-changing scene on non-supersession clauses, that can present difficulties. We have tried to deal with these things throughout.

We have used a domestic transaction as our basic model. There are two reasons for this. The first is that the law and practice in domestic transactions is in many instances applicable also to commercial and other transactions. The second is that it would be impossible to cover the missive clauses in even ordinary commercial transactions without increasing the size of this book by a very considerable degree. However, in our last chapter we introduce some of the specialities in commercial and other transactions, more as an initial guide or checklist, rather than as an in-depth study.

We should like to take this opportunity of blaming each other for any mistakes. Initially we were to be joined by Colin Miller who was formerly the Convener of the Law Society's Conveyancing

Committee. However, he was appointed as a sheriff shortly before we began to write the book and Colin had to apply his considerable ability and energies to his new post. Nevertheless, we are grateful to him for commenting on all of our chapters. We are also grateful to the other 'D J' – McNeil of Morton Fraser Milligan – for his valuable advice, particularly on Chapter 7. Carolyn Slater, formerly of RICS, Scotland, made helpful comments on the parts dealing with surveys.

We hope that what we have produced fills a gap in the market. To that end we have attempted to state the law as at 1 January 1993.

D J Cusine
Robert Rennie
April 1993

Contents

Abbreviations

Commentaries: G J Bell *Commentaries on the Law of Scotland* (7th edn, 1870)

Contract: D M Walker *The Law of Contract and Related Obligations in Scotland* (2nd edn, 1985)

Dickson: W G Dickson *The Law of Evidence in Scotland* (3rd edn, 1987 by P J Hamilton Grierson)

Gloag: W M Gloag *The Law of Contract* (2nd edn, 1929)

Halliday: J M Halliday *Conveyancing Law and Practice in Scotland* (4 vols, 1985, 1986, 1987, 1990)

Erskine: John Erskine *An Institute of the Law of Scotland* (8th edn, 1871)

McBryde: W W McBryde *The Law of Contract in Scotland* (1987)

Principles: G J Bell, *Principles of the Law of Scotland* (10th edn, 1899)

Walker & Walker: A G Walker and N M L Walker *The Law of Evidence in Scotland* (1964)

Walker: D M Walker *The Law of Civil Remedies in Scotland* (1974)

Table of Statutes

Table of Cases

CHAPTER 1

Introduction

The role of the solicitor

1.01 The role of the solicitor is crucial to most contracts for the purchase and sale of domestic heritable property in Scotland. Scots lawyers are justly proud of the fact that contracts can be concluded more speedily than in England. Even with the advent of the 35 clause offer and 20 clause qualified acceptance it is still true that the actual process of concluding a binding contract with speed and certainty remains one of the best features of Scottish conveyancing law and practice. One of the resons for this is that it is generally the solicitor acting on behalf of the purchaser or the seller who signs the offer and acceptance and any other formal letters necessary to conclude the bargain, taking instructions from the parties as the negotiations proceed to conclusion. Because of the special trust placed by clients in their solicitors it is necessary to examine the pre-missive stage of a domestic conveyancing transaction and highlight various stages in the combined negotiation and instruction process up to the point of the lodging and accepting of a formal offer.

The financial arrangements for purchase – surveys

1.02 When a client approaches his solicitor with a view to house purchase the first questions to be addressed relate to the finance for the purchase and the nature of any survey to be carried out over the property itself. In the event that a loan has been arranged by the client without help from his solicitor it is prudent for the solicitor to ensure that the finance is in place and subject to no more than normal loan conditions before an offer is lodged. It is preferable for the solicitor to contact the lending institution directly to ascertain that the funds will be available in time for the proposed date of entry. Similarly, the solicitor should always advise his client on the need for a survey even where a client is not obtaining a loan, and a survey is not therefore mandatory. If a client states that he or she does not require a survey then the solicitor should put in writing the fact that this advice has been given and disregarded. Where surveys are being discussed between solicitor and client the solicitor should ensure that the client understands the different types of survey which are now available either from surveyors directly or through lending institutions. These surveys now go by different names depending on the lending institution involved but generally speaking they fall into three categories:

1. a report and valuation for loan purposes;
2. a report and valuation for loan purposes and for the home buyer; and
3. a full structural survey.

1.03 The first type of survey is the most limited form of inspection and originates from an agreement between the lending institutions and the Royal Institution of Chartered Surveyors. It is simply a valuation for the lending institution which enables that institution to decide if the property is suitable as a security for the loan involved. Normally a copy of this is given to the purchaser as a courtesy. This type of survey involves a visual inspection of as much of the exterior and interior of the property as is visible and easily accessible. Any major defects which are obvious from this superficial inspection will be reported but most lending institutions are careful to point out that there may be defects in the property which are not reported but which a more rigorous survey would reveal. In some cases retentions from loans are recommended to cover defects but again this is by way of recommendation to the lending institution rather than an indication to the purchaser of the actual or likely cost of repair.

1.04 The second and more onerous type of survey is generally known as a home buyer or house purchasers' report and should combine a mortgage valuation for the lending institution with an actual survey of the property with a note of defects for the purchaser. This type of report is usually based on the standard report form issued by the Royal Institution of Chartered Surveyors and will be subject to the standard conditions of engagement issued by that professional body. The purchaser should, of course, be issued with these conditions of engagement and be aware of any exceptions and exclusions.

1.05 The third type of survey is a structural survey and this is not likely to be required unless there are some obvious structural faults in the property which have been noted from a previous general survey. A structural survey is a technical inspection rather than a valuation although it may be combined with a simple valuation. The scope of this type of survey is normally agreed in advance and may include structural engineers, quantity or building surveyors as well as outside contractors such as builders, plumbers, electricians and timber specialists.

1.06 Naturally, the cost of the survey increases with its complexity as, theoretically at any rate, should the potential liability of the surveyor in the event of defects arising. Not surprisingly the report and valuation is the cheapest form of survey and the structural survey the dearest. Any client who requires a structural survey should enquire as to the likely cost prior to the survey being carried out and ensure that any extra charges from other professionals or contractors are included in the overall charge.

1.07 It is important that the solicitor understands what role he may have to play in this vital stage of the house purchase. If the solicitor is actively involved in arranging the loan then there is no doubt that he must advise his client clearly as to the types of survey available and the rights which the purchaser may or may not have against the surveyor in each case. Similarly, if the solicitor is obtaining the finance then he must follow all the regulations laid down by the Law Society of Scotland in terms of the Financial Services Act 1986[1]. If the client comes to the solicitor with the survey carried out and the loan arranged and instructions to lodge an immediate offer then it would be wise for the solicitor to confirm in writing that he has had no part to play in these arrangements.

1 Solicitors (Scotland) (Conduct of Investment Business) Practice Rules 1989.

1.08 There are many different sources of actual finance for house purchase, the building societies having ceded their exclusive role in this field some years ago. The solicitor must remember that although the beauty of the Scottish conveyancing transaction is that all things flow through him the danger is that all blame may attach to him. A solicitor should, therefore, have some basic grasp of the different types of finance which are available. It is important to know whether a loan is likely to attract tax relief under MIRAS or not and whether the loan is to be taken out on a capital and interest repayment basis, an endowment basis, pension plan basis or linked to a unit trust or personal equity plan.

Capital and interest repayment loans

1.09 This type of loan involves a repayment over an agreed period of years of capital and interest by monthly instalments. During the initial period of the loan the interest element of the loan is high and the capital element low. In the later stages of the loan this pattern is reversed with most of the monthly instalment going to reduce the capital until there is nothing left to repay. Since tax relief is granted in respect of interest repayments only this reduces as the loan nears its final term. It is usual for the client to take out a mortgage protection policy for the term of the loan in case of death. Other policies covering redundancy and incapacity are also available.

Endowment loans

1.10 This type of loan involves an endowment policy with a guaranteed death benefit covering at least the initial capital of the loan. The policy should be assigned to the lending institution and the assignation intimated to provide proper security although in modern practice many lending institutions rely on deposit of the policy alone[1]. Solicitors should be aware that the deposit of a policy does not give the lending institution proper security over the policy and there may well be a case where another party such as a child claiming legitim or a trustee in bankruptcy or a factor in an insolvent estate of a deceased person will assert a better claim to the proceeds of the policy with disastrous results for a surviving spouse. The monthly instalments payable to the lending institution only comprise interest on the loan because the capital is covered by the endowment policy. On death of the borrower, or one of them in the case of joint life policies, or on the maturity date of the policy the whole of the capital is paid to the lending institution to repay the loan. In some cases there may be a surplus available for the borrower or his estate. In addition to paying monthly interest the borrower pays premiums to the insurance company. Endowment policies are either full endowments covering the whole capital of the loan as endowment from the start or low cost endowments with a lower profit return but a guaranteed death benefit equal to the amount of the loan. A low cost policy however does not always guarantee full repayment if it runs its full term. Tax relief on the interest paid to the lending institution remains constant.

1 Cusine *Standard Securities* (1991) para 2.07.

Pension plan loans

1.11 This type of loan can be used by the self-employed or those in pensionable employment. The pension itself is not assigned but there is a separate life policy as back-up security capable of assignation. In essence the lending institution 'corners' a part of the pension fund (usually 20 per cent and never more than 25 per cent) and the borrower undertakes to use the proceeds of the capital lump sum from the pension when due to repay the loan. This can be an expensive type of loan to fund from the pension because of the percentages of the fund involved but tax relief is available not only on the premiums paid for the pension but also on the interest on the loan up to the current maximum of £30,000. As with an endowment loan, capital is not repaid until the end of the loan term when there is a lump sum capital payment made from the pension fund. The life policy covers the situation should the borrower die before the date the pension becomes payable.

Unit trust and personal equity plan loans

1.12 The borrower does not make repayment of the capital of the loan directly to the lending institution but, as with endowment or pension loans, pays interest only. The borrower invests in a unit trust or personal equity plan on a monthly basis hoping that the capital growth in the plan will eventually be more than is necessary to repay the loan at the end of its term. Only the personal equity plan method is free of capital and income taxes because unit trusts pay tax internally and the personal equity plan limit is currently £9,000 per annum. Any borrower should, of course, be advised that the investments can go down as well as up and there are no guarantees that the capital will be available to repay the loan.

Investment bond loans

1.13 With this type of loan a lump sum is invested at the outset in the hope that growth over the period of the loan will prove sufficient to effect repayment of the total capital at the end of the loan term. Interest is paid monthly to the lending institution but life cover is also required to cover the gap between the loan and the bond value in the early years.

Fixed interest and low start loans

1.14 Nowadays many lending institutions offer fixed interest and low start loans sometimes for a limited period only depending on the movement of national and international interest rates. When interest rates are high and look set to go higher, fixed interest rate loans can appear very desirable. Similarly, low start loans where the initial instalments and sometimes premiums on a life policy are deliberately scaled down in the first few years of the loan, are attractive to first-time purchasers. In both these cases, however, it is important that the client understands the basis of the loan and his or her likely obliga- tions in the future. Interest rates are generally only fixed for a set period and thereafter can rise and fall in accordance with normal lending institution rates. This can work to the client's advantage or disadvantage depending on interest rates in general. It is important that the client understands that if interest rates fall during the fixed period he or she will suffer. Similarly, with low start loans the client must be made aware that the terms of repayment become increasingly more severe as the loan progresses. The hope with a low start loan is of course that the borrower's employment prospects will improve suffi- ciently to enable him to meet the higher commitment in the middle and later years of the loan.

Loan percentages

1.15 The matter of the amount of the loan available to any purchaser is, of course, one for negotiation depending on various factors. All lending institutions take into account the security value of the property as disclosed in the survey and, of course, the ability to repay the loan measured against the current income of the borrowers. It is usual for lending institutions to apply a multiplier to the annual salaries of the borrowers and work out the amount of the loan available in that way. This, of course, is subject to the security value being enough to cover the amount borrowed. It should be noted however that under the Building Societies Act 1986 a building society cannot lend more than 80 per cent of the valuation of the loan without some form of additional security[1]. Most first-time purchasers require more than this percentage and, indeed, some require a loan of the total purchase price. The normal maximum available is 95 per cent. Per- centages, of course, are expressed as percentages of the mortgage valuation of the house, or the price, whichever is the lower figure. Where more than 80 per cent is required the additional security usually takes the form of a guarantee for the shortfall (sometimes referred to as mortgage indemnity policy) given by an insurance company to the lending institution. The insurance company charges a single premium to the lending institution for this amount and this cost is passed on to the borrower and, generally speaking, deducted from the advance before it is received by the solicitor. In some cases the additional security can be taken in another manner but this is very unusual. It is advisable for the solicitor, especially in high percentage cases, to work out what deductions will be made from the loan before settlement. First-time purchasers are often on a very tight budget and it is unfair to ask them for cheques to cover shortfalls caused by insurance guarantee premiums the day before settlement. While it forms no part of a solicitor's professional duties to advise clients on the level of the commitments they undertake, recent history in the house market has shown clearly the dangers of taking 100 per cent loans in a high market. There are many borrowers who have been made redundant and found that when they tried to sell their house the value had dropped below the amount of the loan. It is always worthwhile pointing out to clients who borrow at this level that there is a personal obligation to repay the loan no matter what the value of the property may be from time to time.

1 Building Societies Act 1986, s 13.

Income tax relief – MIRAS

1.16 At the present time income tax relief is allowed on interest paid on loans up to a maximum of £30,000 provided the loans are for certain qualifying purposes. The allowable purposes are that the loan must have been used for the purchase of certain types of land or buildings or to replace an original loan for these purposes. The land or buildings must be used within 12 months as the only or main residence of the borrower or a dependent relative or a former or a separated spouse or, alternatively, let at a commercial rent for more than 26 weeks out of any period of 52 weeks. Under previous fiscal arrangements the interest was paid gross to the lending institution and the borrower obtained a tax allowance in the normal way against his income. Under the Mortgage Interest Relief at Source scheme (MIRAS) the interest is now paid under deduction of tax. This scheme of course applies only for loans of £30,000 or under. Where the loan exceeds this amount (which is quite normal nowadays) the whole loan is sometimes taken outwith the MIRAS scheme or that part of it which exceeds £30,000 is dealt with separately.

Instructions for a purchase

1.17 When the financial arrangements have been made and the survey carried out, the client, if he still wishes to proceed, is ready to instruct the solicitor to lodge the offer. The instruction to the solicitor is, of course, a matter of the law of agency but the solicitor should never forget that he is one of those professionals who enjoy an ostensible authority as well as an actual authority. The client can therefore be bound by the solicitor's own actions within the scope of ostensible as well as actual authority. It follows from this that the solicitor must ensure that he or she has clear and detailed instructions before lodging the offer. Nowadays it is common for instructions to be taken over the telephone rather than by writing or at a meeting and it is more than usually important for the solicitor to keep detailed notes. The solicitor should not simply rely on what he or she is told by the client but should also ask appropriate and, indeed, sometimes searching questions in relation to the property. Clearly, the solicitor will wish to know the price and the date of entry and any moveable items such as carpets or curtains which are included in the price. Most solicitors use a pro forma offer with a schedule of standard conditions and the Law Society of Scotland have now broken with tradition and provided a House Purchase and Sale Guideline with Standard Clauses[1]. Even, however, in the simplest domestic conveyancing transaction the solicitor would be unwise to rely entirely on his own pro forma offer or standard conditions without making further enquiry in relation to the particular property to be purchased and the parties involved.

1 See Ch 4 below.

1.18 In the first place it is important to know the names of the parties who are to take title to the property. If title is to be taken in a single name the availability of any consent from a non-entitled spouse to any loan document should be canvassed at this stage. The question of a survivorship clause should also be discussed fully if title is to be taken in joint names. Survivorship clauses can cause difficulties years later and it should never be assumed that a survivorship clause is wanted by the purchasers or desirable in every case[1]. Prudent solicitors would be well advised to ensure that they have properly documented instructions before inserting a survivorship destination in any deed.

1 See Gretton 1989 34 JLSS 299; Law Society Update Courses on General Conveyancing, November 1988 and March 1989.

1.19 The difficulties which have arisen over extensions and alterations to domestic property and the existence or non-existence of building warrants, planning permissions, completion certificates and superior's consent are legend. Most solicitors have a standard clause in their offer which provides that such consents must be made available prior to settlement. It is still, however, extremely worthwhile to ask the purchaser whether there are any obvious extensions, alterations or outbuildings and to note, carefully, the purchaser's response. If the solicitor has in his possession a copy of the survey report then he should verify from this whether the surveyor has noted any such alterations or extensions. If actual alterations of this type are disclosed then the general clause in the offer should be modified to specify the particular alterations or extensions for which permissions will be required as well as dealing with the matter generally. All too often purchasers or their solicitors rely on the standard clause followed by a routine confirmation from the seller's solicitor in answer to observations on title that there have been 'no alterations or extensions so far as the seller is aware'.

1.20 The question of roads, footpaths and sewers should not simply be left to the standard clause contained in most offers, especially in rural areas. The position should be clarified at the start. Enquiry should be made of the purchaser prior to the lodging of the offer as to the existence of any private roads, accesses, rights of way, septic tanks and outfalls. If there are private roads used to gain access to the property the offer should stipulate that the title will contain either ownership of the solum of the road or valid servitude rights of access and also that the subjects will only be burdened with an equitable share of maintenance costs if the private road is used by more than one party. If there is a septic tank then provision should be made in the offer for the seller to provide wayleaves not only for the septic tank (if it is situated outwith the property) but also in respect of laying, maintaining and renewing pipes to and from the tank. If the outfall discharges into a water course and thence into a river a consent from a purification board may be required. Such consents are usually given subject to conditions. Some rural properties are served by private water supplies from natural springs. If this is the case provision should be made in the offer for all necessary wayleaves for supply pipes. Enquiry should also be made as to whether the supply has the appropriate certificate of fitness from the water authority. The Scottish Office issue an invaluable guide to the laws controlling private water supplies[1].

1 HMSO 6/92; and see the Water (Scotland) Act 1980, ss 38 and 76 F-J; the Water Supply (Water Quality) (Scotland) Regulations 1990, SI 1990/119; the Water Supply (Water Quality) (Scotland) Amendment Regulations 1991, SI 1991/1333; the Private Water Supplies (Scotland) Regulations 1992, SI 1992/575; the Scottish Office Environment Department Circular No 20/1992.

1.21 It is always useful at this stage to find out from the purchaser what garages or other outhouses, sheds or greenhouses are included in the price. These seemingly innocuous items can be the subject of debate as to whether they are moveable or heritable depending on the degree of fixation to the ground.

1.22 It is also useful prior to the offer being lodged, especially in older and rural properties, to make enquiry from the purchaser as to the basic extent of any ground which pertains to the dwellinghouse. In modern estates this may be of little or no significance because the garden ground will be well defined but with older properties, especially those in the country, many purchasers make assumptions regarding the areas involved which are not borne out by the description contained in the title deeds. The purchaser can sometimes let his solicitor have early warning of any potential difficulty of this type. The solicitor should therefore ask the purchaser whether he is aware of the approximate surface area of any ground which he is purchasing and also whether the ground pertaining to the property is well defined by fences, hedges, walls or other enclosures. It can be useful at this stage to make some general enquiries in relation to boundaries and enclosures such as fences and walls. If there is doubt then further enquiries as to liability for maintenance may be worthwhile.

1.23 Quite apart from the question of the permanent finance for the purchase transaction, the overall financial situation and the timing of settlements should be discussed before the offer is lodged. This is especially important where the purchaser will also be selling his own property. It is important to enquire from the purchaser at the outset whether or not he or she has made any temporary bridging arrangements with a bank should his or her own property fail to sell. Further it is always useful to go over the potential sale price with a view to ensuring that there will be enough surplus to fund the purchaser's own share of the purchase price.

1.24 Once the preliminary matters have been discussed and proper and full instructions taken the offer can be framed for submission. As a general rule solicitors now seem to take the view that the more clauses included in the offer the better the protection afforded not only to their clients but also to themselves. In some cases, this may be the case but a vast amount of clauses, some of which are wholly inapplicable to the transaction, can sometimes mean less certainty at the end of the day. If the purchasing client has been more than unusually detailed or verbose in his description of what is to be purchased it is better to include such matters of detail in the offer where appropriate, especially if the client is to be sent a copy. It is now common practice for solicitors to send copies of the offer to their clients even although the clients can hardly be expected to understand every clause. If the solicitor does this then he must, of course, be prepared to explain the meaning of the various legal clauses to his client. The general obligation or duty of care on a solicitor is to frame the offer exercising the skill and care expected of a normally competent solicitor at that time. Simply sending a copy of the offer to the purchaser does not in any way protect the solicitor if he fails in that duty in the particular circumstances. It is more important to discuss the purchase fully with the purchaser prior to the offer being lodged so as to get a full understanding of what is required, than to send copies of offers and schedules to the purchaser none of which have actually been discussed or explained. The same caveats apply to qualified acceptances and other formal letters as apply to the offer itself; all of these documents should be explained to the purchaser. It is perfectly proper to send copies of the documents to the purchaser and indeed if a copy of the original offer has been sent then copies of all other formal letters should also be sent to the purchaser but with appropriate explanations. Where the Law Society of Scotland Standard Missives are used the client's guide, which is designed to be read along with the missives, should be sent to the client[1].

1 See Ch 4 below.

Insurance

1.25 At common law the risk of accidental destruction passes to the purchaser on conclusion of missives, provided there are no unfulfilled suspensive conditions[1]. This is not the case, however, where the loss or damage is due to the seller's negligence[2]. In practice most offers reverse this position leaving risk with the seller until the date of entry. This is certainly the better way of dealing with the matter. Where a purchaser is purchasing with his own funds insurance should still be effected as at the date of conclusion of missives. Where a lending institution is involved insurance is usually dealt with by that institution. Some solicitors have a temporary insurance cover for all properties passing through their hands. It is important that a purchasing client has cover at the appropriate time and a prudent solicitor should ensure that proper cover exists from some insurance source.

1 *Sloans Dairies Ltd v Glasgow Corporation* 1977 SC 223, 1979 SLT 17.
2 *Meehan v Silver* 1972 SLT (Sh Ct) 70.

Taking instructions for a sale

1.26 At first glance a sale transaction should produce fewer dificulties or dangers than a purchase. The client is selling a property for a known or agreed price and with a known and agreed date of entry. The selling solicitor has simply to ensure that the offer which is accepted reflects these essential elements. There are, however, various matters which can and should be dealt with where possible prior to the offer being received. Obviously the amount of work which a solicitor can do before the conclusion of missives depends to a large extent on the timing of the instruction for the sale. If the solicitor is simply telephoned the day before the offer arrives there is little that he or she can do.

1.27 Prior to the acceptance of any offer, the seller's solicitor will wish to have the title deeds of the sale property in his possession. As soon as the solicitor is aware the property is being marketed then he should obtain these from the seller's lending institution or other custodian. In cases where the property is in an operational area for land registration and the seller's own application for first registration has not been completed, it may be necessary to obtain copies of the deeds at the Land Register from the Keeper together with confirmation that there are no unanswered requisitions from the Keeper. Sale transactions can appear straightforward but a problem at the start in obtaining title deeds or copies can produce delays later on in the transaction. It is a sad fact of professional life that a transaction which goes off the rails at the start often stays off the rails resulting in delayed settlements, delayed entries and consequential exasperation and loss. Clients by and large do not understand why titles 'cannot be traced' or 'are still at the Register'. Any likely delays and their consequences should therefore be explained fully to the clients at the outset.

1.28 Again, especially in rural properties, it is important to ascertain from the seller prior to the missives being concluded whether there are any particular specialities in relation to private roads, accesses, footpaths, septic tanks, water rights and fishing and sporting rights. If the seller's solicitor is forewarned that certain aspects of his title may cause delays or difficulties in the conclusion of missives, information can be obtained in advance of the offer being lodged which makes the framing of a qualified acceptance much easier.

1.29 Before missives are concluded it is important to ascertain from the seller whether a non-entitled spouse will be prepared to sign any necessary consents in terms of the Matrimonial Homes (Family

Protection) (Scotland) Act 1981. At this stage the brave solicitor may also wish to canvass whether there is any matrimonial dispute which would be likely to involve any Transfer of Property Order in terms of the Family Law (Scotland) Act 1985. Clearly, if there is liable to be some sort of dispute, then the solicitor concerned could not continue to act for both husband and wife.

1.30 It is generally thought professionally desirable to apply for property enquiry certificates dealing with planning and redevelopment matters from the district council and roads certificates dealing with the road, footpath and sewer from the regional council as soon as the solicitor is made aware that the property is on the market. Delays in the obtaining of these certificates are inevitable and if the certificates are not available, then a qualified acceptance may leave the missives subject to a suspensive condition in relation to the production of a certificate. There is a growing practice whereby missives are concluded on the basis that a purchaser can resile if he intimates dissatisfaction with the contents of a certificate within a set time from the date of receipt or despatch of the certificate. There are no doubt cases where purchasers who wish to be free from a transaction for completely unrelated reasons attempt to use this suspensive condition as a ground for repudiation. If the certificates are available at the time an acceptance is issued then they can be forwarded with the acceptance on the basis that the purchaser is bound to accept them. Again, if the certificates are obtained in good time prior to the receipt of an offer then difficulties disclosed by the certificates can in some cases be sorted out well in advance. It is preferable when issuing a qualified acceptance to give the purchaser as much information in relation to any outstanding statutory notices disclosed by the certificates as is available. The difficulty of obtaining certificates too far in advance is of course that they are regarded as 'out of date' by purchasers' solicitors. This is a considerable problem when the house market is poor and properties take months and sometimes years to sell. The Law Society of Scotland's standard clause B7 stipulates for a planning certificate dated 'not earlier than twenty eight days prior to the conclusion of the bargain'[1]. It is difficult to see how this counsel of perfection can be met in every case given the vagaries of the house market. Sellers are unhappy at the cost of certificates in general and are unlikely to wish to pay for second certificates obtained to meet deadlines of this type.

1 See para 4.36 below.

1.31 In cases where the property is situated in an operational area for land registration purposes Form 10 (for unregistered titles) or Form

12 reports (for registered titles) should be obtained prior to missives being concluded. Similarly, if the property is not registered but will be the subject of an application for first registration on conclusion of the sale, a P16 boundary comparison report should be obtained where appropriate[1]. If the P16 report shows a likely difficulty with boundaries, then it is prudent to try and sort this out by way of a section 19 boundary agreement prior to any offer being received[2]. If the P16 report discloses something more serious than a discrepancy between the direction of the title boundary and the ordnance survey map then corrective conveyancing to acquire an additional area of ground may be required. In such cases, the seller should be advised to take the property off the market until matters have been resolved. Alternatively, if the seller does not wish to become involved in corrective conveyancing to acquire title to a piece of ground he is possessing then at least any purchaser viewing the property should be made aware that title will not be given to the whole ground as possessed and the qualified acceptance framed accordingly.

1 P16 reports are not available for flatted properties.
2 Land Registration (Scotland) Act 1979, s 19.

1.32 It is important in a sale transaction to ascertain as early as possible the amounts due to be repaid to any secured lender. If there are second charges then clearly it is essential to know the amounts to be redeemed in these cases also. It is important that the seller understands the import of a second charge. Some sellers who take out loans which are not related directly to the property but are for secondary purposes, do not realise that these will require to be repaid on the sale of their property. It is important that a seller is made aware of these facts at the outset. There are a great many different forms of standard security in circulation at the present time some of which, it has to be said, do not make it clear that they are in fact securities at all. When the appropriate redemption figures are to hand, a calculation should be made and the seller advised as to the likely surplus. This is especially important if the seller is purchasing property at the same time. There is little point in informing a seller the day before the date of entry to the property he is purchasing that he is £5,000 short because of a third charge on the sale subjects for double glazing. If it is apparent that the seller is selling because of financial hardship it is prudent to enquire of the seller whether there are inhibitions lodged and to obtain confirmation by obtaining a personal search.

1.33 As has already been noted in this chapter, alterations and additions to property and building warrants and consents are a source of great difficulty in current conveyancing practice. A seller therefore should be asked at the time the property is put on the market whether or not he or any previous owner has carried out any such alterations or additions. Warrants, planning permissions and superior's consents should if possible be gathered prior to any offer being received. If no permissions are available, then the appropriate letters of comfort should be sought from local authorities or, in extreme cases, attempts should be made to obtain building warrants and permissions retrospectively[1]. It is important not to forget the superior at this time. A superior's consent can also be sought retrospectively where appropriate.

1 Not all local authorities will grant retrospective warrants or permissions.

1.34 When the offer eventually arrives, the selling solicitor will hopefully be in a position to deal with it having taken full instructions from the seller. In many cases nowadays the offer will be received from an estate agent who has been acting for the seller with a note that the seller has advised the estate agent that the offer is to be accepted. Under no circumstances should the selling solicitor accept this reassurance from an estate agent or indeed any third party. It is the selling solicitor who will bind the seller and therefore it is the selling solicitor's responsibility to take instructions on the offer in all respects from the seller. It is common practice to send the seller a copy of the offer and ask for instructions. It must be borne in mind that the seller will be concerned with the price, the date of entry and possibly what is included in the price by way of moveable items. The seller will not be interested in such niceties as the *actio quanti minoris*, the non-supersession of the missives by the disposition or whether the clauses in the schedule attached to the offer are deemed to be material. The offer is a contractual document to which the seller is a party and the seller's solicitor should not conclude that contract except with the seller's express instructions. The seller's solicitor must go through the offer clause by clause with the client dealing with such matters as alterations and additions, matrimonial homes consents, NHBC agreements or the lack of them, architects' certificates, the status of the road, footpath and sewer, the knowledge of the client in relation to planning proposals or notices, the knowledge of the client in relation to the existence of specialists' guarantees, the existence or otherwise of hire purchase agreements on moveable items and the state of the client's marriage in relation to transfer of property orders. When the instructions are received to accept the offer, it is important that the seller is made aware of the fact that the acceptance will be qualified. Many sellers are proud of the Scottish system and assume that when they give instructions to accept the offer, the bargain will be concluded. It is important that the solicitor advise the seller that the bargain will not be concluded until the qualified acceptance is itself accepted by formal writing. It should be borne in mind that if the seller has been sent a copy of the offer, he or she should also be sent a copy of the qualified acceptance and any other formal documentation so that he has a complete picture. In any covering letters the seller should be warned where appropriate that there will be no concluded contract until all the qualifications have been accepted. As with purchase transactions however, the sending of copies to the client does not absolve the solicitor from his paramount duty to explain the nature of the contract and all the clauses therein contained.

Closing dates

1.35 Where more than one purchaser offers for a residential property, the seller's agents, be they estate agents or solicitors, usually fix a closing date at which offers will be considered by the seller. The object of this exercise is, of course, to encourage competition with a view to obtaining the highest possible price for the seller. The theory behind closing dates is that every potential purchaser will offer without any inside information from the seller or the seller's agents as to what will be accepted. Once the offers are in, the seller should select the best offer and instruct his solicitor to forward an acceptance. Closing dates as such have no more legal status than fixed price adverts and an unscrupulous seller can if he or she so wishes, disclose the highest offer to one of the other purchasers in the hope that that purchaser will be persuaded to increase his price. Similarly, there is no law which prevents a purchaser who has been advised that he is unsuccessful from directly contacting the seller and trying to negotiate afresh after the closing date has come and gone. Solicitors who are involved in transactions involving closing dates should however bear in mind the professional practice guidelines in relation to closing dates issued by the Law Society of Scotland on 11 September 1991. These guidelines are in the following terms:

Selling solicitor

(1) In taking instructions from the selling client to fix a closing date for offers a solicitor should advise the client that, although not bound to accept the highest or indeed any offer, if the client instructs the solicitor to enter negotiations with a view to concluding a bargain with a party who submits an offer at the closing date,

the solicitor will not be able to accept any subsequent instructions to enter negotiations with or accept an offer from another party unless and until negotiations with the original offerer have fallen through.
(2) In the event of the selling client subsequently attempting to instruct the solicitor to discontinue negotiations entered into with a party whose offer has been timeously received on the closing date in order solely to enter negotiations with or to accept an offer from another party the solicitor should decline to act further in the sale. Should the solicitor be successful in persuading the client to adhere to the original instructions the solicitor may of course continue to act.

Prospective purchaser's solicitors

(1) Where a prospective purchaser instructs the solicitor to submit an offer in a closing date situation, the solicitor should advise the client that if the offer is unsuccessful the solicitor will not be able to accept subsequent instructions to submit a revised offer or formal amendment unless expressly invited to do so by the seller's agent, as to do so would be to place a fellow professional in a situation where he/she could be called upon to act contrary to good professional practice, which would undermine the closing date system.
(2) In the event of the prospective purchaser subsequently attempting to instruct the solicitor to submit a revised offer or formal amendment after the closing date has passed, in the absence of any express invitation to do so by the seller's agent, the solicitor should decline to implement these instructions. The solicitor may accept instructions to intimate to the seller or the seller's agent that in the event of negotiations with the successful party falling through, the prospective purchaser would be willing to enter into negotiations, but no indication of any increased bid should be given.

1.36 These guidelines are of course for the solicitor to follow and do not bind the seller or purchaser who can presumably instruct another solicitor to conclude a completely separate bargain outwith a closing date situation if he or she so wishes. The terms of the guildlines are clear and if attempts are made either by sellers or purchasers to enter into fresh negotiations after the closing date then these instructions cannot be accepted nor can instructions be accepted to break off negotiations following on the issue of a qualified acceptance to the originally preferred offer solely for the reason of negotiating another price with another party. The Law Society of Scotland issued these guidelines not to promote new rules but to restate what they regarded as the existing rules of practice. It is important for solicitors, however, to advise clients, whether purchasers or sellers, of the existence and content of these rules as soon as the client tells the solicitor to fix a closing date. There is perhaps a slight inconsistency between the rules for selling solicitors and for purchasers' solicitors. The rules in connection with selling solicitors apply where the solicitor has been instructed to fix a closing date and therefore presumably would not apply in cases where the closing date was actually fixed by an estate agent or other party. The rules in relation to prospective purchasers' solicitors, however, merely refer to situations where a prospective purchaser has instructed a solicitor to submit an offer 'in a closing date situation'. It would appear therefore that the guidelines applying to the purchaser's solicitor will apply even where it is an estate agent and not the seller's solicitor who has fixed the closing date. It is of course perfectly fair and proper for any unsuccessful purchaser's solicitor to advise the selling solicitor that if the sale for any reason falls through his client would be prepared to reoffer, but it is not proper to give any indication of any increased price.

1.37 The guidelines do not have the status of practice rules as such and accordingly do not contain the time honoured statement to the effect that breach of the guidelines may be regarded as professional misconduct. Notwithstanding this it is submitted that breach of the guidelines would certainly be regarded as unprofessional conduct and serious or deliberate breach could easily fall within the definition of professional misconduct.

CHAPTER 2

Constitution of missives

The requirement of formal writing

2.01 The contract constituted by missives is a contract which relates to the purchase and sale of heritage. As such, it is a contract belonging to that category of contracts known as *obligationes literis* where formal writing is necessary to constitute the contract. This is of course different from obligations which require writing as a matter of evidence. The distinction between the requirement of writing as evidence and the requirement of writing to constitute a contract is well set out in *Paterson v Paterson*[1].

1 (1897) 25 R 144.

2.02 To satisfy the requirements of the law as to formal writing, missives may either be formally attested or they may be holograph or adopted as holograph as privileged writings. Either of these methods of execution renders the contract probative in the wider sense of that term. In practice 'probative' is used in two distinct senses in Scots law. Strictly speaking a probative deed is a deed which proves itself as a matter of evidence without the need for witnesses to speak as to its contents or execution. However, the term 'probative' tends to be used to define a deed which has been signed before witnesses in accordance with the attestation statutes, and this would include holograph deeds. Missives for the purchase and sale of existing or 'second hand' residential property are normally concluded in writing which is adopted as holograph. Missives for the purchase and sale of new properties in the course of construction are normally constituted by a form of offer provided by the builders or the builders' solicitor which is signed and adopted as holograph by the purchasers themselves and then accepted by the builders' solicitor. Missives for the purchase and sale of an existing domestic property are normally signed and adopted as holograph by solicitors acting for purchaser and seller. In this case the missives must be signed and adopted as holograph by a partner of the firm[1]. A faxed offer or acceptance is merely a copy of what has yet to be despatched and has no legal validity on its own. The requirement for formal writing applies equally to a contract for an option to

19

purchase heritage although the document intimating the exercise of the option need not be attested or privileged[2].

1 *Littlejohn v Mackay* 1974 SLT (Sh Ct) 82. This decision has been the subject of discussion and criticism; see Cusine and Pearson 'Who signs for the firm' (1991) 36 JLS 73.
2 *Sichi v Biagi* 1946 SN 66; *Scott v Morrison* 1979 SLT (Notes) 65; *Stone v MacDonald* 1979 SLT 288.

Privileged writings

2.03 As has already been noted, missives are most commonly concluded in the form of privileged writing. This means that they are adopted as holograph by or on behalf of the parties to the missives. Any writing is entitled to the benefit or privilege of a holograph writing if the party to that writing adhibits the words 'adopted as holograph' in his or her own handwriting immediately before the signature. The words should normally be written above the signature but it has been held to be unobjectionable if the words appear below the signature[1]. It is possible that other words of adoption such as 'I agree to the above' in the handwriting of the signatory may also be sufficient[2]. The basis for this theory is that the docquet renders the document binding in circumstances where it would not otherwise be binding[3]. Most missives nowadays comprise more than one page and indeed also contain one or more schedules. Where a new plot of ground is being acquired or where an existing property is being subdivided it is normal to attach a plan to the missives. In these cases, all the pages, schedules and plans should be adopted as holograph individually or alternatively should be signed and docquetted and adopted by suitable words on the last page of the main writing to indicate that all the pages and the schedules and plans are adopted. Thus an offer containing four pages, one schedule and a plan should be adopted on page four in the following manner, 'This and the three preceding pages are together with the schedule and plan before referred to, Adopted as Holograph'. In these situations it is also preferable but probably not essential to initial each page and to docquet each schedule and plan. The adoptive words should of course be in the handwriting of the signatory although in *McBeath's Trustees v McBeath*[4] a majority of a court of seven judges accepted a typewritten will and codicil as valid where the words 'Accepted as Holograph' were typewritten but were followed by a signature in pen. This, however, was a special case turning on its own facts and involving a testamentary writing as opposed to missives. The will and codicil themselves contained a statement to the effect that they had been typed by the grantor and it was accepted that the grantor had required to use a typewriter prior to his death because of physical disability. In a subsequent case[5] a typed will which was signed but not adopted as holograph was held invalid. It should not be assumed that any decision relating to testamentary writings would necessarily apply to missives for the sale and purchase of heritable property and strict adherence to the normal rules is clearly desirable.

1 *Gavine's Trustee v Lee* (1883) 10 R 448.
2 Dickson *The Law of Evidence in Scotland* (3rd edn, 1887) para 756; *Maitland's Trustees v Maitland* (1871) 10 M 79 at 84.
3 *Campbell's Trustees v Campbell* (1903) 5 F 366 at 372.
4 1935 SC 471.
5 *Chisholm v Chisholm* 1949 SC 434.

The intention and capacity of the grantor

2.04 Normally missive letters are exchanged between solicitors who are of course well aware that the words 'adopted as holograph' are used with the intention of making the documents legally binding. Different considerations may however apply where the parties themselves sign and adopt the writings. It has been held that an offer to purchase property which was adopted as holograph by an illiterate man who did not understand that the effect of the phrase was to render the contract binding did not have that effect[1]. It is difficult to see the logic in this decision[2], given the fact that the principle behind privileged writings is to afford them the status of probative writings properly attested. Parties sign deeds before witnesses without necessarily comprehending the rules for subscription and attestation far less the principle of probativity. Where parties are themselves adopting missives as holograph, it is important that they should understand the nature and meaning of the words. Accordingly solicitors should advise clients who are signing builders' missives or any other missives prepared for them and adopting them, that the whole point of the words 'adopted as holograph' is to render the document legally binding.

1 *Harvey v Smith* (1904) 6 F 511; but see *Maclaine v Murphy* 1958 SLT (Sh Ct) 49, 74 Sh Ct Rep 112.
2 See Gloag *The Law of Contract* (2nd edn, 1929) pp 95, 96.

2.05 In an exchange of missives all letters, be they the offer, qualified acceptance or further formal amending letters should be adopted as holograph by both parties or their solicitors; otherwise the parties may resile unless *rei interventus* or homologation has cured the defect.

It should always be borne in mind that in these circumstances either party can resile, not just the party whose correspondence falls short of the normal formal requirement[1].

1 *Malcolm v Campbell* (1891) 19 R 278.

Rei interventus and homologation

2.06   The normal rule which requires contracts relating to heritage to be attested or adopted as holograph suffers exception where one of the parties to the contract is personally barred by *rei interventus* or homologation. The definitions of *rei interventus* and homologation were set out by Bell in his *Principles*[1]. He defines *rei interventus* in the following manner:

'*rei interventus* raises a personal exception, which excludes the plea of *locus poenitentiae*. It is inferred from any proceedings not unimportant on the part of the obligee, known to and permitted by the obligor to take place on the faith of the contract as if it were perfect; provided they are unequivocally referable to the agreement and productive of alteration of circumstances, loss or inconvenience, though not irretrievable.'

Bell defined homologation in the following terms:

'Homologation (in principle similar to *rei interventus*) is an act of the obligor or his legal representative approbatory of a preceding engagement, which in itself is defective or informal or unauthorised, either confirming it or adopting it as binding. It may be express, or inferred from circumstances. It must be absolute, and not compulsory, nor proceeding on error or fraud, and unequivocally referrable to the engagement; and must imply assent to it, with full knowledge of its extent, and of all the relevant interests of the homologator.'

Rei interventus is normally argued in an attempt to validate an improbative agreement but it has also been applied in circumstances where the missives do not disclose complete consensus but actings have followed which are themselves either evidence of consensus or are taken to complete the consensus and bar *locus poenitentiae*[2]. This aspect of *rei interventus* is discussed more fully in relation to the conclusion of missives[3].

It will be seen from the classic definition of *rei interventus* set out by Bell that for the doctrine to apply various requirements must be met.

1 Bell *Principles* §§26, 27.
2 See *Gloag* pp 46–47; *Colquhoun v Wilson's Trustees* (1860) 22 D 1035; *Wight v Newton* 1911 SC 762; *East Kilbride Development Corporation v Pollok* 1953 SC 370; *Errol v Walker* 1966 SC 93.
3 See para 3.33 ff below.

There must be a preceding agreement

2.07 *Rei interventus* does not normally apply unless the actings can be related to a preceding agreement in which there is general consensus[1]. Normally, the antecedent agreement is constituted by an exchange of informal writings clearly evidencing an agreement to buy and sell[2]. Clearly the documentary evidence must show that the parties have gone beyond the state of mere negotiation[3]. Various forms of informal writing have been used in decided cases to evidence the preceding agreement and it has been held that the writ founded on need not be a writ of the party seeking to resile[4]. In some cases various writs have been used to establish an agreement[5]. An adjusted draft[6], a ground burdens receipt containing a statement of an area of ground[7], and a docquet on a building plan[8] have all been accepted as sufficient writings for the purpose of *rei interventus*. Even unsigned documents which set out the basic terms of the agreement may serve to found the plea[9]. *Rei interventus* can still be pled in cases where the antecedent agreement is constituted by both oral agreement and informal writings[10] or even in cases where the agreement is purely oral but in this latter circumstance the agreement must be proved by the oath of the defender[11]. An admission on record[12] or some combination of writ, oath and admission is also sufficient[13]. If *rei interventus* is being pled in a court case it is important to remember that the antecedent agreement by its very nature is improbative in the evidential sense of the term and will require therefore to be proved and spoken to in court[14]. Similarly, where the documents are not signed by the parties themselves but by agents on their behalf it will be necessary to prove that the agents concerned had the appropriate authority[15].

1 *Mitchell v Stornoway Trustees* 1936 SC (HL) 56 at 63 per Lord MacMillan; *Stobo Ltd v Morrisons (Gowns) Ltd* 1949 SC 184; *East Kilbride Development Corporation v Pollok*, above.
2 See *Secretary of State for Scotland v Ravenstone Securities Ltd* 1976 SC 171.
3 *Temperance Permanent Building Society v Kominek* 1951 SLT (Sh Ct) 58.
4 *Emslie v Duff* (1865) 3 M 854.
5 *Wilson v Mann* (1876) 3 R 527.
6 *Bathie v Lord Wharncliffe* (1873) 11 M 490.
7 *Stodart v Dalzell* (1876) 4 R 236.
8 *Mitchell v Stornoway Trustees*, above.
9 *Bell v Goodall* (1883) 10 R 905 at 908; *Wares v Duff-Dunbar's Trustees* 1920 SC 5.
10 *Stodart v Dalzell*, above.
11 *Walker v Flint* (1863) 1 M 417; *Allan v Gilchrist* (1875) 2 R 587; *Mulhern v Mulhern* 1987 SLT (Sh Ct) 62.
12 *Church of England Fire and Life Assurance Co v Wink* (1857) 19 D 1057.
13 *Paterson v Earl of Fife* (1865) 3 M 423.
14 *Pollok v Whiteford* 1936 SC 402.
15 *Danish Dairy Co v Gillespie* 1922 SC 656.

The actings must be unequivocally referable to the agreement

2.08 It is important to distinguish between actings which take place prior to the agreement and actings which take place subsequent to the agreement and in reliance on it. Where a party incurs expense making enquiries about a property or arranging a loan to finance the purchase of the property these are not referable to the agreement because they generally take place prior to any agreement to purchase[1]. Lord Cameron has stated that the word 'unequivocally' in Bell's definition does not mean 'exclusively'. On that basis, although the actings must be referable to the agreement which is being set up and not to another agreement, the fact that the actings may have the additional effect of furthering other transactions between the same parties does not prevent them being used to establish *rei interventus* in respect of one of the transactions[2]. It appears that the actings can be active or passive[3] and also that it is irrelevant that the acts themselves, apart from the contract, are illegal[4].

1 *Mowat v Caledonian Banking Co* (1895) 23 R 270; *Pollok v Whiteford*, above.
2 *Secretary of State for Scotland v Ravenstone Securities Ltd*, above.
3 *Danish Dairy Co v Gillespie*, above.
4 *Graydon & Co v Pollux Properties Ltd* 1957 SLT (Sh Ct) 54.

The actings must be 'not unimportant'

2.09 Bell's delicate double negative has been the subject of a great deal of judicial debate. It is, of course, a question of fact and degree to be decided in each particular case. In the leading case of *Mitchell v Stornoway Trustees*[1] there were many connected actings. Site and building plans had been prepared and then approved by the defenders' factor. They were then submitted to the Dean of Guild Court by the pursuers. While the proceedings were still before the court the defenders' factor gave assistance to the burgh surveyor by explaining the details of the building plans. Before the proceedings in the Dean of Guild Court were concluded the defenders withdrew their grant of the feu and the petition for a lining from the Dean of Guild Court was refused. Three judges in the House of Lords took the view that the Dean of Guild Court proceedings were 'not unimportant' and one judge (Lord MacMillan) went as far as to say that the standard of 'non unimportance' was 'not very exacting[2]'. However, two other Law Lords doubted whether the standard had been met on the particular facts of the case. It is likely that 'not unimportant' is slightly less onerous a standard than 'important' but each case has to be decided on its own merits. In cases of heritable property such actings as taking possession[3], paying part of the price or feuduty[4], and commencing to build or alter[5] are usually sufficient. However, making a token payment to account of £5 on a price of £6,000 has been held to be insufficiently important to constitute *rei interventus*[6]. Where a person is buying from a builder it is usual for a deposit to be paid but as the deposits in such cases are usually a very small part of the price, such an action would probably not be sufficient in itself to constitute *rei interventus*. Payments of substantial deposits in transactions before delivery of a disposition are rare because of the risk of the builder going into liquidation[7]. In some cases both parties' actings can be looked at given the fact that missives are a bilateral contract involving obligations on both sides[8]. Thus where one party removed a sale ticket and the other laid out the ground it was held that these actings taken together amounted to *rei interventus*[8]. In relatively modern cases instructing architects to prepare plans for a hotel, seeking the appropriate building and planning permissions and commencing the actual development on the ground have been held to amount to *rei interventus*[9] whereas examination of title and preparation and submission of a draft disposition by the purchasers' solicitor in a purported purchase have been held not to be sufficiently important in a case involving a shop worth £215,000 where there had been extensive negotiations between the parties' agents for over six months[10].

1 1936 SC (HL) 56.
2 At 66.
3 *Smith v Marshall* (1860) 22 D 1158.
4 *Stodart v Dalzell* (1876) 4 R 236.
5 *Forbes v Wilson* (1873) 11 M 454; *Graydon & Co v Pollux Properties Ltd*, above.
6 *Maclean v Scott* (1902) 10 SLT 447.
7 *Gibson and Hunter Home Designs Ltd* 1976 SC 23; and see Halliday *Conveyancing Law and Practice* (1985) vol II, para 15–82.
8 *Westren v Millar* (1879) 7 R 173.
9 *Secretary of State for Scotland v Ravenstone Securities Ltd*, above.
10 *Rutterford Ltd v Allied Breweries Ltd* 1990 SLT 249.

The actings must be known to and permitted by the other party

2.10 Since *rei interventus* is really part of the wider doctrine of personal bar it is essential that the party founding on the actings can show that the other party knew of these actings for 'it is his permission or encouragement of such acting or abstention which is the kernel of the evidence of his presumed consent, in other words, the root of the personal bar pled against him'[1]. In certain cases actual knowledge is presumed if the actings 'must necessarily be held to be in the contemplation of that party when he entered into the agreement – actings which are in the proper pursuance of the agreement, and which the other party to the agreement would naturally expect should take place in pursuance of it'[2]. It is obvious that presumed or implied knowledge is difficult to establish. It has been held that giving up an existing business in anticipation of the implementation of the contract is not something which the other party to the contract could have anticipated[3] nor is the failure to look for other premises on the assumption that an imperfect contract has secured the desired property[4]. It is important for solicitors or other agents involved in the conclusion of missives to realise that their own knowledge can be imputed to their clients in circumstances where they have actual or ostensible authority to enter the agreement or sanction the actings founded on[5]. There will be circumstances where solicitors or other agents will require to advise a client that certain actings which the client wishes to perform (such as carrying out repair work on the property at a surveyor's request) may have the effect of perfecting an agreement which that client thinks as yet has no legal validity.

1 *Danish Dairy Co v Gillespie*, above, at 664 per Lord President Clyde.
2 *Gardner v Lucas* (1878) 5 R 638 at 656 per Lord Shand.
3 *Gardner v Lucas*, above.
4 *Danish Dairy Co v Gillespie*, above.
5 *Danish Dairy Co v Gillespie*, above; *Heiton v Waverley Hydropathic Co* (1877) 4 R 830.

The actings must be productive of alteration of circumstances, loss or inconvenience

2.11 It has already been noted that the actings upon which the *rei interventus* is based must be 'not unimportant'. It naturally follows from this that the actings must themselves produce some alteration in the circumstances of the party who seeks to uphold the agreement resulting in loss or inconvenience[1]. Unimportant circumstances, it might be supposed, are unlikely to result in such loss and so these two aspects of *rei interventus* are closely connected. Many of the decided cases in this area turn on both points. Presumably the consequent loss or inconvenience need not be catastrophic since in terms of Bell's definition the loss need not be 'irretrievable'. Consequently the size of the loss or inconvenience necessary to justify *rei interventus* will depend on the overall nature and value of the transaction[2]. In one case[3] it was held that there had not been sufficient loss where the purchaser formed a joint venture to work minerals following on an imperfect agreement to acquire a mineral lease and plant and machinery. In another case[4] it was held that giving up existing businesses on the strength of an improbative lease for new premises was too remote. In the recent case of *Rutterford Ltd v Allied Breweries*[5] it was held that the fact that the solicitor acting for the party seeking to enforce the contract had examined titles, drafted documents and generally carried out some conveyancing work was not sufficient alteration of circumstance, loss or inconvenience to found *rei inter- ventus* in the context of the proposed purchase of a shop at £215,000. In that case Lord Caplan pointed out that there was some distinction between the 'not unimportant procedures' and the 'alteration of circumstances, loss or inconvenience'. He stated 'Thus it is not the mere fact that the obligee has incurred some loss that constitutes *rei interventus* but the fact that such loss results from an important step[6]'. In the *Rutterford* case the carrying through of some standard conveyancing was neither important enough nor costly enough in terms of legal expense to constitute *rei interventus*.

1 *Keanie v Keanie* 1940 SC 549.
2 *Kinear v Young* 1936 SLT 574.
3 *Rigg v Mather* (1902) 10 SLT 426.
4 *Gardner v Lucas*, above.
5 1990 SLT 249.
6 At 253.

Homologation

2.12 Homologation is the mirror image of *rei interventus*. *Rei inter- ventus* arises where the party who seeks to enforce the contract founds upon his own actings to perfect the contract; homologation arises where the party seeking to enforce the contract founds upon the actings of the other party who seeks to repudiate. In many cases relating to imperfect missives, *rei interventus* and homologation will both arise because of the bilateral nature of the contract which involves obligations on both sides. While the doctrines are similar and both, of course, derive from the general principle of personal bar, they are not identical. Homologation is a wider aspect of per- sonal bar than *rei interventus* and has a wider application. It can validate properly drawn up contracts which are liable to reduction on the ground of error[1] but unlike *rei interventus*, homologation cannot be used to conclude an agreement where full consensus is lacking[2]. Again, one must look to Bell's *Principles*[3] for the classic definition[4].

To establish homologation the following conditions must be fulfilled.

1 *Gloag* p 544.
2 See para 3.37 below; *Law v Thomson* 1978 SC 343.
3 § 27.
4 See para 2.06 above.

An antecedent engagement

2.13 In the first place it is necessary to prove that there is an agreement between the parties. Normally the agreement will be set out in an informal writing[1] but as with *rei interventus* it can be established by oath[2]. It must be shown that there is an agreement and not simply negotiations or proposals towards an agreement[3]. Plans,[4] an improbative offer to lease[5] and an improbative set of missives for a lease[6] have all been accepted as informal antecedent engagements for the purpose of homologation. The writ to be founded on must involve all the parties who seek to deny the agreement. Thus averments of an agreement by two *pro indiviso* proprietors to sell heritage which referred to the writ of only one of the proprietors were held to be irrelevant[7].

1 *Mitchell v Stornoway Trustees* 1936 SC (HL) 56.
2 Walker & Walker *Law of Evidence in Scotland* para 284.
3 *Temperance Permanent Building Society v Kominek* 1951 SLT (Sh Ct) 58.
4 *Mitchell v Stornoway Trustees,* above.
5 *Forbes v Wilson* (1873) 11 M 454.
6 *Danish Dairy Co v Gillespie* 1922 SC 656.
7 *Stewart's Executors v Stewart* 1993 SLT 440.

The actings must be referable to the engagement

2.14 As with *rei interventus* there must be a clear connection between the actings and the actual agreement, and in point of time the actings must be subsequent to the agreement[1]. There is authority for the view that whereas in *rei interventus* silence can be relevant, homologation requires a positive action[2].

1 *Mitchell v Stornoway Trustees,* above, at 62, 63.
2 *Clark's Executor v Cameron* 1982 SLT 68.

The actings must imply voluntary assent to the engagement in full knowledge

2.15 The state of mind and capacity of the homologator are important. To validate the contract the homologation must be by a party who has the legal capacity to give consent to the contract in accordance with the law[1]. The homologator must act knowing that he has the legal right to repudiate the contract[2]. It has been held that an act done or carried out after court action has been raised has no effect since it cannot be regarded as voluntary[3]. Similarly, any actions carried out under reservation or protest are not regarded as voluntary and have no

effect[4]. Unlike *rei interventus* the actings do not need to be known to
the other party nor result in any actual loss in a financial sense nor
need they be 'not unimportant'[5]. In so far as the actual actings
themselves are concerned, it has been held that an application for
transfer of a licence by a purchaser of a licensed business infers
homologation[6] and in the leading case of *Mitchell v Stornoway
Trustees*[7] it was held that the actings of the superiors' factor in assisting
the feuar in having building plans approved by the Dean of Guild
Court amounted to homologation which prevented the superior from
repudiating the imperfect agreement to grant a feu. Similarly an
application for renewal of an hotel licence has been held to be homologation of a lease[8]. The actings of an agent such as a solicitor can
amount to homologation if the agent has express or ostensible
authority[9].

1 Erskine *An Institute of the Law of Scotland* (8th edn, 1871) III, 3, 47; *Brodie v Brodie*
  (1827) 5 S 900.
2 *Shaw v Shaw* (1851) 13 D 877 per Lord Cockburn; *Gardner v Gardner* (1830) 9 S 138.
3 *Harkness v Graham* (1833) 11 S 760.
4 *Miller & Son v Oliver & Boyd* (1906) 8 F 390.
5 *Mitchell v Stornoway Trustees*, above, at 67.
6 *Charles v Shearer* (1900) 8 SLT 273.
7 Above.
8 *Station Hotel Nairn Ltd v MacPherson* (1905) 13 SLT 456.
9 Contrast *Danish Dairy Co v Gillespie* 1922 SC 656 with *Forbes v Wilson* (1873) 11 M 454.

Adoption

2.16   The word 'adopting' is used by Bell in his definition of homologation. It should, however, be noted that adoption and homologation
are distinct concepts[1]. Adoption validates essentially void contracts
but from the date of adoption only and, generally speaking, in a fresh
document. Homologation perfects contracts from the date of the
contract as opposed to the date of the actings[2]. Adoption can be used
to validate imperfect missives as in the case of *McGinn v Shearer*[3]. In
that case a seller replied to an offer to purchase his house by trans-
mitting a typewritten acceptance which was signed but not adopted as
holograph and an accompanying letter which was in his own handwriting and therefore holograph. The typewritten acceptance was in
the following terms:

'Dear Sir,
I am in receipt of your letter of the 27th inst. for which I thank you.
I note that you are prepared to purchase, on your wife's behalf, the dwellinghouse known as Cedar Lea, Kirkwall belonging to me, on the terms laid down
in your letter, for the sum of £2,000 (Two thousand pounds).

I agree to the terms of your letter and should be glad if you would accept this letter as a formal acceptance.'
Signed but not adopted as holograph.

The accompanying handwritten letter was in the following terms:

'Dear Frank,
I enclose my acceptance of your offer for the purchase of Cedar Lea and I trust you will find it in order.
I am very grateful for the generous terms you have given us for occupation as I cannot see that we could possibly be ready to hand over until Nov.
I hope that you will both have many happy years in your new home – it is a grand house and it will always hold many happy memories for me.
With kindest regards to you both.'
Holograph and signed by defender.

Lord Sorn in the Outer House held that there had been no holograph acceptance and therefore that there were no valid missives. The Inner House with exception of Lord Carmont held that there had been a probative acceptance of the offer in respect that the second holograph letter was a probative acceptance in its own right or alternatively that the informal acceptance was adopted by the holograph letter.

1 For a general discussion on adoption see McBryde *The Law of Contract in Scotland* (1987) para 26-05 and *Walker and Walker* para 285.
2 Bell *Principles* § 27.
3 1947 SC 334.

Scottish Law Commission proposals

2.17   The Scottish Law Commission published proposals and a draft Bill in relation to the legal requirements for writing in 1988[1]. The Bill itself came before Parliament but encountered procedural difficulty. It may be that the Bill will be reintroduced and accordingly it is appropriate to give some consideration to the proposals as they relate to missives.

1 Report on Requirements of Writing (Scot Law Com no 112).

Abolition of common law rules relating to writing

2.18   In *McGinn v Shearer*[1] Lord President Cooper referred to the requirement that contracts relating to heritable property be constituted in probative writing in the following terms:

'It is useless to disguise that the further we recede from the far distant days when land was the substance of the private wealth of the community the more clearly does this rule stand revealed as a fossil relic of feudalism, explicable if confined within the field of strict conveyancing, but completely out of touch with realities when it intrudes into the field of mutual contract.'

One of the fundamental proposals of the Scottish Law Commission is the abolition of any rule requiring a contract to be constituted by formal writing. This proposal relates to the formalities for the constitution of the contract and does not attempt to interfere with the concept of a probative (ie self-proving) deed as a matter of evidence. The recommendations and the draft Requirements of Writing (Scotland) Bill do, however, state that a written document shall be required for the constitution of any contract or voluntary obligation for the creation, transfer, variation or extinction of an interest in land[2]. While writing would still be required under the new proposals it would not require to be probative. Attestation by one witness would, however, be necessary if the deed is to be recorded in the Register of Sasines, Books of Council and Session or Sheriff Court Books[3]. The Land Register is not mentioned because the Keeper himself has discretion as to what documents are acceptable[4]. In so far as missives are concerned these are, of course, not normally recorded or registered and are seldom attested but derive their current privileged status because they are adopted as holograph. Under the new proposals missives would not require to be attested but would require to be in writing. The Scottish Law Commission considered carefully the status of privileged writings and decided to abolish that status[5]. While it is difficult to argue against the view of the Scottish Law Commission that those who are asked to write the words 'adopted as holograph' may have difficulty understanding their meaning or the need for such words, nevertheless letters which are 'adopted as holograph' are easily identifiable as 'missives'. That marking out feature will disappear if the Scottish Law Commission proposals are implemented.

1 1947 SC 334.
2 Clause 1(2)(a) of the draft Bill and recommendations 3(a), 4 and 5 of the report.
3 Clause 11 of the draft Bill and recommendation 29.
4 Land Registration (Scotland) Act 1979, s 4(1).
5 Clause 22(b) of the draft Bill and recommendation 13(e).

Probativity as an evidential matter

2.19 The Scottish Law Commission's recommendations still allow parties to draw up writings which are self-proving in the evidential sense if they conform to the recommended attestation requirements set out in clause 5 of the Bill. In terms of that clause, where a document bears to have been subscribed by the granter and bears to have been signed by a person as a witness of the granter's subscription and states the name and address of the witness, then the document shall be presumed to have been subscribed by that granter, provided that nothing in the document or its testing clause or equivalent indicates that it was not so subscribed or was not validly witnessed. Clause 5, however, deals purely with probativity in the evidential sense and not validity. Even where, as with missives, writing is required to constitute a contract, the contract will still be valid in terms of clause 4 of the Bill if it is simply subscribed by the granter or an agent and no witnesses are required.

Missives under the new proposals

2.20 These recommendations leave missives in rather an awkward position. On the one hand they are a contract relating to an interest in land and even under the new recommendations must be constituted in writing[1]; on the other hand they are not normally recorded or registered for preservation and so need not be attested. The status of holograph writings having been abolished, if the parties wish to constitute missives which are probative in the evidential sense then they would require to be attested in terms of clause 5 of the proposed Bill. The benefit of a probative writing is of course that it proves itself in court without the need to call witnesses to speak to the documentation. The recommendations of the Scottish Law Commission do provide that where a document bears to have been subscribed by the granter then a court can order the document to be endorsed with a certificate to that effect[2]. The procedure involved would be likely to be by summary application to the sheriff supported by affidavit evidence. If the recommendations become law then offers, qualified acceptances and other documentation evidencing the contract would require only to be subscribed by the parties or their solicitors. There would be no point in adding the words 'adopted as holograph' because these words would have no effect. The contract itself would be valid and binding but if it were relied on in court proceedings then it would have to be set up in court in terms of clause 7 or spoken to by witnesses as part of the court process. It is fair to say that many legal bodies who were consulted by the Scottish Law Commission in relation to their proposals opposed the abolition of holograph status for missives and other documents[3]. The Law Society of Scotland among others held the view that it was necessary to set missives apart from other items of correspondence relating to a proposed purchase and sale of heritable property so that it would be clear which documents were intended to be part of the contract and which documents or letters were intended simply to be part of the correspondence. The Scottish Law Commission strongly held to the view that archaic phrases such as 'adopted as holograph' had no place in a modern legal system. Indeed the Commission went to some length to justify their position by quoting Lord President Cooper in *McGinn v Shearer*[4]. Further, the Commission were not even happy that missives should be endorsed with modern wording such as 'intended to be binding' to set them apart from other correspondence. The result of the recommendation if enacted would therefore be that missives would not require to be attested or holograph to be binding but would not have probative status unless they were attested in terms of clause 5 although they could be granted a certificate by the court in terms of clause 7.

1 Clause 1(2)(a) of the draft Bill.
2 Clause 7 of the Bill and recommendation 26 of the report.
3 See para 4–26 of the report.
4 1947 SC 334 at 344, 345 and see para 2.18 above.

Criticisms of the proposals

2.21 Scottish lawyers have been justly proud of the ability of the conveyancing system to achieve a concluded contract in a relatively short space of time. The system of concluding missives by solicitors has afforded clients a certainty not available in the English system where the clients themselves sign the contracts which are then exchanged when it suits both parties to do so. The new proposals bring two risks to the Scottish system. Firstly, solicitors may persevere with missives which are not probative and have to label all other correspondence 'subject to contract' or 'not intended to be binding' or, secondly, they may decide that missives are important enough as evidence of contract to require probative status in the evidential sense in which case they may require missives to be signed by the parties themselves and attested. Theoretically, however, there would be nothing to prevent a solicitor or a firm of solicitors signing missives as agent before a witness and it may be that this will be the solution adopted by the legal profession. One has to wonder however whether the proposals would push the Scottish system of exchanging binding and probative missives closer to the English system of exchanging contracts signed by clients and making correspondence 'subject to contract' with all the uncertainties and delays which this necessarily involves.

Scottish Law Commission proposals on *rei interventus* and homologation

2.22 As has already been noted *rei interventus* and homologation can, under the present law, validate missives for the purchase and sale of heritable property which are defective in form because they are not attested or adopted as holograph. Naturally, if the main recommendation of the Scottish Law Commission were to come into effect there would be no need to have attested or holograph missives and it might be thought that the need for such aspects of personal bar would disappear. However, the Scottish Law Commission proposals retain the twin concepts of *rei interventus* and homologation in relation to contracts for the purchase and sale of heritage although not the specific nomenclature. The new concept is laid out in clause 1(3) of the Bill and in recommendation 6. It is proposed that:

'Where a contract, obligation or trust mentioned in subsection (2) above is not constituted in a written document complying with section 4 of this Act but one of the parties to the contract, a creditor in the obligation or a beneficiary under the trust ("the first person"), has acted or refrained from acting in reliance on the contract, obligation or trust with the knowledge and acquiescence of the other party, the debtor in the obligation or the trustee ("the second person"):
(a) the second person shall not be entitled to withdraw from the contract, obligation or trust; and
(b) the contract, obligation or trust should not be regarded as invalid
on the ground that it is not so constituted if the position of the first person:
(i) as a result of so acting or refraining from so acting has been affected to a material extent, and
(ii) would be adversely affected to a material extent by such withdrawal.'

These new proposals would apply where contracts had been made orally or presumably partly in writing and partly orally and actings had taken place on the faith of the imperfect agreement. The proposals may cause difficulties for estate agents and others engaged in oral negotiations. Apart from this, however, there seems little difference between the new proposals and the existing law. It is perhaps not surprising that even the combined genius of the Scottish Law Commission has been unable to improve much on the classic definitions of *rei interventus* and homologation laid down by Bell[1]. It is amusing, however, to note that the Commission proposes in clause 1(4): 'In relation to the constitution of any contract, obligation or trust mentioned in subsection (2) above, subsection (3) above replaces the rules of law known as *rei interventus* and homologation.'

1 *Principles* §§ 26 and 27.

CHAPTER 3

Conclusion of missives

Unilateral promises

3.01 Most contracts for the sale and purchase of heritable property
are concluded in bilateral agreements between purchaser and seller
generally executed on their behalf by solicitors. In the normal course
of events there will be an offer on behalf of the purchaser followed by a
qualified acceptance on behalf of the seller, possibly some further
formal communications and finally a letter concluding the bargain on
behalf of one of the parties. It is, however, theoretically possible (but
in practice rare) for a party to bind himself to convey heritable property
to another person by a unilateral promise. The promise must be
contained in an attested or holograph writing[1]. Scots law has always
recognised the binding nature of a promise even without an acceptance on the part of the promisee[2]. However, for a uniltateral promise
to be binding, it must be construed as a promise and not as an offer
which would of course require an attested or holograph acceptance in
the normal way. In one case[3] a party brought an action for declarator
that a house had been sold on the basis of the following document
which had been subscribed by the defender before witnesses and then
delivered by the defender to the pursuer:

'I have agreed to sell my house . . . for One hundred and fifty Pounds
(£150.00) to Miss A C Malcolm.'

The court held that the document did not import a unilateral obligation to sell the house at a certain price and was not effectual without
writing on the part of the pursuer. The document was merely one side
of a bilateral contract of sale of heritage which had no effect until
completed by an acceptance in attested or holograph writing from the
other party. In another case[4], the following document was
considered:

'I as the owner of the house Two Millburn Street, Aberdeen, hereby
undertake to sell to Mr Haldane and Miss Cameron, the middle flat
occupied by me at the above address at a price of Six hundred and
twenty five Pounds (£625.00) Sterling when I vacate the said flat.'

The undertaking was adopted as holograph and signed by the owner Mr Watson. Mr Haldane and Miss Cameron attempted to interdict another sale of the same flat to another party on the ground that the holograph letter was a legally binding unilateral promise. The sheriff held that the document founded upon fell to be construed as no more than the record of one side of a contract to sell with no corresponding acceptance. Accordingly it did not bind the seller. The obvious difficulty in granting a unilateral undertaking to sell is that by its very nature a conveyance of property requires certain positive actions on the part of the promisee such as paying the price, taking entry and the recording or registration of the title. While the older authorities[5] all acknowledge the possibility of a binding unilateral promise to sell heritage it is extremely difficult to see how this can be framed standing the decisions already referred to. Even Gloag expresses his doubts: 'but though the competency of such an obligation is recognised, as a general rule a document expressed as an obligation to buy or sell will be construed merely as an offer requiring acceptance, and acceptance by probative writ[6].'

The message to any solicitor involved in the transfer of heritable property is clear. No attempt should be made to contract for a sale or transfer of heritable property by unilateral undertaking. Binding missives constituted by attested or holograph writing should be concluded in each case. It is, however, interesting to note that a unilateral obligation granting an option to purchase a property is more easily enforced than a promise to sell[7].

1 *Govan New Bowling Club v Geddes* (1898) 25 R 485.
2 Stair *The Institutions of the Law of Scotland* 1, X, 3; 1, X, 4.
3 *Malcolm v Campbell* (1891) 19 R 278.
4 *Haldane v Watson* 1972 SLT (Sh Ct) 8.
5 *Alexander v Kinglassie* 1687 M 8422; *Ferguson v Paterson* 1748 M 8440; *Muirhead v Chalmers* 1759 M 8444; *Fulton v Johnston* 1761 M 8446; *Barron v Rose* 1794 M 8463.
6 Gloag *The Law of Contract* (2nd edn, 1929) p 166.
7 *Sichi v Biagi* 1946 SN 66; but see *Hamilton v Lochrane* (1899) 1 F 478, a case construed in the context of a unilateral promise.

Representations and negotiations

3.02 A detailed discussion concerning representations inducing the contract of missives is beyond the scope of this work[1]. Statements in particulars of sale whether issued by agents or by the seller are more likely to be treated as *verba jactantia* rather than representations in relation to the property. A statement in an advert indicating the number of animals which could be supported for grazing on a hill farm has been treated as an expression of opinion and not as a warranty[2]. It is common practice for agents to state in particulars of sale that the description of the property is not intended to form part of any contract nor to be legally binding in any way. Estate agents or property developers may, however, be guilty of a criminal offence if a false or misleading statement is made in the course of estate agency or property development business[3]. The commission of such an offence has no effect on the validity of any contract of sale of itself[4]. As the law stands at the moment missives must be constituted by attested or holograph writing and accordingly there is not the same scope for confusion between representations and terms of the contract. Similarly as the number of conditions and warranties included in offers for the purchase of heritable property increases, so the importance of representations made prior to the conclusion of the missives decreases. Having said that, missives are a contract and are subject to the law of contract in all its aspects. The principles of the law in relation to capacity to contract[5], error[6], fraud[7] and facility and circumvention and undue influence[8] all apply. It should be noted however that the Unfair Contract Terms Act 1977 does not apply to sales of heritage[9]. Solicitors are unlikely to be involved in relation to extraneous matters except perhaps in relation to capacity unless the contract is challenged in some way or there is some question over the extent of the subjects[10]. Questions in relation to capacity involving consents of third parties are likely to be raised during the examination of title stage after the missives are concluded rather than during the negotiations or the adjustment of missives. Where solicitors are acting for a trustee in bankruptcy or in other circumstances where an act and warrant or the consent of some outside party such as a heritable creditor is required, then the missives should be made conditional on such warrant or consent being forthcoming[11].

1 For a general discussion of the contrast between representations and terms of contract, see *Gloag* Ch XXVII; McBryde *The Law of Contract in Scotland* (1987) Chs 3 and 9; Walker *The Law of Contracts and Related Obligations in Scotland* (2nd edn, 1985) Ch 14.
2 *Hamilton v Duke of Montrose* (1906) 8 F 1026 on the meaning of 'as advertised' (a term to be avoided); see *Nisbet v Smith* (1876) 3 R 781; *Mossend Theatre Co Ltd v Livingstone* 1930 SC 90.
3 Property Misdescriptions Act 1991, s 1(1). See Property Misdescriptions (Specified Matters) Order 1992, SI 1992/2834.
4 Ibid 1991, s 1(4); for a general discussion of the Act see Styles 'The Property Misdescriptions Act 1991' (1992) 37 JLS 486.
5 See *Gloag* Ch V; *McBryde* Ch 8; Halliday *Conveyancing Law and Practice in Scotland* (1985) vol I, para 2–40; Walker *The Law of Contracts and Related Obligations in Scotland* (2nd edn, 1985) Ch 5; Age of Legal Capacity (Scotland) Act 1991.
6 See *Gloag* Ch XXVI; *McBryde* Ch 9; Walker *Contract* Ch 14; and see *Steel's Trustees v Bradley Homes (Scotland) Ltd* 1974 SLT 133.
7 See *Gloag* Ch XXVIII; *McBryde* Ch 10.

8 See *Gloag* Chs XXVIII and XXIX; *McBryde* Ch 11; Walker *Contract* Ch 15.
9 For a general discussion of the Unfair Contract Terms Act 1977 see Walker *Contract* p 258 ff.
10 See para 5.03 below; see *Houldsworth v Gordon Cumming* 1910 SC (HL) 49; *Johnston's Trustees v Kinloch* 1925 SLT 124; *Anderson v Lambie* 1954 SC (HL) 43.
11 For a general discussion on purchasing from trustees in bankruptcy, liquidators and receivers see Gretton, Lecture, Law Society of Scotland General Conveyancing Course, October 1991.

Alternatives to missives

3.03 While the conclusion of a sale by a private bargain constituted in missives is by far the most common method of selling heritable property in Scotland, it is not the only one and for completeness it is appropriate to mention the two other methods of contracting which are open to parties. The two are (a) public roup and (b) minute of sale.

Public roup

3.04 Public roup involves the property being exposed in a public auction. Prior to the actual roup or auction, articles of roup are prepared and these set out not only the procedure which will be adopted at the auction but also the terms and conditions of the sale. The articles are equivalent to an offer to sell by the seller. The articles of roup set a date for the auction or roup and the subjects which are to be sold are then advertised. As in any other auction, the subjects are sold to the highest bidder. The articles of roup are then endorsed by the successful bidder and the seller's agent and this written endorsement constitutes a minute of sale or enactment. The articles and the minute of enactment are the contract, the equivalent in missives of the offer and the acceptance respectively. Sale by public roup is the reverse of the normal procedure in that the seller and not the purchaser dictates the terms at the outset. One of the terms which will almost always be contained in articles of roup is that the purchaser will be deemed to have satisfied himself as to the validity and marketability of the title. This means that every bidder, even if ultimately unsuccessful, will have to incur the pre-sale expense of instructing his solicitor to examine the titles prior to the roup. Sale by public roup has become common where a number of subjects are being sold by one seller, as where a public utility such as British Rail or Scottish Enterprise sells off surplus land. So far as the seller is concerned the system is somewhat cumbersome and expensive in that a person has to be engaged to act as an auctioneer. Finding a date for the roup which suits every potential purchaser is also difficult and it may also be that the date which has been selected is not the most opportune from the point of view of obtaining the best price. For these reasons, public roup is now very unusual. At one time, the only way of exercising a power of sale under a bond and disposition in security was by public roup but following upon the 1970 Act[1] this restriction to sale by public roup, even in its application to the bond and disposition in security, disappeared. Exposure by public roup is essential now only in connection with foreclosure.

1 Conveyancing and Feudal Reform (Scotland) Act 1970, s 35.

Current practice

3.05 The procedure of sale by public roup has been used occasionally for the sale of commercial property because it has been regarded as the way of achieving the best price when there are likely to be only two or three major competitors offering in respect of one substantial property. Roups have also become common where a number of subjects situated in different parts of the country are being sold by one seller. Public utilities such as British Rail often sell off surplus land in this manner. More recently sales of domestic property by public roup were tried in Aberdeen when the property market was poor but the experience of most solicitors who exposed properties in this way was not the most fortunate.

Minute of sale

3.06 This is extremely unusual and if the procedure is adopted it is used only in relation to properties which are not openly marketed. Properties sold in this manner tend to be very large or very expensive. The price is usually agreed between the parties and the terms of the sale embodied in a minute of sale which both parties sign before witnesses. Once again the minute is the equivalent of offer and acceptance. Both Menzies[1] and Montgomerie Bell[2] say that the minute of sale is used only in transactions of considerable importance. Montgomerie Bell goes on to say that it is useful where, for any reason, a disposition cannot be framed at once and the transaction settled. He goes on to say that it is often resorted to in these transactions 'because it is explicit in regard to all the particulars of the transaction; whereas the missives of sale leave sundry details to be understood, or settled according to legal construction'. No one would deny that missives have altered in their form and content and that is perhaps one of the reasons why the minute of sale is rarely encountered in practice.

Where a solicitor intends to act for both parties within the rules laid down by the Law Society of Scotland[3] it is often preferable to have the parties sign a sale agreement of this type rather than conclude the sale by offer and acceptance[4].

1 *Conveyancing According to the Law of Scotland* (4th edn, 1900 by J S Sturrock) p 937.
2 *Lectures on Conveyancing* (3rd edn, 1882) vol II, p 698.
3 Solicitors (Scotland) Practice Rules 1986.
4 See para 3.10 below.

The offer

3.07 Since an offer for the purchase of heritable property must be probative or in holograph writing there is not usually the same scope for dispute or litigation as to what does or does not constitute an offer. Thus the formal writings which constitute the agreement are easily identifiable, an advantage which may be lost if the Scottish Law Commission's proposals in relation to holograph writings are implemented[1]. This is especially true where, as is normal, the offer is framed and signed by a solicitor on behalf of the purchaser. Having said that, the law of contract applies and as with any contract constituted by offer and acceptance there must be *consensus in idem*. *Consensus* is a matter which is judged objectively rather than subjectively and has been described by Bell in the following manner[2]:

'To a perfect obligation (besides the proof requisite), it is necessary that there shall be a deliberate and voluntary consent and purpose to engage; excluding, on the one hand, Incapacity by nonage, disease or imbecility; and, on the other, Error, Force and Fraud.'

Generally speaking, what the parties are actually thinking in their own minds at the time the contract is being concluded is not relevant. Thus there still is *consensus* where a person argues that the contract which has been concluded was neither read nor understood by him[3]. As against this general principle the decision in *Harvey v Smith*[4] to the effect that a party must understand the meaning of the words 'adopted as holograph' for them to be effective is difficult to accept. It is perhaps the better view that the case has been wrongly decided[5].

1 See para 2.17 ff above
2 *Principles* §10.
3 *Young v Clydesdale Bank Ltd* (1889) 17 R 231.
4 (1904) 6 F 511.
5 See para 2.04 above; *Gloag* pp 95 and 96; *McBryde* para 5–17; *Maclaine v Murphy* 1958 SLT (Sh Ct) 49.

Offers by agents

3.08 Given the fact that a solicitor is generally involved in the conclusion of missives by offer and acceptance, extraneous factors relating to *consensus* are unlikely to arise. The solicitor is clearly qualified to understand the nature of the offer which he lodges or the acceptance which he despatches and if one of the parties has been unwilling to be bound in the contract the question is more likely to be between that party and his legal advisor. As a matter of agency a solicitor is a member of that class of agents who have ostensible authority to conduct business on behalf of their client so that in some cases a client can become bound without express authority. As a matter of strict law, however, a solicitor does not have ostensible authority to bind his client to any contract without express instructions[1]. Where a firm of solicitors signs an offer on behalf of a client, that offer should be signed and adopted as holograph by a partner of the firm[2]. It may be possible for the firm to give a power of attorney or specific authority to an assistant to sign offers on behalf of clients but this practice is not desirable. Apart from this, proof of actual authority on the part of the solicitor as agent may be proved by parole evidence[3]. The offer should, of course, disclose the name and address of the principal. If the solicitor chooses to offer without disclosing the identity of the principal there is some doubt in the law of agency as to whether or not the other party to the contract can hold the solicitor liable if the principal fails to implement the contract[4]. In one case[5] a firm of solicitors obtained a delay in the execution of diligence against a client by stating that they had authority from an undisclosed friend of the client to offer payment. They were found liable to pay when the so-called friend refused to pay. Where an agent contracts ostensibly as principal then the result will be that both the principal and the agent are liable to implement the contract[6]. As a matter of practice it is important that the solicitor should have proper and complete instructions in relation to any offer which is lodged. Nowadays it is very unusual to obtain written instructions in relation to the purchase of domestic property and it would be stretching credulity too far to either expect or believe that every single clause in a modern offer was the subject of detailed instruction. As has already been noted the solicitor has a pivotal role in the Scottish system of house purchase dependent on trust and expertise[7].

1 *Danish Dairy Co v Gillespie* 1922 SC 656.
2 *Littlejohn v Mackay* 1974 SLT (Sh Ct) 82. But see Cusine and Pearson, 'Who signs for the firm' (1991) 36 JLS 73.
3 *Cameron v Lewis* 1948 SLT (Notes) 2.

4 See *Gloag* p 138; *N & J Vlassopulos Ltd v Ney Shipping Ltd* 1977 1 Lloyd's Rep 478; *H O Brandt & Co v H N Morris & Co* [1917] 2 KB 784; *Fenwick v Macdonald, Fraser & Co* (1904) 6 F 850.
5 *Dores v Horne & Rose* (1842) 4 D 673.
6 Bell *Commentaries on the Law of Scotland* (1870), I, 540.
7 See para 1.01 above and Ch 1 in general.

Documents 'subject to contract'

3.09 The proposals of the Scottish Law Commission to abolish the need not only for probative or attested documentation for the purchase of heritage but also the privileged status of holograph documents have been criticised on the grounds that they may lead to various documents being stamped 'subject to contract' or 'not intended to be binding[1]'. As the law stands at present the bare words 'subject to contract' have very little meaning in Scots law. Where the parties conclude a contract in probative or holograph writing and agree all the terms the mere stamping of the words 'subject to contract' on the correspondence is unlikely in itself to have the effect of a suspensive condition[2]. The matter was discussed at length in the leading case of *Stobo Ltd v Morrisons (Gowns) Ltd*[3]. Lord Cooper stated:

'The only rules of Scots law which it appears to me to be possible to extract from past decisions and general principles are that it is perfectly possible for the parties to an apparent contract to provide that there shall be *locus poenitentiae* until the terms of their agreement have been reduced to a formal contract; but that the bare fact that the parties to a completed agreement stipulate that it shall be embodied in a formal contract does not necessarily import that they are still in the stage of negotiation. In each instance it is a matter of the construction of the correspondence in the light of the facts, proved or averred, on which side of the borderline the case lies.'

There can be writing which indicates purely that the parties are willing to contract to sell and purchase heritage but does not result in a concluded bargain of itself. It is particularly this type of situation which founded much of the criticism of the Scottish Law Commission's proposals to abolish holograph status[4].

1 See paras 2.20 and 2.21 above.
2 *Erskine v Glendinning* (1871) 9 M 656.
3 1949 SC 184 at 192.
4 For examples of the 'subject to contract' doctrine in general contracts see *Stobo Ltd v Morrisons (Gowns) Ltd* above; *Alexander v Montgomery* (1773) 2 Pat 300; *Van Laun & Co v Neilson Reid & Co* (1904) 6 F 644; *Bakers of Edinburgh v Hay* (1868) 6 SLR 144; *Gordon's Executors v Gordon* 1918 1 SLT 407; and see *McBryde* para 4–13 ff. For a discussion of the Scottish Law Commission's proposals see para 2.17 ff above.

Acting for both parties – Practice Rules

3.10 The question of whether solicitors should be allowed to act for purchaser and seller in the conclusion of missives for the purchase and sale of heritable property has been the subject of much debate over the years. There is one school of thought within the legal profession which is firmly of the view that there should be an absolute prohibition of this practice. There is another school of thought which takes the view that solicitors are perfectly capable of acting for both parties in the conclusion of a contract where the main essentials of that contract have already been agreed. It is fair to say that solicitors who practice in small towns or rural areas often have little choice but to act for both parties. The Law Society of Scotland laid down written Practice Rules to deal with this matter in 1986[1]. These Rules came into effect in respect of transactions commenced on or after 1 January 1987. The Rules do not supersede the original unwritten rule that a solicitor cannot continue to act for both parties when a conflict of interest arises and indeed this rule is confirmed in rule 3. In terms of rule 5 a solicitor or two or more solicitors practising either as principal or employee in the same firm or in the employment of the same employer are not allowed to act for both seller and purchaser in the sale or purchase or conveyance of heritable property, or for both landlord and tenant or assignor and assignee in a lease of heritable property for value, or for lender and borrower in a loan to be secured over heritable property, unless they fall under certain exceptions. It should be noted that the exceptions only apply however, where no dispute arises or might reasonably be expected to arise between the parties. There is an absolute prohibition of acting for both parties in the case of residential property where the seller or the landlord is a builder or developer. The excepted categories are:

(a) Where the parties are associated companies, public authorities, public bodies or government departments or agencies;

(b) where the parties are connected one with the other within the meaning of section 533 of the Income and Corporation Taxes Act 1970 (now section 839 of the Income and Corporation Taxes Act 1988);

(c) where the parties are related by blood, adoption or marriage, one to the other, or the purchaser, tenant, assignee or borrower is so related to an established client; or

(d) where both parties are established clients or the prospective purchaser, tenant, assignee or borrower is an established client of the firm or solicitor in question; or

(e) there is no other solicitor in the vicinity whom the client could reasonably be expected to consult; or

(f) in the case of a loan to be secured over heritable property, the terms of the loan have been agreed between the parties before the solicitor has been instructed to act for the lender, and the granting of the security is only to give effect to such agreement.

1 Solicitors (Scotland) Practice Rules 1986.

3.11 In cases falling within exceptions (c), (d) and (e) in the paragraph above there is an additional requirement laid down by the Rules that both parties must be advised by the solicitor at the earliest practicable opportunity that the solicitor or his firm has been requested to act for both parties and that if a dispute arises they or one of them will require to consult an independent solicitor or solicitors. This advice must be confirmed by the solicitor in writing as soon as practicable thereafter[1]. The legal ombudsman is particularly vigilant in this regard. An established client is defined as a person for whom a solicitor or his firm has acted on at least one previous occasion[2]. A solicitor is presumed, for the purposes of the Rules, to be acting for a party for whom he prepares a pro forma offer, whether completed or not, in connection with a missive[3]. This provision is intended to prevent a solicitor denying that he has acted merely because the prospective purchaser signs a prepared offer which is not typed on the solicitor's own notepaper. A solicitor acting on behalf of a party or prospective party to missives cannot issue any pro forma offer or other document requiring the signature of any party without informing that party that the signature may have legal consequences and that he should seek independent legal advice before signing[4]. Where a solicitor or a firm intend knowingly to act on behalf of two or more prospective purchasers or tenants then these clients must be informed of such intention and where a solicitor gives advice to any one of such clients in respect of the price or rent to be offered or any other material condition he cannot then offer advice on the same matter to the other clients[5]. This rule is designed to take account of circumstances where a solicitor may have several interested parties wishing to purchase the same house and the solicitor simply issues pro forma offers for each to sign. In appropriate circumstances the Council of the Law Society of Scotland can grant waivers in respect of any of these rules[6] but breach of the rules may be treated as professional misconduct[7].

1 Rule 5(a).
2 Rule 2(1).
3 Rule 6.
4 Rule 7.
5 Rule 8.
6 Rule 9.
7 Rule 10.

Acting for both parties – practice

3.12 There is no doubt that where a solicitor intends to act for both parties he must be continually on the alert for a conflict of interest or a potential conflict and must follow the Rules laid down by the Law Society of Scotland to the letter. In so far as the actual missives themselves are concerned the solicitor or the two solicitors in the firm acting for both parties, should not attempt to conclude missives with themselves as agents. If they do so this may give rise to the argument that there is no contract because a party cannot contract with himself. In all probability, however, missives concluded in this manner would not be invalid. Provided each solicitor is clearly acting for an independent and disclosed client then under the law of agency it would be deemed to be the parties who were contracting with each other despite the fact that the same firm or same solicitor was agent for both. However that may be, it is not good practice to conclude missives in this manner. It is preferable for any offer and acceptance to be signed by the respective clients themselves and attested or adopted as holograph[1]. At the very least one of the parties to the contract should sign one half of the missives with the other being accepted by the solicitor or solicitors on behalf of the other party. In these cases the process of concluding missives by offer, qualified acceptance and letter concluding the bargain can turn into something of a charade. It makes a great deal of sense for the parties to agree all the terms in relation to price, date of entry and extras and for the solicitors then to prepare a minute of agreement embodying these terms and such technical clauses as are agreed between the solicitors which the parties sign before witnesses[2].

1 See *Mitchell v Scott's Trustees* (1874) 2 R 162 where it was doubted whether it was competent for one man acting for two persons to conclude a contract between them; See also *Gloag* p 26, footnote, where this opinion is doubted.
2 See para 3.06 above.

Incorporation of standard terms

3.13 In the past, missives for the purchase and sale of heritable property have been concluded by express terms contained in the offer and acceptance. Indeed, when the writers of this work were apprentices offers were very often accepted without qualification. In those dark and far-off days an offer seldom ran to more than seven or eight clauses. Nowadays most offers have a schedule attached to them, the terms of which are incorporated into the missives by a clause in the offer. Some firms of solicitors have pro forma qualified acceptances where standard qualifications relating to penalty interest and the right to resile are included. The Law Society of Scotland have gone further than this and have produced a standard form of offer with a client's guide[1] The Law Society's standard clauses are enshrined in a deed registered in the Books of Council and Session which can be referred to and incorporated into the missives. As a matter of contract law it is clear that it is perfectly competent to incorporate extraneous condition in this manner[2]. The general rule that any standard conditions must be brought to the notice of the other contracting party does, of course, apply[3]. Difficulties such as this are unlikely to arise in the case of missives for the purchase and sale of residential property because any incorporated conditions are likely to be attached to the missives or well within the knowledge of the contracting parties or their agents. Solicitors should, however, be careful to advise their clients that standard clauses like those produced by the Law Society of Scotland apply to the contract. Clients' instructions are required in respect of standard clauses in the same way as they are required in respect of express clauses. Incidentally, the fact that the price is not actually specified in an offer does not render the missives invalid provided there is a method of ascertaining it set out in the contract[4].

1 See Ch 4 below.
2 *Stewart, Brown & Co v Grime* (1897) 24 R 414 (the rules of a trade association); *Goodwins, Jardine & Co Ltd v Brand & Son* (1905) 7 F 995 (arbitration clause incorporated into a sub-contract); *Smith v U M B Chrysler (Scotland) Ltd* 1978 SC (HL) 1 (printed conditions); and see generally *McBryde* Ch 13.
3 *McConnell & Reid v Smith* 1911 SC 635; *McCutcheon v David MacBrayne* 1964 SC (HL) 28.
4 *Earl of Selkirk v Nasmith* (1778) Mor 627; on incremental and escalating offers see *Halliday* vol II, para 15–13.

Time for acceptance and time limits

3.14 It is normal practice for an offer to contain a time limit for acceptance. This is not to bind the offerer to keep the offer open for a set period but to ensure that the acceptor must accept within a set period. Care must, however, be taken in the framing of such a clause otherwise the offerer can be held bound to keep the offer open during the period of the time limit with the effect that he is precluded from withdrawing[1].

Assuming that the time limit is properly drafted then the offer can be withdrawn at any time before acceptance. The general rule as to timing is that the offer is effective when it is received but an acceptance is effective from the date of posting[2]. This apparently applies even although the acceptance is held up by postal delay[3]. This of course assumes that the acceptance is a clear and complete acceptance of the offer and not a qualified acceptance setting out new terms. Qualified acceptances are, of course, new offers. If an offer contains no time limit then it must be accepted within a reasonable time. The question of what is a reasonable time is a question of fact and circumstance to be decided in each particular case[4]. It is clear that it is preferable to include a time limit in any offer. Where an offer stipulated that an acceptance was required 'in course of post' it was held that an acceptance after a lapse of six days was of no effect[5]. It would, however, be unwise to rely on vague words of that type. Phrases like 'this offer is open for immediate acceptance only' should be avoided as there is no judicial definition of 'immediate acceptance'. The correct way to frame a time limit is to make it clear that it does not preclude withdrawal within the time limit but will preclude acceptance after the time limit has expired[6]. Professor Halliday in volume II of *Conveyancing Law and Practice in Scotland* has suggested the following wording, 'This offer if an acceptance is not received by us by (hour and date) will be deemed to be withdrawn'. As Professor Halliday notes, loose wording such as 'This offer will remain open up to' should be avoided[7].

1 *Littlejohn v Hadwen* (1882) 20 SLR 5 where the words 'it is understood that Mr Littlejohn has the offer of the estate of R for ten days from this date' were held to preclude withdrawal within that period. And see Bell *Principles* § 73; *Gloag* p 35.
2 *Thomson v James* (1855) 18 D 1.
3 *Dunlop v Higgins* (1848) 6 Bell's App 195; *Jacobsen v Underwood* (1894) 21 R 654.
4 *Hall-Maxwell v Gill* (1901) 9 SLT 222 per Lord Stormonth Darling; Stair *Institutes* I, 3, 9; *Thomson v James* above, at 10 per Lord President McNeil.
5 *Hall-Maxwell v Gill* above.
6 *Heys v Kimball & Morton Ltd* (1890) 17 R 381 at 384.
7 *Halliday* vol II, para 15–05; *A & G Paterson v Highland Railway Co* 1927 SC (HL) 32 at 38.

Withdrawal of offers

3.15 In so far as the mechanics of withdrawal are concerned, these are apparently subject to less formality than the rules relating to offers and acceptances. To be effective in point of time a withdrawal of an offer must reach the recipient before despatch of an unqualified acceptance[1]. Although offers and acceptances in relation to the purchase and sale of heritable property must be in probative or privileged writing it appears that a withdrawal can be made by informal writing, telephone, telex, Fax or word of mouth. Professor Halliday indicates that this is certainly the case where there has been a mistake in a material matter in the offer such as where the solicitor offers a higher price than his client has authorised[2]. In the case of *McMillan v Caldwell*[3], however, this proposition was extended to cover the situation of simple withdrawal even where there had been no error. In that case a formal offer to purchase property was sent by the purchaser's solicitors. The offer was then formally amended and the seller's agents issued a qualified acceptance containing 15 modifications. In an attempt to take matters forward the parties and their solicitors met. At the meeting, after some discussion, the solicitor for the sellers orally withdrew the qualified acceptance as the sellers were no longer prepared to conclude missives on those terms. The purchaser's solicitor, having returned to his office, considered the matter, obtained instructions and issued a formal acceptance of the qualified acceptance, which had not been withdrawn in writing, purporting to conclude missives on the same day as the meeting. The purchaser then sought implement of the missives arguing that there were completed formal missives which could not be qualified or contradicted by an oral withdrawal. The sellers argued that there was no completed contract because there was no *consensus in idem*. The purchasers contended that the withdrawal could only be effective if it was in formal writing following the same rules which relate to constitution of the contract. Lord Kirkwood in the Outer House held that a formal written offer to purchase or sell heritable property could be withdrawn orally even if error was not an issue so long as notice of withdrawal was communicated in some manner to the other party before an acceptance of the offer had been sent. Accordingly in his view no valid contract had been concluded and he reduced the missives *ope exceptionis*. As a matter of equity the decision is undoubtedly fair. After all, one party had indicated that he no longer wished to proceed with the contract so there was no *consensus*, at least in the minds of the parties. However, it is perhaps a little incongruous to have one set of rules for the formation of a contract which require the contract to be in formal or privileged writing and another set of rules in relation to withdrawal. Counsel for the pursuer submitted that an oral withdrawal was insufficient. It was also pointed out that the purchaser who wished implement of the contract was founding on apparently completed missives which were *prima facie* valid and probative. The retention of the requirement of formal writing in relation to every aspect of missives certainly makes the system 'clear and certain[4]'. Counsel for the pursuer also referred to the general principle of the law of contract which lays down that *consensus* is a matter which is to be tested objectively[5]. In fairness, however, this is a principle which is applied generally to contracts most of which need not be concluded in writing, far less formal writing, and there was no direct authority on the point before the court. Perhaps it is best left to Gloag to sum up the position[6]:

'It is remarkable that there is no definite authority on the question whether an acceptance can be recalled or revoked by adopting some channel of communication (eg telegraph or telephone) which brings the fact of the recal(sic) to the notice of the offerer before he has actually become aware of the acceptance. Common sense would seem to dictate an affirmative answer to the question.'

If a withdrawal is made orally it is good practice to follow this up with a formal written withdrawal at the earliest opportunity. The onus of proof still rests firmly on the party seeking to show that the offer or acceptance has been withdrawn[7].

1 *Thomson v James* (1855) 18 D 1; *Henthorn v Fraser* [1892] 2 Ch 27.
2 *Halliday* vol II, para 15–06.
3 1990 SC 389.
4 See *Rutterford Ltd v Allied Breweries Ltd* 1990 SLT 249 at 252 per Lord Caplan.
5 See *McBryde*, para 5–14.
6 *Gloag* p 38.
7 *McMillan v Caldwell*, above at 398.

Discharge of completed missives

3.16 Although an offer or a qualified acceptance can be withdrawn orally, a concluded set of missives in attested or holograph writing cannot be discharged by oral agreement. In *Inglis v Lownie*[1] missives were concluded for the sale of heritable property but thereafter a dispute arose between the parties regarding the content of the disposition. The parties agreed to discharge the contract. It was orally agreed between the parties that the purchaser would accept repayment of the price with no interest or damages in full and final settlement of all claims he might have. Subsequently, however, the purchaser changed his mind and raised an action for declarator that he was entitled to resile from the contract by reason of the seller's repudiation and for repayment of the price with interest and damages in addition. The sellers resisted the claims for interest and damages contending that the parties' oral agreement barred the pursuer claiming these items. The sheriff granted decree in the pursuer's favour and the defenders appealed. The Sheriff Principal held that the primary purpose of the agreement was to discharge the contract constituted by missives and that such a contract could only be discharged by a writing or its equivalent. The oral agreement was held to be of no legal effect. Sheriff Principal Ireland, QC made the following comments:

'The agreement (to discharge the contract) was constituted by word of mouth. If it were allowed to receive effect it would revoke a contract relating to heritage and constituted by probative writing. This would contravene the principle contained in the maxim *unumquodque eodem modo dissolvitur quo colligatur*, unless it can be brought within some exception to the rule.'

In some ways it is rather difficult to reconcile this approach to missives with the approach taken in *McMillan v Caldwell*.

1 1990 SLT (Sh Ct) 60.

The acceptance

3.17 Nowadays it is extremely unusual to receive a clean acceptance of an offer without further qualification, although on 'Black Wednesday' when the pound went through the floor and interest rates looked like going through the roof one of the authors was expressly instructed to issue one for fear of a withdrawal of the offer. Again, the normal rules governing offers and acceptances apply to missives. For there to be *consensus in idem* and therefore a concluded contract the acceptance must meet the offer[1]. Thus a qualified acceptance is in effect a new or counter offer which in itself must be accepted by the offerer before the bargain is complete[2]. Where a Minute of Agreement for the sale of land was responded to by the purchaser with a written consent to the terms but subject to the addition of certain matters relating to the amount of the feuduty for the area of the subjects and the minerals, it was held there was no concluded contract[3]. Again it should be noted that the test of *consensus* is generally objective and even where the parties themselves aver there is a contract, the court can decide there is no *consensus*[4]. Certain matters can be mentioned in an acceptance which are not in themselves regarded as qualifications because they do not require the offerer's assent. Thus a statement in an acceptance of an offer to purchase heritage to the effect that a disposition must be delivered does not prevent consensus[5]. The reasoning here, of course, is that the law implies that a valid disposition must be delivered in exchange for the price. Similarly an acceptance which is conditional on the purchaser's solicitor approving the title has been held to bind the parties unless the purchaser's solicitor finds the title invalid or unmarketable[6]. Qualifications, however, which have the effect of reversing the implied obligations to deliver a good title[7] or a clear search[8] or which imposed an obligation on a purchaser to pay a deposit on the price before settlement[9] are counter offers which require formal acceptance in their turn.

1 *Mathieson Gee (Ayrshire) Ltd v Quigley* 1952 SC (HL) 38.
2 *Dickson v Blair* (1871) 10 M 41.
3 *Johnston v Clark* (1853) 18 D 70.

4 *Mathieson Gee (Ayrshire) Ltd v Quigley*, above.
5 *Thomson v James* (1855) 18 D 1 at 14 and 23.
6 *Hussey v Horne-Payne* (1879) 4 App Cas 311.
7 *Nelson v Assets Co* (1889) 16 R 898.
8 *Dickson v Blair*, above.
9 *Jones v Daniel* [1894] 2 Ch 332.

Further qualification – the right to withdraw and conclude

3.18 It is not uncommon nowadays for the conclusion of missives to extend beyond the stage of formal offer, qualified acceptance and letter concluding the bargain. In some cases there are further formal letters from both purchaser and seller which are themselves to be regarded as counter offers. The question has arisen in a number of cases as to whether it is open to a party to withdraw one qualified acceptance and accept the previous offer or previous qualified acceptance unconditionally. The matter has been canvassed judicially in three leading cases.

3.19 The first case to deal with this matter was *Wolf and Wolf v Forfar Potato Co*[1]. This is a decision of the Second Division of the Inner House and while the facts did not relate to missives for the sale and purchase of heritage the decision is equally applicable to that type of contract. The chain of events was as follows:

(1) A Forfar merchant telexed an offer to an international merchant in Amsterdam on 29 November 1977 to sell potatoes subject to certain conditions regarding delivery dates and sizes and imposing a time limit for acceptance. (The offer.)

(2) By telex dated 30 November 1977 the international merchant purported to accept the offer subject to additional conditions. (The first acceptance.)

(3) Following a telephone conversation between the parties to clarify the position the international merchant sent a further telex also dated 30 November 1977 within the time limit purporting to accept the original offer unconditionally. In that telex there was a request that additional conditions telexed in the first acceptance should be given consideration. (The second acceptance.)

1 1984 SLT 100.

3.20 The Forfar merchant refused to supply the potatoes on the basis that there was no concluded contract. The Inner House held that the first acceptance from the international merchant was a qualified acceptance and a counter offer and that the offer fell on receipt of that counter offer and was no longer open for acceptance. Two of the judges referred to a passage in *Gloag*[1] where he states:

'An offer falls if it is refused. If the refusal is not peremptory but combined with a request for better terms the general construction is that the offer is gone, and that the party to whom it was made, on failure to obtain the terms he requests, cannot fall back on an acceptance of the original offer.'

As authority for this proposition Gloag cites two cases[2].

1 *Gloag* p 37.
2 *Hunter v Hunter* 1745 M 9169; *Hyde v Wrench* (1840) 3 Beavan 334.

3.21 It should be noted that there was no attempt in this case to withdraw the first acceptance before issuing the second acceptance. The first acceptance on its own was treated as a rejection of the original offer. As a matter of commercial practice, however, a qualified acceptance is not generally to be regarded as a rejection of an offer. It is normally thought to be an acceptance of an offer subject to the adjustment of the terms, or simply a stage in the process of arriving at *consensus*. Straightforward rejection of an offer generally arises over the question of price. A qualified acceptance on the other hand generally deals with the matters of a more technical nature. In the context of missives a qualified acceptance has been described in the following manner[1]: 'A reply which commences "I accept the offer subject to the following conditions . . ." is not a rejection of the offer, although at the stage of the reply the bargain is inchoate'. While this statement is a correct reflection of how parties see the process of conclusion of missives from a commercial point of view it is questionable how far it can be regarded as a correct reflection of the law in the light of the cases decided. Given the fact, however, that the original qualified acceptance sent out in *Wolf & Wolf* was never withdrawn the decision must be regarded as correct[2].

1 *McBryde*, para 5–35.
2 See *McBryde*, para 5–86 ff.

3.22 The next case dealing with the matter of withdrawal and conclusion is *Rutterford Ltd v Allied Breweries Ltd*.[1] This is an Outer House case before Lord Caplan and it follows the decision in *Wolf & Wolf v Forfar Potato Co*[2] closely. The *Rutterford* case involved missives for the purchase of a shop in Greenock and in that case the timetable of events was as follows:
(1)   The purchaser's solicitors sent an offer dated 5 May 1988 to the seller's solicitors at a price of £215,000.
(2)   The seller's solicitors sent an acceptance dated 9 June 1988 to the purchaser's solicitors containing 14 qualifications.

(3)   The purchaser's solicitors sent a further formal letter dated 9 September 1988 to the seller's solicitors accepting the preceding qualified acceptance but imposing further qualifications.

(4)   The seller's solicitors sent a further formal letter dated 29 September 1988 to the purchaser's solicitors accepting the previous qualifications of 9 September but imposing seven further qualifications.

(5)   The purchaser's solicitors sent a further formal letter dated 11 October 1988 to the seller's solicitors accepting the previous qualifications but once again setting out further qualifications. By this time the gap between the parties was narrow and related to the manner of implementing the bargain rather than to its substance.

(6)   The purchaser's solicitors sent a formal letter to the seller's solicitors dated 11 January 1989 withdrawing the last qualified acceptance dated 11 October 1988 which had been sent by them and purporting to accept the qualifications contained in the previous letter from the seller's solicitors of 29 September 1988 holding the bargain to be concluded by virtue of the letters of 5 May, 9 June, 9 September and 29 September 1988 and 11 January 1989.

(7)   The seller's solicitors then wrote to the purchaser's solicitors on 11 January 1989 by way of informal writing acknowledging the letter concluding the bargain and sending draft Form 12 Application and draft Letter of Obligation. The tenor of this correspondence was indicative of a bargain which was to proceed.

(8)   The purchaser's solicitors examined the titles and prepared a draft disposition submitting the same with the appropriate Land Register forms to the seller's solicitors on 13 January 1989.

(9)   Various other conveyancing matters were referred to in correspondence but by letter dated 16 January 1989 the seller's solicitors wrote to the purchaser's solicitors indicating that they did not accept there was a concluded contract under explanation that the solicitor who had been dealing with the transaction had been on holiday when the conveyancing correspondence dealing with the various forms had taken place.

(10)   The sellers argued there was no concluded contract but the purchasers argued that they were entitled not to insist on some of their own qualifications, to accept previous qualifications set out by the sellers and hold the bargain as concluded.

1   1990 SLT 249.
2   1984 SLT 100.

3.23 In the course of the debate before Lord Caplan, various authorities were referred to[1]. Various cases were also referred to, the most important on the question of conclusion of the bargain being *Wolf & Wolf v Forfar Potato Co*[2] and on the question of possible *rei interventus* or homologation evidenced by the conveyancing having proceeded to some extent, the leading cases of *Mitchell v Stornoway Trustees*[3], *Errol v Walker*[4] and *Law v Thomson*[5]. Basically the question before the court was whether or not the character of the missives was that of a travelling set of negotiations which changed from time to time as the parties sought *consensus* or whether each formal letter was a rejection of the previous formal letter and a counter offer which then became the only offer on the table. Gloag's position is clear[6]; a qualified acceptance changes the nature of the bargain and in his opinion the original offer cannot then be accepted *de plano*. The alternative view is set out by McBryde[7].

1 Bell *Principles* § 26; Craigie *Conveyancing* (3rd edn) pp 246–248; *Gloag* pp 37 and 39; *McBryde*, para 5–86 ff.
2 1984 SLT 100.
3 1936 SC (HL) 56.
4 1966 SLT 159.
5 1978 SC 343.
6 *Gloag* p 37 and para 3.20 above.
7 Paras 5–35 ff and 5–86 ff.

3.24 Lord Caplan, having reviewed all the authorities, followed the decision in *Wolf & Wolf v Forfar Potato Co*[1] and decided:
(1) That the effect of the qualified acceptance of 11 October 1988 was to set up a counter-offer which cancelled the offer represented by the seller's acceptance of 29 September 1988.
(2) That in relation to acceptance or rejection of terms there was no distinction to be drawn between essential and inessential or technical conditions in a contract as this could only lead to confusion and uncertainty for contracting parties.
(3) That the continuing of negotiations after an offer was refused could only be regarded as keeping that offer alive where the offerer effectively so represented through these negotiations.
(4) That it could not be inferred from the pursuer's averments that simply because between September 1988 and 11 January 1989 the party's agents corresponded 'on certain matters' relating to the contract of sale the defenders were representing that their previous qualified acceptance had been restored.
(5) That what the pursuers claimed to have done in preparing the draft disposition and conveyancing forms did not amount to *rei interventus*, in the context of a transaction having a value of £215,000.

(6) Therefore that it was not open to the purchasers to attempt to conclude the bargain by withdrawing their own latest qualifications of 11 October 1988 and accepting the seller's previous qualifications of 29 September 1988.

1 1984 SLT 100.

3.25 Lord Caplan in coming to this conclusion, took the view that a qualified acceptance was in effect a statement that the offer was not acceptable and the focus then shifted to the original offerer who had to consider a fresh set of proposals. The offerer did not require, in Lord Caplan's view, to consider whether or not to withdraw his original offer for he already had a response. Lord Caplan was influenced in his decision by the fact that to take another position would be to accept that two offers affecting the same property could be on the table at the same time, namely, the original offer which could be accepted by the sellers without qualification and a qualified set of proposals set up by a qualified acceptance or other correspondence which could be accepted simultaneously by the purchasers. In other words, there could conceivably be two contracts with differing terms concluded at the same time in relation to the same subjects. There was a supplementary argument put before his Lordship based on *rei interventus* in relation to the correspondence and conveyancing work which had followed the purported conclusion of the bargain, but his Lordship had no difficulty in holding that the difficult case of *Errol v Walker*[1] did not apply because the work done could not be regarded as 'substantial' or 'not unimportant' in terms of Bell's classic definition of *rei interventus*[2]. Lord Caplan also noted that homologation could not complete an unconcluded contract[3]. The decision in the *Rutterford* case is logical and follows the previous authority but it may have come as a surprise to many legal practitioners who had assumed that qualifications were not rejections of previous offers but stages in a process of formal negotiation leading to a concluded bargain. This is a reasonable commercial view of the situation where the qualifications are of a technical nature and do not go to the root of the contract. Lord Caplan refused to accept any distinction between so-called essential conditions and non-essential or technical conditions.

1 1966 SLT 159.
2 *Principles* §§ 26, 27; para 2.06 above.
3 *Law v Thomson* 1978 SC 343.

3.26 The most recent case relating to withdrawal of one part of a missive and conclusion on another part is the infinitely more complicated case of *Findlater v Maan*[1]. In that case the timetable of events was as follows:

(1) The purchaser's solicitors made an offer for a dwellinghouse in Glasgow in formal writing on 25 March 1988.

(2) The seller's solicitors issued a qualified acceptance to the purchaser's solicitors on 28 March 1988.

(3) The purchaser's solicitors issued a further formal letter to the seller's solicitors on 29 March 1988 accepting the previous qualified acceptance subject to one further qualification.

(4) The seller's solicitors under reference to the letters of 25 and 28 March 1988 (but not to the letter of 29 March 1988) intimated by formal letter of 30 March 1988 one further qualification to the purchaser's solicitors.

(5) The purchaser's solicitors by formal letter dated 6 April 1988 accepted the terms of the seller's solicitors formal letter of amendment of 30 March 1988 and withdrew the qualification contained in his own (the purchaser's) letter of 29 March 1988 and held the bargain to be concluded.

1 1990 SC 150.

3.27 The seller (who had simply changed his mind about selling) argued that there was no concluded bargain. The purchaser raised an action craving declarator that the letters comprised a binding contract. The sheriff dismissed the action holding that there was no concluded bargain on the basis that the circumstances were indistinguishable from the circumstances in *Wolf & Wolf v Forfar Potato Co*[1]. The purchaser appealed to the Sheriff Principal who allowed the appeal holding that the correspondence could not be construed as a series of offers and counter-offers but as a series of letters in continuing negotiations reflecting both parties' willingness to contract and both parties' expectation that *consensus* would be ultimately achieved. The Sheriff Principal chose to view the exchange of missives in a commercial sense[2]. The seller appealed to the Inner House of the Court of Session where it was submitted that it was not open to the purchaser to withdraw the letter of 29 March 1988 in order to conclude a bargain without the prior consent of the seller. It was also argued that the letter of 6 April 1988 from the purchaser's solicitors did not make it clear what the bargain was and that the purchaser was not entitled to waive the provisions of the letter of 29 March 1988, although these provisions were conceived solely in his favour – a distinction falling to be drawn between the terms of a contract and the terms of an offer.

1 1984 SLT 100.
2 See para 3.21 above.

3.28   The Inner House held that although the Sheriff Principal had erred in his approach, the case was in fact distinguishable from *Wolf & Wolf v Forfar Potato Co*[1]. The court took the view that the letter of 28 March 1988 as a qualified acceptance fell to be regarded as a counter-offer as did the letters of 29 and 30 March 1988. Where the letter of 30 March was written without reference to the letter of 29 March, there were in effect two offers on the table and according to the Inner House it was open to the purchaser to withdraw the offer of 29 March and accept the seller's offer of 30 March, there being no principle of law which required the seller to consent to such withdrawal. This decision is of course very difficult to reconcile with the decision in *Rutterford v Allied Breweries Ltd*[2]. In the latter case, Lord Caplan was clearly of the view that it was contrary to principle for there to be two contracts on different terms capable of conclusion at the one time whereas the Lord-Justice Clerk, Lord Ross, who delivered the only written judgment in the *Findlater* case, appeared to find no difficulty in accepting such a proposition. Lord Ross accepted that a qualified acceptance of an offer fell to be regarded as a new offer or counter-offer and indeed expressly referred to the passage in *Gloag* supporting this proposition[3]. Lord Ross follows the chain of correspondence carefully in his judgment and takes up the point that the letter of 30 March 1988 from the seller's solicitors refers to the offer of 25 March and the qualified acceptance of 28 March, but does not refer to the letter of 29 March. In his judgment he states:

'In my opinion, the true approach to be made in the present case is as follows. The letter of 29th March and the letter of 30th March were two offers which existed at the one time, one at the instance of the seller and one at the instance of the purchaser. They were not written under reference to one another and neither of them superseded the other, they both co-existed. In that situation, I am of the opinion that it was open to the Pursuers to accept the offer contained in the letter of 30th March 1988. It was not disputed that that letter fell to be regarded as an offer and it was an offer which was open for acceptance. The Pursuers did accept that offer by their letter of 6th April 1988. Of course so long as the other offer of 29th March 1988 remained in existence, there could be no final *consensus in idem*. However, there was no reason why the Pursuers should not withdraw the letter of 29th March 1988.'

Lord Ross then went on to quote another passage from *Gloag* to the following effect[4]: 'Except in cases where there is an undertaking to hold the offer open for a definite time, it may be withdrawn at any time before acceptance'.

1 1984 SLT 100.
2 1990 SLT 249.
3 *Gloag* pp 37 and 39.
4 *Gloag* p 37.

3.29 There are clear differences between *Findlater v Maan* and *Wolf & Wolf v Forfar Potato Co*. In the latter case, it was a straightforward matter of an offer, a qualified acceptance and then an attempt to accept the original offer without a withdrawal of the qualified acceptance. There was no lengthy chain of correspondence as there was in *Findlater v Maan*. It is however extremely difficult to distinguish *Rutterford Ltd v Allied Breweries Ltd*, and *Findlater v Maan*. It may be significant that there is no discussion of the *Rutterford* case in Lord Ross's judgment. It may also be significant that in the *Findlater* case there was some doubt as to whether the letter of 29 March had actually been received before the further letter of 30 March had been transmitted and the court probably accepted that there were no grounds to assume that this was the case. The court may have felt that at the crucial time the letter of 29 March was somehow out of the reckoning and this may have been the vital difference in the reasoning in the two cases. The kernel of the judgment is found when Lord Ross sums up what he regards as the proper way to look at the correspondence[1]:

'On 25th March 1988, the Pursuers made an offer to purchase the subjects. On 28th March 1988 the Defender's solicitors sent a qualified acceptance of that offer and that qualified acceptance falls to be treated as a new offer. It then appears that on 29th March, 1988, the Pursuer's solicitors sent a qualified acceptance of the acceptance of 28th March 1988. This in turn also fell to be treated as a new offer. Likewise, on 30th March 1988 the Defender's solicitors, *under reference to the offer and the qualified acceptance dated 28th March*, added a further qualification. This in turn meant that the letter of 30th March, 1988 also fell to be regarded as a new offer. This meant that there were, as Counsel put it, two offers on the table at the same time, namely, the letter of 29th March, 1988 and the letter of 30th March, 1988.'

1 1990 SC 150 at 161.

3.30 It is perhaps difficult to state exactly where the law now stands in relation to the vexed question of the travelling missive. It is probably correct to say that *Wolf & Wolf v Forfar Potato Co*[1] is different from *Rutterford Ltd v Allied Breweries Ltd*[2] and it can probably be argued that the *Rutterford* case is marginally different from *Findlater v Maan*[3]. What cannot be denied, however, is that Lord Caplan's reasoning that there should never be two offers capable of acceptance at the one time on different terms is not accepted by the Inner House according to the *Findlater* case. It would undoubtedly have been

easier for all those attempting to conclude missives if the three cases
had all come to the same conclusion.

1 1984 SLT 100.
2 1990 SLT 249.
3 1990 SC 150.

3.31 The authors submit that the position in relation to withdrawal
and conclusion as a result of the current case law is as follows:

(1) An offer or a qualified acceptance can be withdrawn in writing
     (formal or informal), by Fax, telex, telegraph, telephone call or
     generally orally[1].
(2) In the case of a straightforward offer for the purchase of heritable
     property followed by qualified acceptance from the seller, it is not
     open to the seller to issue a further unqualified acceptance of the
     offer and attempt to conclude a bargain[2].
(3) The same principle will apply if there is a chain of correspond-
     ence where every formal letter in that chain accepts in its terms the
     immediately preceding letter and refers to that preceding letter as
     part of a travelling missive. In such a case, a party cannot go back
     down the chain withdrawing one qualifying letter and accepting
     terms contained in a previous qualifying letter[3], but
(4) if there is an apparent break in the chain of correspondence and a
     letter is somehow isolated, a situation can arise where two formal
     letters are issued independently of each other in relation to the
     same contract and in that case there will be two possible contracts
     which can be concluded and the first party to conclude will
     conclude on these terms[4].
(5) If missives have been concluded they cannot be discharged except
     by formal writing[5].

1 *McMillan v Caldwell* 1990 SC 389.
2 *Wolf & Wolf v Forfar Potato Co* 1984 SLT 100; *Gloag* p 37.
3 *Rutterford Ltd v Allied Breweries Ltd* 1990 SLT 249.
4 *Findlater v Maan*, above.
5 *Inglis v Lownie* 1990 SLT (Sh Ct) 60; as to alterations to concluded missives and
   variations see paras 3.40 and 3.41 below.

Suggestions for practice

3.32 The lessons for solicitors should be clear. Although an oral
withdrawal is sufficient to preclude a concluded bargain this should be
followed up in formal writing in the context of the travelling missive.
If parties wish to avoid being caught in a *Findlater v Maan* type of
situation every formal letter must clearly refer to the immediately

preceding letter in the chain, accepting the terms of that preceding letter and importing new terms into the contract. Accordingly, if acting for a purchaser, the following, it is suggested, may be the last letter in the chain:

'On behalf of our clients Tie Up Quick & Co Ltd, we hereby accept the formal modifications contained in your letter on behalf of your clients Flannel Slither & Withdraw Ltd, dated 30 June 1992, relative to our formal letter of 25 June 1992, relative to your formal qualified acceptance of 23 June 1992 of our formal offer of 22 June 1992 and we now hold the bargain to be concluded on the basis of these formal communications.'

The position in relation to this matter is difficult enough where the correspondence is clearly isolated as formal correspondence intended to be part of the missives. If the Scottish Law Commission proposals were to become law[1] and any writing became capable of concluding a contract, then the position may become even more complicated and difficult to determine.

1 See para 2.17 ff above.

Conclusion of missives by actings

3.33 In the normal course of events missives are concluded in writing either by formal writing or sometimes by informal writing followed by *rei interventus* or homologation[1]. The twin principles of *rei interventus* and homologation are both aspects of personal bar and at least in the case of *rei interventus* there are suggestions and indeed decisions to the effect that actings which follow missives which do not disclose complete *consensus* may bar *locus poenitentiae*. This application of *rei interventus* was set out by Gloag in the following terms[2]:

'But the term *rei interventus* is also applied, though not so frequently, to the case where parties have been in negotiation for a contract, and one of them has acted, and been known and allowed to act, on the mistaken assumption that the negotiations had reached the point of a completed contract. . . But when *rei interventus* is relied upon in cases where parties have not arrived at any agreement, verbal or written, the rule that actings may bind them to a contract is not an exception to the general rule that contract requires agreement. What is really meant is that the actings in question are evidence that agreement has been actually reached, though it has not been indicated in words or in other ways than by actings. In the former case (normal *rei interventus*) the actings render an agreement binding; in the latter they prove that an agreement was reached.'

Gloag cites two cases as authority for this proposition[3]. A close examination of these cases shows, however, that the parties had actually reached agreement on the essential points of the contract. Generally speaking, for there to be a pre-existing agreement in terms of Bell's classic definition of *rei interventus* in the ordinary sense[4], it is not necessary for there to be express agreement on every single term normally found in a contract relating to heritage[5]. It may be that Gloag is to be criticised for extending the definition of *rei interventus* by referring to cases which do not really justify such an extension.

1 See para 2.06 ff above and Ch 2 generally.
2 *Contract* (2nd edn) pp 46–47.
3 *Colquhoun v Wilson's Trustees* (1860) 22 D 1035; *Wight v Newton* 1911 SC 762.
4 *Principles* §§ 26, 27.
5 *Walker & Walker* para 282; *Westren v Millar* (1879) 7 R 173 at 178.

3.34   In the case of *East Kilbride Development Corporation v Pollock*[1] it was held quite clearly that as the essentials of a contract were lacking in certain items of correspondence, *rei interventus* could not be used to complete the contract. In that case, there was a reference to the passage in *Gloag* already cited and also to one of the cases referred to by Gloag[2]. That case however was distinguished in the following manner by Lord Strachan[3]:

'Whatever reservations there may be about *Colquhoun's* case[4], it is obviously binding on me; and I would require to follow it if it were applicable to the present case. I have, however, come to the opinion that it is not applicable, for the reason that in the present case the necessary contractual basis in writing is absent. The passage which I have quoted from the judgment of Lord Justice-Clerk Inglis in *Colquhoun* proceeded on the basis that there was in writing an offer and an acceptance. The acceptance was conditional, but it is clear that Lord Justice-Clerk Inglis regarded the writings as containing the essentials of a contract. Similarly, Lord Cowan held that the correspondence which had passed contained all the essentialia of a Feu Contract . . . applying that test, I am of opinion that in the letters in the present case, the essentials of a contract are lacking . . . in my opinion, Colquhoun's case is not an authority for holding that in such circumstances, a contract may be completed by *rei interventus*.'

1 1953 SC 370.
2 *Colquhoun v Wilson's Trustees* (1860) 22 D 1035.
3 1953 SC 370 at 375.
4 *Colquhoun v Wilson's Trustees*, above.

3.35   If matters had rested with the *East Kilbride Development Corporation* case, one might be forgiven for thinking that Gloag's proposition that *rei interventus* could be used to complete a contract was fundamentally unsound and indeed had been discredited. However, in the case of *Errol v Walker*[1], the Second Division held that *rei interventus* could indeed complete a contract and further, that because *rei interventus* could be proved by parole evidence, proof of the contract by writ or oath was unnecessary. The case involved an action of declarator and removing where the defender averred that he had purchased leasehold property from the pursuer. He averred that he had delivered to the pursuer's solicitor a probative offer to purchase the leasehold, had been put in possession of the property, had paid instalments to account of the price in terms of the offer, and had to the pursuer's knowledge, carried out extensive improvements on the property. It was also averred that he had received no written acceptance. In coming to their decision to allow a proof that the actions were capable of constituting acceptance of the offer, the Inner House of the Court of Session relied heavily on the passage already cited from *Gloag*[2].

1 1966 SC 93.
2 *Contract* (2nd edn) pp 46–47.

3.36 The decision in *Erroll v Walker*[1] itself is extremely hard to reconcile with any previous authority apart from *Gloag* and has been the subject of criticism in articles and textbooks[2]. A reading of the judgments in the case certainly suggests that the three judges did not rely on the same authorities when arriving at their individual decisions and it is likely that in examining some of the cases they failed to appreciate that there were writings evidencing an agreement involved. It seems strange, in a case where there is an imperfectly constituted agreement to require the agreement to be proved by writ or oath and the *rei interventus* by parole, whereas where *rei interventus* is used to prove *consensus* the agreement itself can be proved by parole. There is no one who would question the closing remarks of the Lord Justice-Clerk when he stated 'I have not found this an easy case and I have found the authorities both confused and confusing'. It is respectfully submitted by the authors that *Errol v Walker* is wrongly decided. However, it is an authority which may be used in certain circumstances by aggrieved parties who wish to set up an agreement for the sale or purchase of heritable property in circumstances where there have been actings but no concluded agreement provable by writ or oath. Contracting parties and their legal representatives must therefore always be on their guard to prevent any actings on the part of one of the parties while the contract is still in the negotiation stage. In one very recent case[3] proof *habile modo* was allowed where a solicitor acting for both parties had issued a draft lease and alleged oral agreement followed by actings. It was indicated, however, that proof of any oral agreement would require to be by oath and the question of how the informal agreement could be proved was reserved until after the proof.

1 1966 SC 93.
2 A L Stewart (1966) 11 JLS 263; S C Smith *'Rei interventus* revisited' 1986 SLT (News) 137; Walker *Contract* para 13–36; *McBryde* para 27–44.
3 *Tomorrow's World v Burgess* 1992 GWD 29–1722.

3.37   In so far as homologation is concerned, there is clear authority for the proposition that it cannot be used as evidence of consent to complete an agreement[1].

1 *Law v Thomson* 1978 SC 343.

Scottish Law Commission proposals in relation to *rei interventus*

3.38   As has already been noted[1] the Scottish Law Commission Report on the Requirements of Writing proposes a new law of *rei interventus* and homologation. The question therefore arises as to how far these new proposals take on board the type of situation envisaged in *Errol v Walker*[2]. In fact the new proposals (clause 1.3 of the draft Bill and recommendation 6 of the Report) relate only to 'a contract obligation or trust' in circumstances where one of the parties has acted or refrained from acting 'in reliance on the contract obligation or trust'. Accordingly the new proposals would only apply in circumstances where there was an antecedent agreement. The new *rei interventus* could not be used in terms of these proposals to complete an unconcluded agreement. This does not of course mean that *Errol v Walker* would immediately become a dead letter. In point of fact, the report of the Scottish Law Commission probably accepted that *Errol v Walker* represented the law[3]. In any event, the report really dealt with the requirements of writing in relation to contracts and not personal bar or evidence. *Errol v Walker* is a decision where a contract was concluded by actings and not by writings, so presumably any new Bill would be so drawn in such a way as to leave other aspects of the law of personal bar, including that decision, untouched[4]. It may be that the Scottish Law Commission's view is that *Errol v Walker* is a good decision from an equitable point of view and that the modern trend of law reform is to prefer equity to certainty. It is the authors' view however that lack of certainty seldom brings equity.

1 Para 2.22 above.
2 1966 SC 93.
3 Para 5–12 of the Report on Requirements of Writing (Scot Law Com no 112).
4 See S C Smith *'Rei interventus* revisited' 1986 SLT (News) 137.

Alteration of missives

3.39 The term 'alteration' is often used in two distinct senses when applied to written contracts. In one sense, it refers to a physical alteration in the writing itself, where for example a word is deleted, a word is interlined or a word is typewritten on an erasure. In another sense it refers to a variation in the actual terms of the agreement committed to writing. It is beyond the scope of this work to deal in detail with the law relating to the alteration of writings in the first sense[1]. Suffice it to say that in so far as alterations are concerned, missives which are adopted as holograph are in the same position as attested deeds and the presumption is that any alterations or additions are deemed to have been made after the missives have been executed[2]. Alterations or additions which are not properly authenticated are treated as *pro non scripto*. In so far as erasures are concerned, if the words erased are not legible, it will be presumed they were of importance although a party cannot simply substitute any wording with a view to setting aside the deed[3]. The rules of construction are well set out by Professor Halliday[4] as follows:

(1) If the unauthenticated alteration or addition relates to words which are not of material importance, these words will be disregarded but the whole deed will not be invalid.

(2) If the alteration or addition is to words which are of material importance to only one part of the deed which is deemed to be separable, only that part of the deed will be invalid and the remainder of the deed will be effective[5].

(3) If the alteration or addition is to words which are essential to the validity of the whole deed, then the whole deed is invalid.

1 See *Halliday* vol I, para 3–24 ff.
2 *Kedder v Reid* (1840) 1 Rob App 183; *Boswell v Boswell* (1852) 14 D 378; *Munro v Butler Johnstone* (1868) 7 M 250 at 256.
3 *McDougall v McDougall* (1875) 2 R 814.
4 *Halliday* vol I, para 3–24.
5 *Abernethie v Forbes* (1885) 13 R 263 at 268, 269.

3.40 In so far as missives are concerned, these documents are, generally speaking, holograph rather than attested. If alterations are made to a material part of the missives, however, then their position in the appropriate clause of the missives should be clearly indicated by a caret and any additions or deletions should be sidescribed by the parties signing the missives. If the alterations are not material, then it is preferable to at least initial these alterations. It should be noted by practitioners, however, that an alteration to a material matter such as the price requires to be sidescribed and not simply initialled. The saving provision governing informalities of execution does not apply to holograph writings but only to deeds or writings which are subscribed by the grantor and bear to be attested by two witnesses[1]. In any event, that procedure relates purely to informalities of execution and not to alterations on the actual body of the documentation.

1 Conveyancing (Scotland) Act 1874, s 39.

Variation of missives

3.41 The other sense in which the term 'alteration' is used in relation to written contracts is where the parties decide to vary the written contract after it has been concluded. For the purposes of this work, we will use the term 'variation' when dealing with this type of alteration so that there is no confusion. Apart from the statutory provisions for rectification[1] it is a fundamental principle of Scots law that where a contract requires writings for its constitution, it is incompetent to alter the written contract by oral agreement and not only is parole evidence of the variation inadmissible, but reference to an oath is incompetent[2]. This is certainly the case where one of the parties disputes the oral agreement to vary. It may not be an absolute rule where the parties agree that the formal contract does not reflect the original conditions agreed[3]. This relaxation of course only applies where the parties agree that the contract is inaccurate. 'When both parties are agreed that the writing does not express the contract, and yet differ as to what the real contract is, then, unless evidence were admissible, there would be a complete impasse – no solution being possible[4].' Thus where a disponee admitted that the consideration actually paid was not the price stated in the disposition, the disponer was allowed to prove by extrinsic evidence that the disposition although *ex facie* absolute was truly in security[5]. The difficulties arise normally where one party to the missives does not agree that they have in fact been varied by an oral agreement. If the oral agreement to vary can be established by writ or oath or judicial admission, then *rei interventus* or homologation can be used to prove the variation and *rei interventus* or homologation can be proved *prout de jure*. What this really means is that there is a new agreement established according to the normal rules of *rei interventus*[6]. Where there is no actual oral agreement averred to vary the written missives, but there have been facts and circumstances which can only be explained on the assumption that the missives have been varied, there is some authority for the view that a case may be brought provided the actings are more important and substantial than those required for *rei interventus* or homologation[7].

1 Law Reform (Miscellaneous Provisions) (Scotland) Act 1985, s 8 and see para 3.42, above.
2 *Perdikou v Pattison* 1958 SLT 153; *Walker & Walker* paras 304 and 305.
3 *Halliday* vol II, para 15–01; *Grant's Trustees v Morrison* (1875) 2 R 377; *Grant v Mackenzie* (1899) 1 F 889.
4 *Grant v Mackenzie* above at 894; See Dickson *The Law of Evidence in Scotland* (3rd edn, 1887) para 1035; *Norval v Abbey* 1939 SC 724 at 730.
5 *Miller v Miller* (1905) 12 SLT 743
6 See para 2.06 ff, above
7 *Dickson* para 1029; Erskine *An Institute of the Law of Scotland* (1871) III, 2, 3 note (d); *Carron Co v Henderson's Trustees* (1896) 23 R 1042 at 1049; *Baillie v Fraser* (1853) 15 D 747 at 750; *Walker & Walker* para 307.

3.42 It is perhaps unlikely in the context of missives for the purchase and sale of domestic heritable property that the parties will by oral agreement or by their actings vary the concluded written missives but it is not impossible especially in relation to the date of entry. Clearly any such alteration should be effected by an exchange of formal letters otherwise the change will not be binding on the parties unless *rei interventus* or homologation can be proved. It should be noted, however, that there is a distinction between an averment that an already concluded and agreed missive has been subsequently varied and an averment that the actual written missive does not reflect the intention of the parties. When the statutory provisions for rectification are considered[1] this difference is crucial.

1 Law Reform (Miscellaneous Provisions) (Scotland) Act 1985, s 8.

Rectification of missives under statute

3.43 It is now competent under certain circumstances to vary the terms of a written contract by statute[1]. The provisions relate to the rectification of defectively expressed documents where the contract fails to give effect to the intention of the parties. Obviously if both parties agree that the missives or other contract do not accurately reflect their intention, it is open to the parties to conclude a written agreement amending the missives. Difficulties of course arise where one party wishes to rely on the terms of the written missives and the other seeks to have them rectified. It is in this type of situation that the statutory provisions come into play.

1 Law Reform (Miscellaneous Provisions) (Scotland) Act 1985, ss 8 and 9.

3.44 Before the court can make an order under section 8 of the Law Reform (Miscellaneous Provisions) (Scotland) Act 1985, it must be satisfied either that a document intended to express or give effect to an agreement fails to express accurately the common intention of the parties to the agreement at the date when it was made, or that a document intended to create, transfer, vary or renounce a right fails to express accurately the intention of the grantor of the document at the date when it was executed. Missives would fall into the first category of document being an agreement expressing the common intention of two parties. However, in terms of section 9 of the Act, the court cannot order rectification unless it is satisfied that no innocent third parties are adversely affected to a material extent by rectification. Third parties are unlikely to be affected in the case of missives. Such third parties can of course consent to the rectification if they wish[1]. As a general rule, rectification will take effect from the date of conclusion of the missives but the court does have a discretion to order rectification to have effect from a later date to protect the interest of an innocent third party[2].

1 Law Reform (Miscellaneous Provisions) (Scotland) Act 1985, s 9(1)(b).
2 Ibid, s 9(4).

3.45 For the purposes of rectification, the court is entitled to have regard to all relevant evidence whether written or oral[1]. Where an application is being made under the section, it is competent to register a notice of the application in the Register of Inhibitions and Adjudications specifying the names and designations of the parties to the application and the date when authority for service or citation was granted, and containing a description of the land to which the application relates[2].

1 Law Reform (Miscellaneous Provisions) (Scotland) Act 1985, s 8(2).
2 Ibid, s 8(7) and (8).

3.46 The statutory provisions outlined above are extremely useful in cases where there has been a genuine error in expression in the missives of which one party seeks to take advantage. Some practitioners are still unaware of the existence of the statutory provisions and cling to the old belief that once the missives are concluded in writing, there is nothing that can be done to rectify a mistake, except perhaps to bring an action of reduction on the grounds of error and intimate a circumstance to the professional indemnity insurers. Very often, however, the mere threat of an application under section 8 is enough to persuade the other contracting party to implement the original intention as opposed to what is written down. There are a number of decided cases on the section and it is useful to examine each of them in some detail.

3.47 The first case to deal with the rectification legislation was *Shaw v William Grant (Minerals) Ltd*[1]. This case came before Lord McCluskey in the Outer House. The case is important because Lord McCluskey laid down the matters on which the court has to be satisfied before it can order rectification. These are:

(1) That there is a document to be rectified.
(2) That the document was intended to express or give effect to an already existing agreement arrived at between two (or more) parties.
(3) That there was, when the document was executed, a pre-existing agreement – whether or not enforceable.
(4) That the agreement itself embodied and was an expression of one or more intentions common to (that is to say, shared by) the parties.
(5) That the intentions were actual (not deemed) intentions.
(6) That the agreement itself must have been reached at a definite point in time.

In the particular case his Lordship concluded that there were no sufficient and specific averments that any agreement had been reached prior to the execution of the formal document and that the pursuer's averments were irrelevant. The main point in relation to missives or any other contract to be rectified is that there must be a real and definite agreement pre-dating the defectively expressed document, not just a series of proposals or negotiations.

1 1989 SLT 121.

3.48 The second case to deal with the rectification provisions is *MAC Electrical and Heating Engineers Ltd v Calscot Electrical (Distributors) Ltd*[1]. This was a case brought to rectify a disposition following on missives because the plan attached to the disposition was incorrect. In many cases the disposition and missives will both be involved in this way or indeed may both require rectification. As a procedural matter, the action was defended on the grounds that the 1985 Act was not specifically mentioned in the pleadings. The Lord Ordinary ventured an opinion, however, that if facts and circumstances were relevantly averred to infer that the disposition did not express accurately the common intention of the parties, there was no need to mention the Act as such.

1 1989 SCLR 498.

3.49 The third case to deal with this matter is that of *Oliver v Gaughan*[1]. In that case missives were concluded for the sale and purchase of property by reference to a plan attached to the particulars of sale. When drafting the disposition, the purchasers in error included an additional piece of land which also belonged to the seller and which was not specifically reserved from the sale. In fairness, the purchasers thought that they had actually contracted to acquire the extra piece of ground in terms of the missives. The error in the disposition was not noticed by the seller's solicitors. When the purchaser occupied and acted as owner of the additional piece of the land, the seller sought to rectify the disposition in terms of section 8(1)(a) of the Act. Lord MacLean in the Outer House granted the order for rectification. He held that the parties' conflicting intentions were not relevant to the proper construction of the missives. The court held that it was the parties' common intention only to sell and buy the land shown on the plan attached to the particulars and the petitioner had discharged the onus of proof to leave no fair and reasonable doubt that the disposition did not reflect the agreement reached between the parties. In this case the intention of the parties was partly construed from the missives and the extrinsic evidence of intention.

1 1990 GWD 22-247.

3.50 It appears that the scope of this action and the right to require rectification is wide. In *Bank of Scotland v Graham*[1] it was held that a petition by a heritable creditor to correct a defectively executed standard security was relevant. The deed had been signed by the proprietors of the property who were also designed as the debtors under the personal obligation. Unfortunately the security had been signed once only, in the place appropriate for the signature of the debtors, and the place where the proprietor should have signed was left blank. The trustee in bankruptcy of the proprietors argued that the security was invalid and could not be rectified because the rectification proposed was not correction of a defectively expressed document but the creation of a new right. These arguments were, however, repelled. If, therefore, one had a set of missives where the schedule had not been signed, or perhaps a plan or other annexation had not been signed, then it would look as though rectification would be competent assuming it could be proved that the parties had actually agreed to include such a schedule or plan.

1 1991 SLT (Notes) 879, 1992 SLT 253.

3.51 An example of a case dealing with rectification in relation to missives and a disposition is the case of *Angus v Bryden*[1]. In that case the petitioner raised an action seeking rectification of missives and the disposition relating to the sale of certain fishings. The petitioner owned the exclusive right to river fishings pertaining to his land which he held on one title along with fishings on another stretch of the same river over land owned by a third party and further, some sea fishings at the mouth of the river. The petitioner averred that he agreed informally with the purchaser to sell him the river fishings. The purchaser's solicitors submitted an offer and the petitioner's solicitors sent out a qualified acceptance. There then followed a further formal letter from the purchaser's solicitors and a letter from the petitioner's solicitors concluding the bargain. The petitioner then executed a disposition which granted both the sea fishings and the river fishings and this was recorded. The petitioner averred that neither the offer nor the qualified acceptance had been intended to include the sea fishings. The purchaser averred that he had intended to offer to buy the sea fishings and that the qualified acceptance extended to them as well. The petitioner and seller argued that even if the missives did include the sea fishings, on receipt of the qualified acceptance, the purchaser's solicitors had known that any reference to sea fishings had been included in error. The petitioner further argued that the purchaser had not intended to offer for the sea fishings and had not been in good faith because they had then sent a formal acceptance in the full knowledge of the unintentional error. The court granted a declarator and the case was put out by order for the parties to consider how rectification was to proceed. The formal offer for the fishings described the subjects by reference to the description in the seller's title but did not specifically mention sea fishings which were a separate hereditament in that title. Lord Cameron in the Outer House held that the implication was that the offer referred only to the river fishings. The qualified acceptance described the subjects by general reference to the seller's title but that had to be read subject to the preceding phrase 'certain fishing rights in the river'.

1 1992 SLT 884.

3.52 A good example of a case involving plans is *George Thompson (Services) Ltd v Moore*[1]. In that case the seller concluded missives with the purchaser for the sale of certain estate lands. The particulars of sale contained a plan showing several delineated areas. The sale particulars and the missives themselves expressly excluded the sale particulars from constituting part of the offer or contract. The missives themselves did not mention one of the delineated areas which were held by the seller on a separate title. The disposition followed the missives and again excluded the same delineated area. The purchaser petitioned the court to rectify both the missives and the disposition averring certain facts inferring the existence of a prior common intention to include all the delineated areas on the plan attached to the particulars. The purchaser averred that prior to conclusion of missives the seller had shown him over the whole estate including the excluded area and that after the sale the purchaser had occupied and farmed the excluded area. The seller had left the area and never attempted to exercise any rights of ownership over the excluded area. The purchaser argued that to the extent that the missives and the disposition were at variance with the previously expressed common intention, they should be rectified. The seller, however, argued that the purchaser had to aver the existence of an actual antecedent agreement whether written or verbal showing a common intention and relied heavily on the observations of Lord McCluskey in *Shaw v William Grant (Minerals) Ltd*[2]. The court dismissed the petition and held that for the purposes of section 8(1)(a) there must be an earlier agreement from which a common intention could be discerned and that the purchaser had failed to aver such an agreement.

1 1992 GWD 3–144.
2 1989 SLT 121.

3.53 It is clear from the case law and the observations of Lord McCluskey in *Shaw v William Grant (Minerals) Ltd*[1] in particular, that to successfully petition for rectification, it is necessary to aver and thereafter prove an agreement which predates the missives or other document and which discloses a common intention which is different from the intention of the parties as expressed in the missives, disposition or other documentation. Many of the cases which have been cited above were, of course, dealt with on the basis of relevancy. The averments of prior agreement and common intention would require to go to proof. The standard of proof appears to be on the balance of probabilities[2].

1 1989 SLT 121.
2 See *Rehman v Ahmad* 1992 GWD 31–1800.

CHAPTER 4

Content of missives

Introduction

4.01 When the authors graduated and entered that lowly paid but elite group known as law apprentices, domestic house purchase was very much the commercial backbone of many legal firms. At that time offers consisted of perhaps six to ten clauses and a *de plano* acceptance was common. There is no doubt that the bulk of the work carried out in a domestic transaction was proper conveyancing as opposed to the adjustment of the missives as a contract. Land registration was introduced as a concept in 1979 and has been creeping its way across Scotland since 1981. As titles become registered and transactions involve dealings with registered interests as opposed to first registration applications there is no doubt that the actual conveyancing in the proper sense of that word becomes easier and quicker. When dealing with a registered title a disposition need only refer to the title number and this takes the place of a full particular description or description by reference and the reference to burdens. The same title number can be used in security documents. Surprisingly, however, as the conveyancing side of a domestic transaction becomes less complicated the contractual side of the transaction becomes more complicated. There are those who even fear that the Scottish system of house purchase will evolve to the state where it is similar to the English system, where it takes an eternity to adjust the actual contract and unscrupulous purchasers and sellers take advantage of this elongated process to withdraw or seek an increase in the price. There can be no doubt that missives have become more complicated. What is certain, however, is that this is not the fault of the legal profession. Missives have become more complicated because of many extraneous factors, none of which are really directly related to pure conveyancing. The trail probably starts with certificates in relation to roads, footpaths and sewers, then meanders its way through property enquiry certificates to the provision of NHBC agreements and certificates or letters from architects, through the provision of warrants, planning permission and completion certificates. Thence the profession is diverted into the plumbing trade to examine various central heating systems of different age and design only to be brought back suddenly to the law in relation to matrimonial homes and transfer of property orders. Latterly, we find ourselves up against serious environmental issues with the passing of the Environmental Protection Act 1990.

4.02 It is with hindsight perhaps unfortunate that the legal profession should have sought to deal with so many diverse matters in the context of the purchase and sale of domestic heritable property. The Scottish lawyer has, of course, always been regarded as an all-round man of affairs and it has, no doubt, been the desire to provide the ordinary domestic conveyancing client with the best all-round service which has brought about the current state of affairs in relation to missives as a contract. It is not the purpose of this book to lay down an ideal set of conditions to be included in a modern set of missives and, indeed, there is a very good argument for tailoring the missives to suit each individual property[1]. Commercial considerations, however, dictate that most solicitors have standard forms of offer for domestic property. Qualified acceptances, however, can now sometimes run to as many clauses as the offer. This tendency to send out a complicated offer and then to receive an equally-complicated qualified acceptance has led to some criticism of the profession. With this in mind the Law Society of Scotland set up a working party to see if some standard clauses could be set down. It is fair to say that the Law Society of Scotland has always shied clear of setting down precedents or giving legal advice. There was, however, considerable demand from the profession and from other sources to attempt to standardise missives. Accordingly, following upon the report of the working party, the Law Society promulgated a Deed of Declaration with a style offer and standard clauses, the final version of which was issued in April 1992. Some firms use the standard clauses as the basis of their offer but others do not. Even where the standard clauses are used they are generally met with a qualified acceptance. Accordingly it cannot be said that at the present time the standard clauses have solved the problem of the ever-growing missive. It is fair to state, however, that the standard clauses issued by the Law Society do contain basic terms which are likely to be found in one shape or form in an offer for the purchase of domestic heritable property. Accordingly, the authors in dealing with the content of missives have decided to use these standard clauses as the basis for the discussion.

1 In relation to taking instructions and the framing and submission of offers see 'Keeping the client informed – an exercise in self-preservation' by Dr Robert Rennie, Law Society General Conveyancing PQLE Course, November 1990.

4.03 Before embarking on the detailed consideration of the clauses, it is worth drawing attention to the guideline which precedes the clauses as it contains useful advice which, if followed, should make the conclusion of bargains a quicker process. We realise, of course, that not all of the guidelines may be applicable in every case, but the advice is worth heeding, where possible. The guideline is in the following terms:

'Delays in the conclusion of missives are caused not only by the length and complexity of offers, but not infrequently by reason of the seller's solicitor having insufficient information in his possession to enable him to deal speedily with offers when they are received. The Council therefore accepted the advice of the Working Party which prepared the original and revised versions of the Deed of Declaration and Standard Clauses that the Council should promulgate a series of simple guidelines to be followed by the selling solicitor as soon as he is aware that his client proposed to sell his house. The Working Party was, of course, acutely aware that in many cases the solicitor is not informed about the forthcoming sale which may be handled by an estate agent or by the client himself and in these circumstances there is little or nothing that the solicitor can do to prepare himself in advance if he is suddenly presented with an offer and instructed to accept it. The Council therefore perceives a need for education of the public to the effect of per-suading sellers to advise their solicitors whenever they propose to sell their houses, whether or not the solicitor is instructed to market the property on his client's behalf. The Council nonetheless urges all solicitors who have knowledge of a prospective sale to abide by the Guidelines which the Council perceives must considerably assist in speeding up the conclusion of missives.'

The recommendations in the guidelines are not intended to erode, let alone negate, the principle of *caveat emptor*, but rather are designed to ensure that the seller's solicitor provides the purchaser's solicitor with as much information about the property as possible at the outset of the transaction, and it is anticipated that this will help to shorten the time gap between notification that a particular offer is acceptable and conclusion of missives. The revised guideline is as follows:

(1) Solicitors should treat the matter of conclusion of missives as a priority and should, wherever possible, attempt to meet stipu-lated deadlines.

(2) Whenever a solicitor is aware that his client intends to sell his house the solicitor should obtain the title deeds, familiarise or re-familiarise himself with their terms, and, where appropriate, obtain extracts or quick copies of any missing deeds which a purchasing solicitor may reasonably require to examine.

(3) A selling solicitor should obtain property enquiry certificates at his client's expense as soon as he is aware that the property is to be sold.

(4) On receipt of an acceptable offer a selling solicitor should indentify from the title deeds and other information in his possession how many of the standard clauses in the offer can be accepted without qualification, and the practice of sending the title deeds to the purchaser's solicitor with a qualified acceptance, allowing the latter a period of time within which to satisfy himself as to the terms of the titles, should be discouraged.

(5) A selling solicitor should check and if necessary enquire of his client at the earliest possible stage if there are any matters which might affect a purchaser's decision to buy the house. Examples of such matters are:

  (a) Any alterations which have been carried out to the property within the preceding ten years or such other period as is found in offers in your locality. If there have been any such alterations the solicitor should ascertain whether or not all requisite local authority permissions and, where appropriate, completion certificates, have been obtained.

  (b) Any periodical payments affecting the property such as annual factoring charges.

  (c) If the house is a top flat in a tenement, whether or not liability for maintenance of the roof has been apportioned to all the flats in the tenement or if the client has been solely liable for payment for roof repairs.

  (d) Whether or not the client has any information regarding obligations for maintenance of the property and in particular common amenity areas etc.

  (e) Whether or not there have been any disputes in relation to the use of the property or any adjoining or neighbouring property.

  (f) Whether or not the client has knowledge of any outstanding local authority notices requiring repairs to the property.

  (g) The existence of any guarantees which run with the house against recurrence of wood rot or woodworm infestation.

  (h) The existence of and the level of contribution required in relation to the maintenance of joint facilities such as private access roads, amenity areas etc.

  (i) Whether or not any other party has a right to occupy the property such as a non-entitled spouse or co-habitee, or a tenant.

  (j) Whether or not any of the services (eg water or drainage) is private and, if so, information that the continued existence of these services has been properly constituted in the title deeds.

  (k) Full details of all fittings and fixtures and moveable items which are to be sold along with the property and if they are to be included in the sale price or the subject of a separate offer.

(l) Whether there are any servitudes or wayleave rights affecting the subjects which should be drawn to the attention of the purchaser.

4.04 All of these matters are likely to arise in most transactions and so if the titles and the other pieces of information such as property enquiry certificates can be obtained before conclusion of missives and ideally prior to the subjects being put on the market, this should make life for both parties and their solicitors easier.

One other preliminary matter which is worth mentioning before we deal with the clauses is that the standard missive clauses in common with many other styles of offer deal with some matters which are found in qualified acceptances rather than the offer. For example, it is common for the purchaser to insert a clause dealing with delays in settlement in the hope that it will be accepted without qualification or only minor qualification. In this way the purchaser's solicitor 'calls the tune' by using his or her own style.

4.05 The standard clauses are set out in three sections (parts A, B and C) and are preceded by a short style offer. The initial intention was that clauses contained in part A would be accepted by sellers without qualification as core clauses, that the clauses contained in part B should apply unless the parties had expressly contracted out or agreed to vary the same, and that clauses contained in part C should be adopted, altered or omitted in accordance with the wishes of the parties. As a strictly legal matter of course the conditions do not have the force of law and all of them can be qualified at will. Professor Halliday also deals with the content of missives[1] and he provides various styles of offers for properties ranging from a semi-detached villa to commercial properties and farms[2].

1 Halliday *Conveyancing Law and Practice in Scotland* vol II, para 15–22 ff.
2 *Halliday* vol II, para 15–136 ff.

The style offer

4.06 The style offer contained in The Law Society's Deed of Declaration of Conditions is in the following terms:

'On behalf of and as instructed by our client (design) . . . .
. . . .
("the purchaser") we hereby offer to purchase from your client ("the seller") insert postal address of house, situation in building etc ("the subjects of sale")
. . . .
at a price of . . . . The date of entry shall be . . . .

The Law Society of Scotland's Standard Clauses as registered in the Books of Council and Session on the Third day of April, Nineteen Hundred and Ninety Two shall apply to and are incorporated in this Offer, but subject to the qualifications detailed in the Schedule annexed and subscribed as relative hereto.

The purchase price shall include the following moveable items, namely . . . .

This offer, unless sooner withdrawn, will remain open for acceptance by letter reaching us not later than . . . .,

The style offer provides for the normal variable items for any purchase, namely, the name and address of the client, an adequate description of the property, the price, the date of entry, a list of any moveable items included in the price and a time limit. It is important, obviously, to name and design your client and, indeed, in many cases a qualified acceptance will contain a clause requiring the purchaser's address and a forwarding address if these do not appear in the offer. It is also important, obviously, to insert a proper postal address of the property and if the property is a flat to describe its situation within the building of which it forms part (eg the flatted dwellinghouse known as 59c McDonald Road, Glasgow being the northmost house on the third floor above the ground floor of the tenement of dwellinghouses at 57 to 60 McDonald Road aforesaid). It is tempting when dealing with flatted properties to describe them briefly as one up, right or two up, left. This can, however, be confusing where there are four flats on one landing and where the stairways themselves turn inside the building. Any outbuildings such as garages, greenhouses, sheds or huts should be specifically mentioned in the descriptive section of the offer. In some offers for flatted property it would be normal to include here a list of the common rights which the purchaser expects to obtain but provision is made for this in clause B5 of the standard clauses. Where, however, specific common rights are important a prudent solicitor may wish to include more detail in the offer[1]. In so far as the ground pertaining to the subjects is concerned it may be sufficient in the case of ordinary residential property with an enclosed garden to simply add the words 'with the garden or other ground pertaining thereto'. In older properties, however, where the boundaries are uncertain, or where the property is a new plot or first split-off or where it is known in advance that it is particularly important to a purchaser that he obtain a certain area of ground with the house it is appropriate to describe the ground with reference to a surface area and to attach a plan, possibly based on the ordnance survey, to the offer. In the event that the seller is not willing to pay the cost of a plan the purchaser should still be urged by his or her solicitor to obtain one even at the purchaser's expense. The style offer set out by the Law Society makes no mention of pertinents nor are these stated to be included in the purchase in any of the standard clauses. It can sometimes be useful to include pertinents. The term may extend what is purchased to include rights which have been omitted *per incuriam*[2]. Professor Halliday is clear that pertinents should be included in any offer[3]. The price should be clear and specific although a definitive figure need not be inserted in the missives, provided the offer contains a definite method of ascertaining the price[4]. Normally, a specific price is stated, and an offer which is '£X more than the highest offer received' should not be accepted, because all offers should be confidential and hence one should not be used as a basis for another. If the price is to be apportioned between moveables and heritage such apportionment should be stated expressly, but the apportionment should be reasonable[5]. The date of entry should be a definite date or at least be subject to a definite end date, eg 'such date as may be mutually agreed but not later than . . .' It should be remembered that if the parties subsequently agree to alter the date this should be done by a formal exchange of letters. In so far as moveable items are concerned obvious items such as carpets, curtains, kitchen equipment, fires, light fittings and blinds should be included. There is a very useful list of fittings and fixtures in Halliday's *Conveyancing Law and Practice in Scotland*[6]. It is safer to include a central heating system in the list of moveable items because there is some doubt as to whether radiators are heritable or moveable. As a general rule it is safer to include things which may be heritable rather than exclude them in case they turn out to be moveable. In so far as the time limit is concerned, words like 'immediate acceptance' should be avoided. A particular day and a particular time in that day should be set down[7].

1 See *Halliday* vol II, paras 15–42 and 15–43.
2 *Cooper's Trustees v Stark's Trustees* (1898) 25 R 1160; *Meacher v Blair-Oliphant* 1913 SC 417.
3 *Halliday* vol II, paras 15–41, 18–38 and 18–39.
4 *Earl of Selkirk v Nasmith* (1778) M 627; Gloag *The Law of Contract* (2nd edn, 1929) p 40.
5 DC Coull 'A stamp duty warning for conveyancers' (1987) 32 JLSS 389.
6 Vol II, para 15–37.
7 As to time limits in general see para 3.14 above.

The standard clauses

4.07 As has already been stated the standard clauses are laid out in three sections. The clauses contained in part A are the ones which are generally regarded to be common to all transactions and unlikely to be qualified. The clauses in part B may be qualified depending on circumstances and the ones in part C are regarded as optional depending on the wishes of the parties and the requirements of the particular transaction. It is appropriate to deal with each part separately.

PART A

Clause A1 – Rights of vacant possession and absence of occupancy rights

4.08 'The date of entry shall be as specified in the offer and shall be the date when entry with vacant possession shall be given to the whole subjects of sale in exchange for payment of the purchase price. At that date there will be no subsisting occupancy rights of a non-entitled spouse in terms of the Matrimonial Homes (Family Protection) (Scotland) Act 1981, as amended, and the seller will deliver appropriate evidence to that effect on or before the date of entry. In addition the seller warrants that as at the date of entry (or the date of settlement, whichever is the later) the subjects of sale will not be affected by any court order in terms of the Family Law (Scotland) Act 1985 or any amendments thereto.'

While it has been decided that it is not essential to specify a date of entry in missives[1] it is almost invariable practice to do so. Sometimes, however, the date of entry is not specified with absolute clarity. For example, an offer may provide 'The date of entry shall be 31 July 199– or such other date as may be agreed between the parties.' The obvious question is 'What if the parties fail to agree?' This happened in *Sloans Dairies Ltd v Glasgow Corporation*[2] where the property was burned down before the parties could agree on a date of entry and the issue which arose was where the risk fell. This can be avoided by providing 'The date of entry shall be 31 July 199–, or such other date as the parties shall agree, but, in any event, it shall be not later than 31 August 199–'.

1 See *Gordon District Council v Wimpey Homes Ltd* 1988 SLT 141 and authorities reviewed therein.
2 1977 SC 223.

4.09 What does 'date of entry' mean? It may seem odd to pose the question, but it can mean the actual date provided for in the missives whether entry is taken or the physical date entry is given. The date in the missives can come and go without the transaction being settled. The purchaser may, nevertheless, be given entry at a different date in exchange for a deposit with interest on the balance and that could also be described as 'the date of entry'. If the transaction is finally settled at yet another date, that could be the date of entry, because at that point, the purchaser is in a position to acquire a real right to the subjects, which, prior thereto, he could not[1]. If the date of entry is to be changed by agreement, it is undoubtedly best to record this in a formal amendment to the missives, and, in the situation in which the date of entry comes and goes without settlement, the seller, or the purchaser, should ensure that the party in default, if there is one, appreciates that the agreed date of entry has now passed and that any penalty or interest clause in the missives now applies.

1 *Gibson and Hunter Home Designs Ltd* 1976 SC 23.

4.10 At entry, the purchaser will usually require vacant possession, without occupancy rights and free of any property transfer order. The standard clauses provide for this by clause A1.

There are three points to consider in this provision: (a) vacant possession; (b) the Matrimonial Homes (Family Protection) (Scotland) Act 1981; and (c) the Family Law (Scotland) Act 1985.

(a) *Vacant possession*

4.11 If an offer specifies only that entry will be given that does not imply vacant possession. In *Lothian & Border Farmers Ltd v McCutcheon*[1] the pursuers purchased *inter alia* a small house from the defender. After settlement, they discovered that the house had been let and they raised an action, claiming under the warrandice clause in the disposition, which was in the usual form: 'And I grant warrandice'. The action failed and in the course of his judgment, Lord Birnam said that a lease was one of the ways by which the owner of a property could get a return on his investment and he said, 'The view which I have expressed involves no difficulty or hardship in the purchasers of property, for where vacant possession is to be given this is nearly always stipulated for in the missives of sale[2]'. As it is not unknown for domestic property to be leased, eg to students, it is essential for the purchaser to specify for vacant possession, if that is what is wanted.

1 1952 SLT 450.
2 1952 SLT 450 at 451.

(b) *No occupancy rights*

4.12 The intricacies of the Matrimonial Homes (Family Protection) (Scotland) Act 1981 are, fortunately, outwith our remit[1], but, as conveyancers know, a non-entitled spouse has occupancy rights implied by law and there cannot be any dealing with the subjects which will defeat these rights unless the person in right of them either consents or renounces the rights, or they are dispensed with by the court, or they have prescribed[2]. If the subjects of sale are not a matrimonial home in which a spouse of the seller has occupancy rights, as where the seller is a separated person with a spouse living elsewhere, the seller should produce an affidavit to that effect. The requirements of the Act apply not only to the current transaction, and so the purchaser will require to be satisfied about previous transactions within the previous five years in respect of which such rights might still subsist. The usual type of transaction is a sale, or the granting of a standard security. If the evidence is not available, it is prudent to require the seller to obtain an indemnity against the existence of a spouse who may choose to exercise such a right.

1 See Nichols & Meston *The Matrimonial Homes (Family Protection) (Scotland) Act 1981* (2nd edn), C B Miller, 'The Matrimonial Homes Act' Lecture for Law Society of Scotland PQLE General Conveyancing Course, April 1988; George Gretton 'The Matrimonial Homes Act' Lecture for Law Society of Scotland PQLE General Conveyancing Course, November 1989.
2 The Matrimonial Homes (Family Protection) (Scotland) Act 1981, ss 6–7.

(c) *The 1985 Act*

4.13 Under the Family Law (Scotland) Act 1985 a court may order the transfer of property from one spouse to another[1]. The court order does not have the effect of transferring the title but, equally, there is no provision for recording the decree in either the Property Register or the Personal Registers which would make the existence of the order public and thus put any purchaser on notice[2]. Thus the prudent purchaser will require the seller to warrant that there is no such order. Obviously a warranty from a dishonest seller is worthless.

1 Section 8.
2 DJ Cusine 'Property transfer orders; some conveyancing imponderables' (1990) 35 JLS 52; EM Clive 'Property transfer orders' (1990) 35 JLS 118.

Clause A2 – Mineral reservations

4.14 'The minerals are included in the purchase price in so far as the seller has right thereto.'

This clause is a very straightforward clause which simply indicates that the minerals may be excluded from the title. It should really be read together with clause B4[1]. If clause A2 is not included then it is assumed that the whole of the subjects *a coelo usque ad centrum* are included in the sale[2]. The bare standard clause may well be inadequate in certain circumstances. In certain areas of Scotland, such as Lanarkshire and West Lothian, and for some reason in certain parts of Ayrshire, there are mineral reservation clauses which contain power to enter the surface. Clearly, a power of this nature would render a title unmarketable[3]. When acting for a purchaser, therefore, it is normal to stipulate that although the minerals may be reserved the reservation clause contains adequate provision for compensation for any surface damage and does not contain a right to enter the surface or carry out surface operations. Clause B4 contains such a provision[4]. When acting for a seller in these areas it will be necessary in some cases to qualify the mineral reservation clause contained in the offer (whether clause A2 or A2 and B4) to the effect that the purchaser will be bound to accept the terms of the mineral reservation clause as contained in the title whether or not compensation is payable for surface damage. The matter then may become a question of negotiation between the purchaser and seller depending on the terms of the particular clause and the eagerness of the parties to contract. In the experience of the authors the practice has developed along the following lines:

(1) All solicitors will accept a mineral reservation clause where there are no rights to enter the surface or carry out surface operations and where compensation is payable for surface damage.

(2) Most solicitors (especially those who themselves practice in old mineral areas) will accept a mineral reservation clause even where there is no compensation payable for surface damage, provided there is no right to enter the surface and no evidence to suggest recent mining operations.

(3) There can be difficulty in pursuading purchasers' solicitors to accept a mineral reservation clause which contains powers to carry out surface operations and resume parts of the surface even where compensation is payable for such resumption.

In some cases, of course, the matter can be easily resolved by approaching the superior or other party owning the minerals and asking for either a conveyance of the minerals or a discharge of any rights to enter the surface. In other cases where the party owning the minerals is not prepared to grant such a discharge it may be possible to obtain a letter confirming that there is no present intention to work the minerals. Practical considerations also weigh heavily in deciding whether or not to accept the terms of a particular clause and one must also bear in mind that in the case of coal and minerals worked with coal there are statutory protections and various rights to have subsidence damage rectified or claim compensation in respect of workings by the British Coal Corporation or their statutory predecessor the National Coal Board[5]. The authors offer the following practical suggestions:

(a) It is not safe, where acting for purchaser or seller, to rely on a clause 'that the minerals are included only in so far as the seller has right thereto'. If acting for a purchaser it is important at least to stipulate that the mineral reservation clause will not contain a right to enter the surface. It is also advisable as a first step to stipulate that there will be compensation for surface damage[6]. If acting for a seller, the particular type of mineral reservation clause contained in the title should be disclosed in the qualified acceptance and the purchaser should be invited to accept it.

(b) If for practical reasons a title is to be accepted which contains an onerous reservation clause then the purchaser's solicitor should consider whether it is necessary to take specific instructions from the purchaser and his lender especially if rights to enter the surface are involved.

(c) If detailed instructions are deemed necessary then these instructions should be obtained in writing.

(d) The purchasing solicitor should make himself aware of the character of the surrounding area and consider whether as a practical proposition mining is an active industry or simply a historical fact.

(e) The assessment of the practical risks can be greatly aided by referring to mineral reports available from British Coal or other mineral surveyors. There are many purchasers who will be terrified by the terms of a mineral reservation clause if boldly set out by their solicitor but whose fears can be assuaged by a mineral report indicating that no further workings are likely and that all subsidence is likely to have ceased.

(f) The risk of damage can sometimes be covered by an indemnity policy.

(g) In many cases the superiors or the owners of the minerals are prepared to convey the minerals or at least discharge surface rights.

(h) Even where a conveyance of minerals or discharge of surface rights cannot be obtained most superiors or minerals owners are prepared to confirm that they have no present intention of working the minerals or exercising the surface rights.

There have been attempts to promulgate law reform in relation to mineral reservation clauses by the Law Society of Scotland. A draft clause was proposed for the most recent Law Reform (Miscellaneous Provisions) Bill[7] which would have had the effect of making private mineral owners pay compensation no matter what was contained in the mineral reservation clause. Unfortunately the government of the day had other ideas for that particular Bill and this genuine law reform was, along with many others of merit, jettisoned. The Scottish Law

Commission will be considering mineral reservation clauses as part of its overall review of property law in Scotland.[8] It should be noted that the fact that a land certificate makes no mention of a reservation of minerals does not necessarily mean that the minerals are included. Only where the land certificate specifically includes minerals can the practitioner be sure. It is unusual for the Keeper to grant full indemnity for titles to minerals.

1 See para 4.32 below.
2 *Whyte v Lee* (1879) 6 R 699; *Todds v McCarroll* 1917 2 SLT 127; *Campbell v McCutcheon* 1963 SC 505.
3 See the comments of the Lord President in *Todd v McCarroll* above at 128 where he states that the purchaser is entitled to some sort of assurance that the property will continue to exist.
4 See para 4.32 below.
5 Coal Mining (Subsidence) Act 1991.
6 As in standard clause B4.
7 Now the Law Reform (Miscellaneous Provisions) (Scotland) Act 1990.
8 For further material on mineral rights and reservation clauses see Rennie 'Non oil-related minerals and reservation clauses' Law Society PQLE General Conveyancing Course, April 1988; Rennie, Minerals Seminar, University of Glasgow Legal Education Service, April 1992; Rennie 'Compensation rights for subsidence damage' lecture for University of Strathclyde, Centre for Professional Legal Studies, October 1992.

Clause A3 – Ground burdens

4.15 'The ground burdens, if allocated, will be redeemed at the expense of the seller in terms of the Land Tenure Reform (Scotland) Act 1974 or any amendments thereto and evidence of redemption will be delivered within one month of settlement.'

It is theoretically unnecessary to have such a clause in missives, but it is invariably found. It requires the seller to redeem any allocated feuduty or ground annual or other pecuniary ground burdens affecting the property. Under the Land Tenure Reform (Scotland) Act 1974[1] the payments which are covered are feuduty (including an unallocated cumulo feuduty, or part of a cumulo feuduty which has been allocated), and also ground annuals (whether allocated or not), skat and other perpetual periodic payments, but excluding teind, stipend or standard charge. Although this clause states the obligation expressly, the seller is obliged by law to redeem the periodic payments just referred to. Many such burdens will have been redeemed and so the seller should be able to produce a redemption receipt, or a duplicate, with the titles. This can cause some difficulties where the feuduty may have been redeemed, but it is not known to whom, because many superiors are untraceable; their only interest in the land having been the payment of feuduty. It may therefore be difficult to obtain a duplicate redemption receipt. If the feuduty has not been redeemed, the seller will be required to produce evidence of redemption within one month of the date of settlement. This matter may be added to any letter of obligation to be granted at settlement. The obligation is to redeem only allocated burdens, but there is a mechanism for allocating such burdens if previously unallocated, or only apportioned.[1] The standard clauses impose an obligation to do this on the seller in clause B2: 'There will be no pecuniary burdens affecting the subjects of sale after settlement . . .' Under the pre-1974 law a purchaser could resile if the feuduty turned out to be an unallocated portion of a *cumulo* where the missives provided that the feuduty was a fixed allocated amount[2]. It should be noted that tack duties under long leases cannot be redeemed legally in terms of the redemption legislation.

1 Section 4(7).
2 *Bremner v Dick* 1911 SC 887; *Morrison v Gray* 1932 SC 712.

Clauses A4 and A5 – Maintenance, condition and existence of subjects of sale

4.16 'The seller will maintain the subjects of sale in their present condition (fair wear and tear excepted) until the purchase price is paid or the purchaser takes possession, whichever date is the earlier. In the event of the subjects being destroyed or materially damaged prior to that date either party shall be entitled but not obliged to resile from the contract to follow hereon without penalty and without prejudice to any entitlement to claim damages from the other party.' (Clause A4)

'The risk of damage to or destruction of the subjects of sale will remain with the seller until the purchase price is paid or the purchaser takes possession, whichever is the earlier.' (Clause A5)

In terms of clause A4 if the seller is to remain in possession until the date of entry he or she will be required to ensure that at that date the subjects are in substantially the same condition as they were at the time of the offer. In most cases, a seller will be willing to accept this. Allied to that provision is a declaration that the risk will pass to the purchaser at the same date.

4.17 At common law, risk in a contract of sale, whether for heritage or moveables, passed at the time of conclusion of the contract. The position in relation to the sale of goods was altered by the Sale of Goods Act 1893[1], but the position in relation to heritage remains unaltered as is illustrated by *Sloans Dairies Ltd v Glasgow Corporation*[2]. In that case, Sloans had agreed to sell property to the defenders at a date of entry to be agreed between them. A date was never fixed and the property was damaged by fire. The court held that the risk had passed at the date of the conclusion of missives and so the Corporation were not entitled to have the purchase price reduced to take account of the damage caused. The only exception to the common law rule was where the damage or destruction had been caused by the negligence of the seller.[3] The practice in most cases has been to provide that the risk will remain with the seller until the date of payment or until possession is taken. That will become the law if the Scottish Law Commission's proposals are implemented[4].

In cases like *Sloans Dairies*, when the risk passed to the purchaser on conclusion of the bargain, it might have been possible for his interest as 'purchaser price unpaid' to be noted on the seller's insurance policy. However, this became impracticable where the seller's insurance was part of an institutional lender's block insurance policy. If the risk is to remain with the seller until the date of entry, there may be some duplication of insurance cover, but that is a small price to pay for the sensible provision that the risk should remain with the person in possession.

As has already been said, in most cases the seller will be willing to accept the position both in relation to maintenance and also the passing of risk. In some instances, however, this will not be acceptable. The most common instance is where the subjects are being sold by a heritable creditor who will never have been in *de facto* possession. A heritable creditor will frequently be selling subjects which have been without an occupant for some time, and because there will not be an occupant until the date of the purchaser's entry, the heritable creditor will not undertake to maintain the subjects in their existing condition until entry, because they could be the target of vandals in the interval. Furthermore, the heritable creditor may also expect the purchaser to assume the risk of damage on conclusion of missives for the same reason. The implications for the purchaser are clear. It will be essential for the purchaser's interest in the subjects to be insured at the time of conclusion of the bargain as 'purchaser price unpaid'. In some solicitors' firms, blanket insurance cover exists for clients who are purchasing properties, but whether that cover exists or not, the purchaser's interest must be insured. In most instances the insurance position after entry will be dictated by the purchaser's heritable creditor, but if not, it will be essential to obtain some permanent cover for the subjects.

In the clause quoted above, as in most missives, should the subjects not be in the condition at entry as they were at the time of concluding the contract, either party may resile. If the subjects are destroyed or become a constructive total loss the contract would in any event be frustrated at common law and either party could resile[5]. The fact that one of the parties has been negligent does not automatically rule out the operation of the doctrine of frustration[6], nor does a breach of contract[7]. The clause not only reverses the common law position but is wider in that material damage which is provided for in the clause might not amount to frustration at common law, unless the damage was so extensive that the subjects could no longer be used as a dwelling-house. The clause quoted above does not make any reference to either fault or breach, but it does not preclude any argument on these matters, as the last part of the clause makes clear, at least in relation to breach. One reason why it is desirable to allow both parties to resile is the possibility that the seller's insurance may be sufficient to allow him to build another house on the subjects, which would not be an option if only the purchaser could resile.

1 Section 20, now the Sale of Goods Act 1979, s 20.
2 1977 SC 223.
3 *Meehan v Silver* 1972 SLT (Sh Ct) 70.
4 Report on the Passing of Risk in Contracts for the Sale of Heritable Property (Scot Law Com no 127).
5 *Tay Salmon Fisheries Co v Speedie* 1929 SC 593; *Cantors Properties (Scotland) Ltd v Swears & Wells Ltd* 1978 SC 310.
6 *London & Edinburgh Shipping Co v Admiralty* 1920 SC 309.
7 McBryde *The Law of Contract in Scotland* (1987) para 15–40.

Clause A6 – Statutory repairs notices and repairs generally

4.18 'The seller will be responsible for the cost of any repairs to the subjects of sale instructed prior to the date of entry. In addition, and without prejudice to the foregoing, the seller will be responsible for the cost of any repairs required under Notices issued by the local authority or any other competent body prior to the date of entry.'

This clause covers two situations, one where the repairs are done at the instigation of the seller or someone else, and the other where the repairs are required by some other body, frequently a local authority. The repairs which are carried out at the instigation of the seller will usually be repairs which relate only to his property, a simple example of which would be replacing missing or broken slates, or defective windows. Where the seller's property adjoins others, as in a tenement or block of flats, the seller may have to contribute to the cost of repairs which are carried out on parts owned in common by the seller and others where the seller is obliged to make a contribution to the cost. In a tenement, the repairs may be instructed by all or a majority of the proprietors, or they may be instructed by a factor. Factors are common in tenement properties in Glasgow and the West of Scotland and in some modern flatted and other developments. What the purchaser is seeking to avoid in this clause is being saddled with the cost of repairs which may be instructed prior to entry, but not carried out until after that date. If there are repairs to be carried out after entry the purchaser should suggest that a retention equal to the cost of repairs be made and put on joint deposit, pending completion of the work. If that is not done, while the purchaser's position in terms of the missives would be clear, the person carrying out the repairs might eventually look to the purchaser for payment on the basis that he has benefitted from the work.

4.19 The other type of repairs envisaged in this clause are those carried out at the instance of a third party, usually a local authority. The clause would equally apply to repairs at the instance of a heritable creditor. Local authorities have power to instruct repairs under the Building (Scotland) Act 1959[1], Civic Government (Scotland) Act 1982[2] and the Housing (Scotland) Act 1987[3]. The expenses incurred by the local authority under the 1982 Act are recoverable from the 'owner' at the time when the local authority issues its claim[4], and 'owner' may include the owner of a flat not itself requiring repair[5]. Under the 1987 Act if the local authority is of the opinion that the property is in a state of serious disrepair, it may carry out the necessary work if the owner refuses to do so. In that event, if a purchaser subsequently purchases the property which is subject to the notice the purchaser will be liable for the cost[6]. The local authority may also make a charging order which is recorded in the Register of Sasines or registered in the Land Register[7].

1 Section 10; see *Sowman v Glasgow District Council* 1984 SC 91.
2 Sections 87–98.
3 Sections 108–109.
4 *Purves v City of Edinburgh District Council* 1987 SLT 366.
5 *University Court of the University of Edinburgh v City of Edinburgh District Council* 1987 SLT (Sh Ct) 103.
6 Housing (Scotland) Act 1987, s 108.
7 See McDonald *Conveyancing Manual* (4th edn) paras 19–45 to 19–47.

4.20 It is competent also for a heritable creditor to carry out repairs in the event of the debtor failing to do so[1], but liability for the cost of repairs instructed by the debtor does not transmit to the heritable creditor even where the repairs are under an obligation in the titles[2] nor it is submitted on the same reasoning would the cost transmit to a purchaser.

1 Standard conditions 7 and 10(6) in Schedule 3 to the Conveyancing and Feudal Reform (Scotland) Act 1970.
2 *David Watson Management Ltd v Woolwich Equitable Building Society* 1992 SLT 430.

Clause A7 – Title evidence

4.21 'The seller will produce at his expense (if the subjects of sale are not already registered in terms of the Land Registration (Scotland) Act 1979) all necessary documentary evidence that the title to the subjects of sale is valid and marketable and without prejudice to the foregoing generality he will produce at his expense each writ (or an extract thereof) forming part of the prescriptive progress of titles together with each writ (or a copy thereof) referred to for description or creating any real rights or burdens affecting the subjects of sale.'

This clause relates to sasine transactions only where the *dominium utile* is being sold. If the subjects are held on a long lease then clearly this clause and, indeed, other clauses in the standard missives would require to be radically altered. A purchaser cannot be forced to take a long leasehold title unless the missives expressly provide for this[1]. The clause repeats the common law obligations of a seller of heritable property. These obligations are set out clearly by Professor Halliday[2]. It is interesting to note that the standard missive clause does not place any time limit on the production of a valid and marketable title, whereas there is a time limit in clause B10 relating to the matters covered in part B of the standard clauses. Accordingly the common law rule that a purchaser cannot resile if a marketable title has not been made available by the date of entry but must allow the seller a reasonable time, will apply. A stipulation in the missives laying down a time by which the obligation to produce a marketable and valid title must be implemented will entitle the purchaser to resile if it is not met[3]. Apart from this a seller is entitled to a reasonable time to produce a good marketable title before the purchaser can resile. In this context three years has been held too much[4]. In another case six months was held not unreasonable[5]. Each case would require to be decided on its own facts and circumstances[6]. Where a purchaser is faced with this difficulty then it would be appropriate for him to intimate to the seller that if a valid marketable title cannot be produced by a certain date then he or she will resile from the bargain. The length of period to be stipulated should have regard to the nature of any defect which has to be remedied in the title, the steps which have already been taken by the seller, and how close the seller is to rectifying the defect. It should be noted that where the title which is produced is not merely defective but does not cover the whole of the subjects purchased then the purchaser can resile immediately and the seller is not entitled to any time to rectify the problem[7].

1 *McConnell v Chassels* (1903) 10 SLT 790.
2 Vol II, para 21–01.
3 *Hutchinson & Son v Scott* (1830) 8 S 377.
4 *Fleming v Harley's Trustees* (1823) 2 S 373.
5 *Raeburn v Baird* (1832) 10 S 761.
6 See *Hunter v Carswell* (1823) 1 S 248; *Smith v Aiken* (1829) 8 S 84; *McNeil v Cameron* (1830) 8 S 362; *Carter v Lornie* (1890) 18 R 353; *Gilfillan v Cadell & Grant* (1893) 21 R 269.
7 *Moray v Pearson* (1842) 4 D 1411; *Whyte v Lee* (1879) 6 R 699; *Todd v McCarroll* 1917 2 SLT 127; *Campbell v McCutcheon* 1963 SC 505.

Validity and marketability

4.22 It is the authors' view that there is a distinction to be drawn between a valid title and a marketable title. A valid title is one which covers the whole of the subjects purchased and contains a prescriptive progress of title deeds which are properly executed and not *ex facie* invalid or forged together with all necessary connecting links with evidence of such possession as is necessary for prescription to operate. A title which is marketable is one which in addition to being valid contains no burdens, conditions or reservations in the title or by operation of law which are unduly onerous or burdensome or which contravene any terms of the missives. In the authors' submission it is perfectly possible to have a valid title to a public house, for example, which is rendered unmarketable because it contains a prohibition of the sale of alcohol. Similarly a valid title to a dwellinghouse which contained a reservation of minerals with power to enter the surface and sink pits would not be marketable[1]. For the seller to comply fully with the provisions of standard clause A7 it is necessary to exhibit a title which is both valid and marketable. The purchaser's remedies for breach of the seller's obligation to produce a valid and marketable title are dealt with elsewhere[2].

1 See *Todd v McCarroll* 1917 2 SLT 127 at 128 where the Lord President indicated that the purchaser was entitled to an assurance that the property would continue to exist.
2 See paras 6.03 and 6.09 below.

Clause A8 – In exchange for the purchase price

4.23 'In exchange for the purchase price the seller will execute and deliver a valid disposition of the subjects of sale in favour of the purchaser and will exhibit or deliver:

(a) If at the date of settlement the provisions of sections 2(1) and 3(3) of the Land Registration (Scotland) Act 1979 do not apply to the transfer of the seller's interest, clear searches in the Property Register for a period of 20 years or from the date of recording of the foundation writ, if earlier, and in the Register of Inhibitions and Adjudications for a period of five years against all the parties having an interest in the subjects of sale during the period of positive prescription; further, the searches will be continued at the seller's expense to the date of recording of the disposition in favour of the purchaser and will not disclose anything adverse to the seller's right to grant a valid marketable title in favour of the purchaser and in the event of there being any adverse entry the seller shall be responsible for discharging such an entry at his expense;

OR

(b) If at the date of settlement the subjects of sale are situated in an operational area within the meaning of the Land Registration (Scotland) Act 1979 and the provisions of the said Act relating to a First Registration under the said Act apply, a valid marketable prescriptive progress of titles together with (1) a Form 10 Report brought down to a date as near as practicable to the date of settlement and showing no entries adverse to the seller's interest and (2) such documents and evidence including a plan or plans as the Keeper may require to enable the Keeper to issue a Land Certificate in the name of the purchaser as the registered proprietor of the whole subjects of sale without exclusion of indemnity;

OR

(c) If at the date of settlement the subjects of sale are situated in an operational area within the meaning of the Land Registration (Scotland) Act 1979 and under the provisions of the said Act the subjects are registered, a Land Certificate with all necessary links in title evidencing the seller's exclusive ownership of the subjects of sale together with (1) a Form 12 Report brought down to a date as near as practicable to the date of settlement and showing no entries adverse to the seller and (2) such documents and evidence as the Keeper may require to enable the interest of the purchaser to be registered in the Land Register as registered proprietor of the whole subjects of sale without exclusion of indemnity and to note the Land Certificate accordingly;

AND

(d) Where conditions (b) and (c) apply, the Land Certificate will disclose no entry, deed or diligence prejudicial to the purchaser's interest other than such as have been created by or against the purchaser or have been disclosed to and accepted in writing by the purchaser prior to the date of settlement.'

The obligation to execute and deliver a valid disposition applies to all cases whether the transaction will result in a recording in the Sasine Register or a registration in the Land Register, although the form of the disposition will vary in the case of a dealing in a registered interest. It should be noted that the clause does not provide for delivery of a disposition to 'the purchaser or his or her nominee'. This is a common

extension of the obligation to deliver the disposition. Where a purchaser intends to pass the purchase on to another party the standard
clause will require amendment if a formal assignation of the missives
is to be avoided. In cases where the title is already registered the
disposition will be shorter in form and will simply convey the subjects
by reference to a title number. The title number encompasses the
whole of the dispositive clause including any reference to burdens,
and of the remaining executry clauses only a warrandice clause, a
stamp clause (if appropriate) and a testing clause will follow. A valid
disposition is one which is properly executed by the seller and contains all appropriate clauses, including, in sasine cases a deduction of
title clause where the seller is not infeft[1]. In land registration cases
there is no need for a deduction of title clause but all the links must be
forwarded to the Keeper. In some cases a non-supersession clause is
included in the disposition although this is really a matter of contract
rather than conveyancing and many practitioners prefer to exchange
letters of non-supersession clearly delivered after settlement[2].

1 For an exhaustive discussion of the structure of dispositions see *Halliday* vol II,
 Ch 22.
2 On supersession of the missives generally see Ch 5.

4.24 The remainder of clause A8 deals with the three alternative
situations which arise because of the dual system of sasine recording
and land registration. Clause A8(a) again relates purely to sasine
transactions, clause A8(b) to first registrations and clause A8(c) to
sales of registered interests. Clause A8(d) applies to first registrations
and to sales of registered interests.

Clause A8(a) – Sasine transactions

4.25 Clause A8(a) provides that in addition to the obligation to
produce a valid marketable title in terms of clause A7 and the obligation to execute and deliver a valid disposition in terms of the preamble
to clause A8 the seller will also require to produce clear searches in the
Property Register for a period of 20 years or from the recording of the
foundation writ if earlier and in the Personal Registers for a period of
five years. The searches are to be continued at the seller's expense to
the date of recording of the disposition. Again, the obligation to
deliver a clear search merely restates the common law position[1]. The
obligations to exhibit or deliver a marketable title and to exhibit or
deliver a clear search are separate, so that even where a purchaser
agrees to purchase without the benefit of any search he can still take
objection to the title on some other ground[2]. Professor Halliday

suggests[3] that the period of the property search should be 40 years 'or such lesser period as may be acceptable to the purchaser', whereas the Law Society's standard clause indicates a period of 20 years, provided the foundation writ is recorded within that period. The 40-year period was laid down as a matter of practice many years ago on the basis that a bond and disposition in security would be likely to have been transmitted at some point in that period. In modern times, when on average people change houses every seven to ten years, twenty years is probably reasonable. In so far as the personal searches are concerned, these are for the normal period of five years up to the date of recording of the disposition against all parties having an interest in the subjects during the ten-year period of positive prescription. The standard clause accepts the argument that there is no need to search each individual seller in the prescriptive period up to the date of recording of the conveyance by him to the next purchaser. The standard clause, however, retains the notion of 'clear searches'. It is settled law in sasine transactions that this obligation means that the seller must remove an inhibition which on the face of the register affects the sale even although the inhibition may for some other reason be ineffective[4]. The reason for this is that the search is technically not clear in terms of the obligation imposed by the missives. Accordingly, if an inhibition is registered after the date of conclusion of the missives and thus does not affect the actual sale transaction it is still necessary to ask the purchaser to accept this position and formally amend the obligation in the missives to deliver a clear search. If the purchaser does not agree to this and the inhibitor is not prepared to discharge the inhibition against the sale property because it is ineffective, an action for recall of the inhibition may be necessary. Where the purchaser does accept the position then the missives should be photocopied or registered in the Books of Council and Session to retain proof for all time that the inhibition post-dated the missives and thus did not affect the transaction[5]. Any letter of obligation being granted at settlement would also require modification in such circumstances.

1 See *Halliday* vol II, paras 21–01, 21–03, and 21–73 ff.
2 *McKenzie v Clark* (1895) 3 SLT 128.
3 Vol II, para 21–03.
4 *Dryburgh v Gordon* (1896) 24 R 1.
5 See *Halliday* vol II, paras 21–86 and 23–15.

Clause A8(b) – First registrations

4.26 Where the subjects are in an operational area for land registration purposes and the transaction induces a first registration then clause A8(b) provides that the seller must produce a valid marketable prescriptive progress of titles together with a form 10 report brought down to a date as near as practicable to the date of settlement, showing no entries adverse to the seller's interest, and such other documents and evidence as the Keeper may require to issue a land certificate in the purchaser's name as the registered proprietor of the whole subjects of sale without any exclusion of indemnity. An obligation to provide a valid marketable prescriptive progress of titles in connection with a first registration is exactly the same obligation as for a sasine transaction and the same considerations apply[1]. A form 10 report is the equivalent of a search and it includes a search in the Register of Sasines, the Land Register and in the Register of Inihibitions and Adjudications. It should be noted, however, that a form 10 report will not disclose split-offs from the main parent title. When applying for a form 10 report therefore any exceptions to the title should be detailed in the application. The Keeper's staff do, however, have a policy of contacting agents about exceptions revealed in the sasine search part of a form 10 report. This valuable service is to ensure that both the Keeper and the presenting agent agree on what is to be reported on. It is normal to obtain a form 10 report at the commencement of the transaction and to update this with a continuation form 11 report, possibly including a personal search against the purchaser, immediately prior to settlement. Some practitioners think it advisable to instruct these searches and reports as soon as they know that property is for sale, with a view to ascertaining whether there are any second securities or inhibitions which might affect a sale. The obligation to deliver documents and evidence including plans to the Keeper is similar in many ways to the obligation to produce a valid title. If the title to the property is valid and covers the whole subjects of purchase then the Keeper should have no difficulty in issuing a land certificate without exclusion of indemnity, although it must be borne in mind that the Keeper is concerned with validity of title only. If the title contains onerous burdens and conditions which may in certain circumstances render it unmarketable, the Keeper will simply include these burdens and conditions in the burdens section of the title sheet without comment. The land certificate will be granted without exclusion of indemnity in so far as the actual validity of the title is concerned. This is important when considering land registration transactions where some practitioners tend to the view that if a land certificate has been granted with no exclusion as to indemnity there is no need to assess the impact of the burdens section on marketability. In certain circumstances the Keeper may require a plan to identify the ground to be purchased. This is common with very old properties, the title to which relies on a bounding description with no plan, or where the physical boundaries set out in the foundation writ are no longer identifiable. In cases of this type it is advisable to attach a plan to the disposition being granted and refer to this as an alternative description to that contained in the deed. The Keeper will provide, where possible, a comparison between the title boundaries and the physical boundaries by way of a P16 report. It is not usual in missives to provide that the seller is obliged to produce such a report but in cases of doubt it is recommended that such a report be obtained.

1 See paras 4.21 and 4.22 above.

Clause A8(c) – Registered interests

4.27 The seller's obligation in a transaction involving the sale of property which already has a registered title is to produce a land certificate with all necessary links in title which evidence the seller's exclusive ownership, together with a form 12 report showing no entries adverse to the seller, and such further documents and evidence as the Keeper may require to enable the purchaser to be registered as proprietor of the whole subjects without exclusion of indemnity. At first sight this seems a reasonable stipulation but it should be noted that there is no mention of marketability in the standard clause. A land certificate with no exclusion of indemnity, although valid, may still be an unmarketable title depending on the burdens and conditions which apply. Standard clause A8(c) must therefore be read in conjunction with clause B2 which provides that the titles do not contain 'any other burdens of an unusual or unduly onerous nature'. If clause A8(c) is left as it stands, clause B2 must not be qualified. A form 12 report is a search against a registered interest and it includes a search in the Land Register and Personal Registers. Some practitioners apply for this as soon as they know a property is on the market with a view to ascertaining whether there are any second securities or inhibitions which might affect a sale. A form 13 report is usually obtained closer to settlement to update the situation.

Clause A8(d) – First registrations and dealings in registered interests

4.28 In the case of first registrations and in the case of dealings with registered interests it is provided in the standard clauses that the land certificate will disclose no entry, deed or diligence prejudicial to the purchaser's interest other than such as have been created by or against the purchaser or disclosed to and accepted in writing by the purchaser prior to settlement. The land certificate, therefore, must not disclose any undischarged securities apart from a security to the purchaser's own lender and must not have an exclusion of indemnity in relation to a diligence such as an inhibition. Similarly, a deed of servitude disclosing a right of way across the property would be a deed prejudicial to the purchaser's interest. Unduly onerous burdens and reservations, however, probably do not fall within the definition of 'entry, deed or diligence' and reliance must therefore still be placed on clause B2. In connection with all land registration transactions it should be noted that the obligation to deliver a 'clear search' does not have the same import as it does in sasine transactions[1]. It is up to the Keeper to decide whether a diligence such as an inhibition has any effect on the validity of the title. Accordingly, the Keeper will not exclude indemnity in relation to an inhibition which postdates the conclusion of missives, provided a copy of the missives is furnished to him. In these circumstances the purchaser has no claim against the seller in respect of breach of the obligations contained in the missives because the obligations contained in standard clauses A8(b) and (c) do not provide for the exhibition of 'clear searches' as such but merely require the seller to furnish such documents as the Keeper himself requires to issue the land certificate without exclusion of indemnity.

1 See para 4.25 above.

PART B

Clause B1 – Overriding interests

4.29 'Where the transfer of the seller's interest in the subjects of sale is, or at the date of settlement will be, governed by the Land Registration (Scotland) Act 1979 that interest is not and will not be affected by any overriding interest as defined in section 28(1)(a) to (h) inclusive of that Act.'

Although the concept of an overriding interest has been introduced by the 1979 Act, the concept was not hitherto unknown. Although a title is recorded in the Register of Sasines, it does not follow that everything affecting that property can be ascertained from a search in that Register. Servitudes constituted by prescription are not ascertainable from a search. The same is true of land registration where the purchaser wishes to ensure that the property which he purchases will be free of any such overriding interest. The only item in the list in the 1979 Act which does not appear above is 'common interest', or 'joint or common property'. The reason for that is that every flat will be affected by common property rights and also common interest and the purchaser of such a property will be deemed to have accepted that position.

Clause B2 – Ground and other burdens

4.30   'There will be no pecuniary burdens affecting the subjects of sale after settlement and the Titles do not contain any other burdens of an unusual or unduly onerous nature.'

This clause has already been dealt with as regards ground burdens[1] and as regards unusual or onerous burdens[2].

1 Para 4.15 above.
2 Paras 4.22, 4.23, 4.27 and 4.28 above.

Clause B3 – Implementation etc of conditions of title

4.31   'All conditions of title, except those of a continuing nature, have been fully implemented.'

Before accepting this clause the seller's solicitor should ensure that the seller is in a position to grant such a warranty. Most prudent solicitors in modern practice will ask the seller whether or not he or his predecessors have carried out any alterations or additions to the subjects of purchase. The main purpose of this enquiry is, of course, to ascertain the whereabouts of planning permissions, building warrants and certificates of completion. The position of the feuing conditions and the superior should, however, not be forgotten in connection with these alterations. If there have been alterations neither the seller nor his predecessors may have bothered to obtain the superior's consent. In such a case it may be that clause B3 will require modification on the part of the seller. Alternatively, the seller may feel able simply to accept the clause and thereafter argue that consent is not required or apply for retrospective consent of the superior[1]. Although the standard condition does not provide for the production of a certificate from the superior to the effect that the feuing conditions have been implemented, the purchaser may wish to be satisfied that continuing obligations, eg maintenance, have been implemented. If an offer contains such a clause the seller's solicitor must ensure that the superiors will be prepared to grant such a certificate. Some superiors are prepared to grant certificates easily whereas others are prepared to grant certificates only after an inspection and for a suitable fee, and some superiors are not prepared to grant such certificates at any price for fear of acquiescence. Where clause B3 is expanded to include a demand for a superior's certificate, a seller may wish to delete this requirement while granting a warranty that the seller has received no intimation of any sort from the superiors alleging any breach of the conditions.

1 See Donald's B Reid 'Superior's consents', lecture for University of Strathclyde Centre for Professional Legal Studies, October 1992.

Clause B4 – Reservation and working of minerals

4.32   'In the event of the minerals being reserved to the seller, the superior or some other third party, the titles of the subjects of sale contain a provision affording full rights of compensation to the proprietor in respect of any surface damage, damage to buildings or other damage occasioned by working of the minerals.'

This clause has to be read in conjunction with clause A2[1]. In some areas, as has already been noted, the titles will not provide for rights of compensation and may occasionally allow the superior or other party owning the minerals to enter the surface and carry out surface operations. Accordingly, when acting for the seller in such an area, care must be taken to modify clauses A2 and B4. The mere deletion of clause B4 on its own would not, it is submitted, mean that a purchaser would be bound to accept any type of mineral reservation clause. Mineral reservation clauses have an effect on the marketability of the title and even if the minerals position was governed by clause A2 and nothing else a severe mineral reservation clause could render the title unmarketable. Accordingly, when acting for a seller whose title contains a difficult mineral reservation clause it is important to qualify both clause B4 and clause A2.

1 See para 4.14 above.

Clause B5 – Tenement properties etc

4.33   'If the subjects of sale form part of a larger building, the seller's title includes a right of common property in the solum of the building of which the subjects of sale form part. Furthermore, the liability for the maintenance of the solum, the roof and other common parts and any charges for common services is allocated among all the proprietors of the said building equally or on some other equitable basis. In the event that the subjects of sale comprise the top floor (or part thereof) of such building, evidence will be provided at the seller's expense to the effect that a real burden imposing a share of such maintenance has been validly inserted in the title deeds of all the other flats or houses in the said building.'

The purpose of this clause is to ensure that the purchaser is not forced to accept a title to a tenemental flat where the common rights and obligations are unusual or unduly burdensome. Where titles to flatted property are silent, the common law of the tenement will apply both as to rights of ownership, rights of common interest and obligations. The main principles of the law of the tenement are well set out by Professor Halliday[1]. Clause B5 states that the liability for maintenance of the solum, roof and other common parts, and any charges for common services are allocated equally or on some other equitable basis. Presumably if the flats in the tenement are of differing size it would be equitable to divide the obligations for maintenance with reference to the respective floor areas or the old gross annual values of the properties. It remains to be seen whether conveyancers will in the future use valuations of properties for council tax purposes in the same manner. Liability for maintenance of the solum and the roof are particularly identified in clause B5. If the deeds are silent then the solum and foundations are owned exclusively by the ground flat proprietors so far as below each proprietor's exclusive property, subject to a right of common interest in all the other proprietors of the tenement[2]. Similarly the roof of a tenement is, in the absence of any provisions to the contrary, the property of the owner or owners of the top flat so far as it extends above their respective flats as is the air space or garret between the top floors of the flats and the roof[3]. It is undoubtedly the difficulties surrounding maintenance of roof and foundations which cause the most problems in tenemental properties. There are a number of tenements, especially in Edinburgh, where the titles are silent concerning the roof and in these cases the obligation of maintenance of the roof will fall entirely on the topmost proprietor or proprietors. Clause B5 does, of course, note the difference between common rights and common obligations. It is perfectly feasible to have a situation where the seller's title indicates that the roof is common and that the obligation for maintenance of the roof is shared equally or on some other equitable basis among all the proprietors but where this particular burden has not been inserted in all of the titles to other flats in the tenement. In such circumstances the title to each flat will determine the obligations undertaken by the owner of that flat, and the statement in the title to the topmost flat to the effect that the obligation for maintenance will be shared equally cannot alter the titles to other flats. For this reason clause B5 requires the seller to produce at the seller's expense evidence that real burdens have been validly inserted in the title deeds of all other flats in the tenement where the subjects of sale are the top flat. Obviously, the provisions of clause B5 are for the purchaser's protection and a purchaser's solicitor should not allow them to be qualified without careful enquiry as to the title position. Similarly a seller's solicitor should not accept the terms of clause B5 unless sure that the seller will in fact be able to implement all the obligations contained in that clause[4].

1 Vol II, para 18–20.
2 *Johnston v White* (1877) 4 R 721; *Calder v Merchant Co of Edinburgh* (1886) 13 R 623.
3 *Taylor v Dunlop* (1872) 11 M 25; *Sanderson's Trustees v Yule* (1897) 25 R 211.
4 For a general discussion on the law of the tenement see KGC Reid 'Law of the tenement' (1983) 28 JLS 472.

Clause B6 – Roads, sewerage and water supply etc

4.34 'The seller will provide at his expense a certificate prior to the date of entry from the appropriate local authority confirming (i) that the roads, footpaths, waterchannels and sewer *ex adverso* and serving the subjects of sale have been taken over and are maintained by the local authority (ii) that there are no road proposals which will affect the subjects of sale and (iii) that the subjects of sale are connected to the public water supply. Furthermore, the seller warrants that he is not aware of any proposals by or rights in favour of a public or local authority, statutory undertaker or other party which would affect the subjects of sale.'

This is a fairly straightforward clause in so far as it relates to roads, footpaths, sewers and water supplies. Either these services are public or they are not. Obviously the seller's solicitor should ascertain the position before accepting such a clause. In some cases where the property is situated in a well-known residential area and it is a matter of almost public knowledge that the roads, footpaths, sewers and water supplies are public, the seller's solicitor may qualify this clause by stating that while the seller believes the position to be as stated in the clause no certificates will be exhibited or delivered. While this qualification may be accepted in some cases it should be noted that the question of road proposals is quite separate from the actual status of the services as public utilities. It is worth noting, especially when dealing with rural properties, that where a road is adopted any verge is also adopted[1]. There are, of course, many cases where roads, footpaths, sewers and indeed sometimes water supplies are not public. In such cases this clause will require to be substantially modified by the seller's solicitor. Where a road or footpath is private, the purchaser will wish to know whether he has ownership of the road and footpath or merely a right of access over the same. A purchaser will also wish to know what the precise obligations for maintenance of the road and footpath are and whether these are shared by any other user. Where there is no public sewer and the subjects are served by a septic tank, the purchaser will wish to know whether the septic tank is situated within the subjects of sale or in adjoining property. Similarly the purchaser will wish to know whether the septic tank serves his own property exclusively or whether it is used by any adjoining properties. Where the septic tank is outwith the subjects of sale the purchaser should ensure that there are adequate servitude rights for the positioning of the septic tank in adjoining property and for all pipes leading thereto and therefrom. Where the septic tank drains into a river or into a tributary of a river consents may be required from a purification board. Some rural properties are still served by private water supplies from natural springs. Obviously when acting for the seller this should be disclosed in a modification to clause B6. When acting for the purchaser evidence of the appropriate wayleaves for the water supply and the pipes carrying the same should be sought. Enquiry should also be made as to whether the supply has the appropriate certificate of fitness from the water authority. As has already been noted[2] the Scottish Office issue a guide to the laws controlling private water supplies[3].

1 Roads (Scotland) Act 1984, s 151.
2 See para 1.20 above.
3 HMSO 6/92; and see The Water (Scotland) Act 1980, ss 38 and 76 F–J; The Water Supply (Water Quality) (Scotland) Regulations 1990, SI 1990/119; The Water Supply (Water Quality) (Scotland) Amendment Regulations 1991, SI 1991/1333; The Private Water Supplies (Scotland) Regulations 1992, SI 1992/575; The Scottish Office Environment Department Circular no 20/1992.

4.35 Clause B6 does not just deal with the status of roads, footpaths, sewers and water supplies. It goes on to provide a warranty by the seller that the seller is not aware of any proposals by, or rights in favour of, a public or local authority, statutory undertaker or other party which would affect the subjects. One has to assume that this warranty is meant to relate to roads, footpaths, sewers and water supplies and proposals in connection therewith. However, the actual warranty is drawn so as to cover any proposals which would affect the subjects. The clients' guide to the standard missives issued by the Law Society for the information of clients tends to suggest that this warranty is meant to cover proposals by the local authority or statutory undertaker such as Scottish Power, British Gas or British Telecom which would adversely affect the property, but the warranty is wider than that.

Clause B7 – Planning etc

4.36 '(a) The seller will provide at his expense prior to the date of entry a
certificate (dated not earlier than twenty eight days prior to the
conclusion of the bargain to follow hereon) from the appropriate
local authority confirming that the subjects of sale are (i) in an
area designated in the Development Plan primarily for residential purposes (ii) not within a housing treatment or housing
action area (iii) not adversely affected by any planning schemes,
orders or proposals under the Town and Country Planning (Scotland) Acts or other Statutes (iv) not included in any proposals or
orders under the Housing (Scotland) Acts or other Statutes
(v) not subject to any outstanding matters in the knowledge of
the said local authority and (vi) not designated for compulsory
acquisition for any planning purposes of the said local authority.

(b) The purchaser accepts that the subjects of sale may be
(i) included in a list of buildings of special architectural or histo-
ric interest or (ii) located within a conservation area.

(c) The seller warrants that he is unaware of any proposals by any
public or local authority, statutory undertaker or other party
which would affect the subjects of sale.'

All offers for domestic heritable property contain a clause designed to
protect the purchaser from any unpleasant shocks in relation to
planning, redevelopment or local authority orders. The standard
missive clause states that the seller will provide at his expense a
planning certificate (dated not earlier than 28 days prior to the conclusion of the bargain) from the planning authority confirming that the
subjects are in a residential area, not within a housing treatment or
action area, not affected by any schemes, orders or proposals, not
included in any proposals or orders, not subject to any outstanding
matters and not designated for compulsory acquisition. The purchaser accepts in terms of the standard clause that the subjects may be
included in a list of buildings of special architectural interest or in a
conservation area, presumably because it is accepted that inclusion in
such lists or areas is beneficial to the property. It is fair to say that not
every purchaser would accept that this is the case. Accordingly,
before issuing an offer with that condition, a prudent solicitor should
enquire from the purchaser whether he wishes to make any alterations
to the subjects. Where subjects are on a special list or in a conservation
area, the planning requirements can be very strict especially as regards
external alterations including windows. Apart from this the matters to
be covered in the certificate are fairly standard although what is meant
by 'not subject to any outstanding matters in the knowledge of the
said local authority' is far from clear. One might be forgiven from
wondering whether an idle thought of potential redevelopment in the

mind of a junior officer in the planning department at half past three on a Friday afternoon would be an outstanding matter in the knowledge of the authority. Selling solicitors may well wish to delete or modify this particular paragraph. The timing of the issue of the certificate is problematic. No one has a crystal ball and no selling solicitor can predict with any accuracy the date of conclusion of missives. When a seller advises his solicitor that the property has been placed on the market, it is normally regarded as prudent practice for the solicitor to write immediately for the titles and the planning and roads certificates. Given the cost of these certificates nowadays this course of action may not be economically sensible. It seems to the authors that the selling solicitor will have one of two problems:

(a) Either he will apply for the certificates immediately and find that the house is not sold until after the 28-day period, in which case he may be faced with having to obtain up-to-date certificates at extra cost to the seller; or

(b) he will wait until an offer is received before applying for the certificates, in which case he may have to insert a suspensive condition in the missives regarding the content of the certificates and in addition run the risk that the certificates are not actually available at the date of entry.

A 28-day time limit may be reasonable in a buoyant market where one might expect a house to sell within a month of its being exposed for sale, but not otherwise. Depending on market conditions, selling solicitors may well be forced to qualify this time limit or delete it altogether.

4.37   In terms of clause B7(c) the seller warrants that he is unaware of any proposals by any public or local authority, statutory undertaker or other party which would affect the subjects of sale. The words 'other party' are worthy of note in this clause. It seems that this clause would certainly cover a proposal by a next-door neighbour to erect an extension. If this sub-clause is accepted as it stands, however, one can conceive of a situation where a purchaser, who does not wish to proceed for completely unrelated motives, seeks to resile on the ground that a proposal to build a school or widen a road half a mile away may 'affect' the subjects of sale. It might have been better had the word 'adversely' been inserted before the word 'affect' in the clause. This type of clause also presents difficulties in relation to the seller's state of knowledge. If it can be shown that the seller has been served with notification of a planning application, then the knowledge is clear. If, however, a planning application has only been advertised in the local press, there may be arguments as to whether the seller either knew of the planning proposal or at least ought with reasonable diligence to have known about it. There may well be cases where the seller's agents will wish to delete or substantially qualify this particular branch of clause B7.

Clause B8 – Structural alterations, etc

4.38 'If the subjects of sale have been converted or altered in the [10] year period prior to the date of conclusion of the bargain to follow hereon the seller will provide at his expense such evidence as may reasonably be required by the purchaser that (i) the relevant works were carried out and completed in conformity with all necessary local authority permissions and warrants, and (ii) all other necessary consents and permissions, including that of the superior were obtained and any conditions attaching thereto were fully implemented.'

While this clause is obviously concerned to identify any structural alterations which have been carried out with the necessary permissions, it is also designed to identify those which have not.

It is outwith the scope of this book to identify those situations in which planning permission and/or a building warrant may be required. Under the most recent Building (Procedure) (Scotland) Regulations of 1991[1] some works may be carried out without the need to obtain a warrant, but the works must comply with the relevant regulations. A purchaser has to consider primarily the necessity of planning permission, a building warrant or at least work complying with the regulations and the title conditions.

The purchaser will be concerned, therefore, to ensure that the seller exhibits all of the permissions and warrants which are required and, in the case of works requiring a building warrant, a completion certificate which is evidence that the work was carried out in accordance with the warrant and approved plans. The consent of the superiors where appropriate should also be exhibited unless acquiescence can be established. In recent years, more emphasis has been placed on these matters than formerly, if only because of the increased interest in DIY. It is particularly important for the purchaser to be assured that the work has been completed in accordance with any building warrant granted or if completed under the new regulations where a warrant is not required, that the completed work complies with the regulations. Even where a building warrant has been granted and a completion certificate issued, theoretically the purchaser may not be entirely safe, simply because the completion certificate is granted after inspection and the relevant statutory provision is somewhat guarded in its terms.

1 SI 1991/159.

4.39 The clause quoted above suggests a period of ten years. This is proposed as a sensible 'cut-off' point, but every purchase has to be considered in the light of the approach taken by the relevant local authority. Some insist on going back further than that, even although their records may not still be extant. It follows that unauthorised alterations cause infinitely more problems than the authorised ones with or without the documentation.

4.40 Unauthorised alterations may already have been drawn to the purchaser's attention by his surveyor, but even so, the clause is designed to require the seller to reveal them. It would obviously be prudent for the selling solicitor to consider this matter with the seller prior to the property being put on the market. The seller may be able to identify a potential problem which the selling solicitor can solve in advance. Even where the appropriate documentation cannot be obtained, a letter of comfort may be available from the local authority prior to any offer being lodged. There will undoubtedly be a large number of properties which have been altered in some way without the appropriate permission or warrant. Some sellers may have employed tradesmen to do work without either party realising that planning permission and/or a building warrant was required. A good example of this type of work is double glazing which may require such permissions.

4.41 The position in England, as we understand it, is that a local authority building control department may not take steps to investigate such alterations if they have been carried out more than one year previously, unless the alteration is a danger to the public, or affects the structural stability of the building[1], but there is no such limitation period in Scotland. In relation to planning, there is a cut-off period of four years[2]. Thus, in theory at any rate, any building control authority in Scotland may insist that any unauthorised alteration has the necessary permission, if the alteration was carried out after the coming into force of the Building (Scotland) Act 1959. Some attempt has been made to persuade local authorities to take a consistent view of the problem of unauthorised alterations. From a strictly legal point of view it is likely that retrospective completion certificates cannot be granted in terms of the legislation although some local authorities are actually prepared to issue retrospective warrants followed by completion certificates. The irony of the situation is that legally it is probably impossible to do this when the work complies with the regulations but possible to do this where rectification work has to be carried out prior to the issue of the warrant and completion certificate. Apart from this, local authorities are generally prepared to issue 'letters of comfort'. These letters are issued by the relevant official and confirm that the authority do not propose taking any action. Often this is sufficient to persuade a doubting purchaser, his surveyor and lender that the problem if not insoluble can at least be ignored for practicable purposes. However, the letter will usually make it clear that the stance taken will not bind the council in future should an actual problem arise. Some local authorities, (eg Aberdeen, Dundee and Edinburgh) have introduced an inspection system under which they will inspect the property for a fee and issue a letter as a result. While the fee may be quite high such an inspection followed by a letter does provide greater comfort for all concerned. Practical considerations should always be balanced with legalities when dealing with unauthorised alterations. It should always be borne in mind that the terms of a completion certificate make it clear that there is no guarantee that there is nothing wrong with the property. The completion certificate relates only to what could be seen on inspection.

1 Building Act 1984, s 36.
2 Town and Country Planning (Scotland) Act 1972, s 84(3), as amended by the Local Government and Planning (Scotland) Act 1982, Sch 2, para 19(a).

4.42 It may be that while the seller is willing to provide evidence in connection with alterations carried out during the seller's occupancy he or she is not prepared, or able to provide evidence or documentation, in relation to previous periods. In this event, the clause will be met by some kind of qualification which will attempt to put the responsibility on to the purchaser. This situation may occur in a normal sale but will certainly occur where the subjects are being sold by a heritable creditor, or trustee in bankruptcy or some other person who has never been in occupation of the property and cannot give assurances about structural alterations. In such cases, because the seller has no knowledge, the purchaser's clause may even be deleted in its entirety.

4.43 In any discussion of alterations, it is important not to lose sight of the relevance of the title conditions. Although the seller may have obtained planning permission, building warrant and a completion certificate for converting a self-contained house into two flats, there may be a prohibition in the title against the subjects being sub-divided or being occupied by more than one family. In such a case the consent of the person entitled to enforce the title condition should be produced where required and it should be remembered that the consent of the superior may not be the only consent required if there is a *ius quaesitum tertio*.

Clause B9 – Subjects of sale erected within last ten years

4.44 'If the subjects of sale were constructed within ten years prior to the date of conclusion of the bargain to follow hereon (i) they were constructed by a contractor who was at the time a member of the National House Builders Council ('the NHBC') (ii) the subjects of sale were registered with the NHBC and are currently covered by all NHBC warranties available at the date of registration, and (iii) the seller will deliver at his expense all relevant documentation pertaining to the said warranties together with the appropriate local authority certificate of completion.'

This clause may seem innocuous enough at first sight but selling solicitors should not forget the last few words of the clause 'together with the appropriate local authority certificate of completion'. Presumably in the case of a house erected within ten years, the completion certificate will be readily available. The clause only deals with recently-built houses which are covered by the NHBC. It does not cover those houses which although built within that period, do not have the benefit of the NHBC guarantee. There are many houses which are covered by certificates from architects as alternatives to the NHBC guarantee. These certificates if granted by qualified persons and in appropriate terms are generally accepted by lending institutions. A selling solicitor will require to qualify the terms of clause B9 if in fact the house is covered by an architect's certificate and not by an NHBC guarantee. In these circumstances it is sensible to forward the architect's certificate with the qualified acceptance and invite the purchaser to accept the terms of the same.

Clause B10 – Time limits

4.45 'The seller will provide all relevant documentary evidence of the matters specified in conditions B1 to B9 inclusive of Part B of the Schedule to the foregoing offer within . . . weeks of the date of conclusion of missives. If the said documentary evidence does not implement the obligations of the seller hereunder or discloses matters materially prejudicial to the purchaser's position, the purchaser shall be entitled to withdraw from the missives to follow hereon without penalty by delivering written notice of that fact to the seller's solicitors within five working days from the date of receipt of the last of said items of documentary evidence. In the event of the purchaser failing to give notice as aforesaid within said period of five working days he will be deemed to be fully satisfied in respect of all such matters.'

Clause B10 inserts a materiality factor into some of the seller's obligations in part B of the standard clauses although oddly enough not into the more important clauses in part A. As has already been noted[1], the seller has a reasonable time within which to produce a valid marketable title before the purchaser can resile. If clause B10 is accepted in its entirety, then unless the seller can implement all of his or her obligations in terms of conditions B1 to B9 within a certain period of weeks, the purchaser will be entitled to resile. It should, however, be noted that clause B10 appears to go further than this in that it states that the purchaser shall also be entitled to resile if any of the documentary evidence in terms of conditions B1 to B9 discloses 'matters materially prejudicial to the purchaser's position'. It seems to the authors that this introduces a new and slightly dangerous obligation on the part of the seller which is not specifically covered anywhere else in the missives. Presumably the 'matters materially prejudicial' must bear some relation to the other matters canvassed in conditions B1 to B9 because the prejudicial matters must at least appear in the documentary evidence to be exhibited in terms of these conditions. It is to be hoped that these words do not have the result of allowing a purchaser to withdraw from a bargain because of some unconnected statement in a document produced in terms of one of the conditions from B1 to B9. The purchaser requires to intimate repudiation by delivering written notice within five working days from the date of receipt of the 'last of said items of documentary evidence'. This rather unusual wording presumably does not mean that intimation of repudiation on the grounds of a bad planning certificate cannot be made until the seller has exhibited the roads certificates and all other items mentioned in conditions B1 to B9. What it probably does mean, however, is that a seller cannot assume that a planning certificate or a roads certificate has been accepted merely because five days have elapsed from the receipt of one of those documents. The purchaser is not bound to proceed until the seller has delivered or exhibited all other documentary evidence relating to clauses B1 to B9 and five days have elapsed from receipt of the last of these to be delivered. In some qualified acceptances the five-day limit is related individually to each piece of evidence to be exhibited. Where standard clause B10 applies, it is suggested that the seller's agents should ask the purchaser's agents for written confirmation that the purchasers accept the terms of each item of evidence as implementing the seller's obligation as it is delivered.

1 See paras 4.22 and 4.23 above and 6.03 and 6.09 below.

Clause B11 – Non-supersession clause

4.46 'This offer and the missives following hereon will form a continuing and enforceable contract notwithstanding the delivery of the disposition in favour of the purchaser except insofar as fully implemented thereby. The missives, however, will cease to be enforceable after a period of two years from the date of delivery of said disposition, except insofar as they are founded upon in any court proceedings which have been commenced within said period. A clause to this effect will, at the option of the purchaser, be included in the disposition in his favour.'

This clause is dealt with in Chapter 5 which deals with the relationship between the missives and the disposition. Although the standard missive clause provides for a clause of non-supersession in the disposition it is probably preferable to exchange letters of non-supersession after settlement.

Clause B12 – The *actio quanti minoris*

4.47 'Notwithstanding any rule of law to the contrary the *actio quanti minoris* will be available to the purchaser.'

It is probably settled law that the *actio quanti minoris* is not available to the purchaser unless provided for in the missives[1].

1 See para 6.28 below.

PART C

Clause C1 – Fittings and fixtures

4.48 'The purchase price includes all fittings and fixtures in and upon the subjects of sale and any items the removal of which would cause damage to the fabric of the property including all growing trees, flowers, plants and shrubs in any garden ground pertaining to the subjects of sale.'

This clause has to be read in conjunction with the list of moveable items included in the offer itself. It is perhaps unfortunate that the word 'heritable' does not preface the words 'fittings and fixtures'. Fixtures are recognised in law as moveable items which have become part of the heritage by accession. However, the word 'fittings' tends to suggest moveable items. In *Jamieson v Welsh*[1] Lord Low ventured the opinion that the use of the term 'fixtures' in an offer added nothing to it because the whole heritage was already purchased. He did, however, go on to state: 'The word "fittings", however, is in a different position, and presumably means such things as ordinary grates or gas brackets, which in the absence of a special agreement, the seller would be entitled to remove'. The Lord President appeared to agree with this definition. The difficulty with the standard clause is that it appears to include all fittings and fixtures in and upon the subjects of sale without restricting this to heritable fittings and fixtures. It seems to the authors therefore that unless clause C1 is in some way modified, a purchaser might conceivably make a claim for all manner of moveable items which were never intended to be part of the bargain. Shrubs, trees and garden stock are also included in terms of the standard clause. As Professor Halliday himself states[2], a purchaser should include specifically any item which he wishes to include in the purchase whether it be regarded as heritable or moveable and likewise, the seller, if he wishes to remove an item which might be heritable, should specifically exclude it. Reference may be made to Professor Halliday's very useful list of items which have been the subject of judicial decision in this regard[3].

1 (1900) 3 F 176.
2 Vol II, para 15–35.
3 Vol II, para 15–37.

Clause C2 – Interest on price

4.49 'It is a material condition of the bargain to follow hereon that (a) the purchase price will be paid on the date of entry and (b) the seller will give entry with vacant possession to the subjects of sale. Without prejudice to the foregoing if (but only if) at the date of entry the seller has (a) implemented all obligations incumbent on him in terms of the bargain to follow hereon and (b) is in a position to give possession of the subjects of sale to the purchaser, the purchaser will pay to the seller interest on any part of the purchase price outstanding at said date at a rate of 4% per annum above the lowest base rate for lending charged by any of the Scottish clearing banks during the period of non-payment (together with any arrangement fee or other charges incurred by the seller on any borrowing by him necessitated by the purchaser's failure to pay the purchase price timeously); and that notwithstanding consignation and whether or not the purchaser shall have taken occupation of the subjects of sale; and in the event of any part of the purchase price remaining unpaid on the expiry of a period of four weeks from the date of entry, the seller will be entitled but not obliged, forthwith to resile from said bargain to follow hereon and to resell the subjects of sale, under reservation of all claims which may be competent to the seller to recover from the purchaser all loss and damage sustained by the seller on any such resale and interest as aforesaid.'

The consequences of a breach of contract are dealt with in Chapter 6 but it is useful to identify the main features of this default clause.

4.50 It is now very common for the offer to contain this type of clause, whereas formerly, the clause was inserted by the seller in a qualified acceptance. As has already been said, the advantage to the purchaser's solicitor in inserting the clause is that he can choose his own words and should know what his own clause means. If the clause is clear to the seller, it is less likely that the clause will be altered, except perhaps in relation to the rate of interest payable, or the period of the 'long stop' after which the seller may resile.

4.51 The clause also makes payment of the price a material condition of the contract. At common law, payment on the due date is not deemed to be of the essence of a contract for the purchase and sale of heritage[1] but it is now almost invariable practice to make it so. The basic reason for so doing is to allow the seller the option of resiling if the purchase price is not paid on the due date. Normally that is not a course which a seller would take immediately but the clause makes the legal position of the seller clear. The clause also avoids having to define what is a reasonable time to give to the purchaser for making payment under the common law. It is now almost universal practice for missives to contain such a provision, and the prime purpose is to draw to the purchaser's attention the possible consequences of failing to make punctual payment.

1 *Rodger (Builders) Ltd v Fawdry* 1950 SC 483.

4.52 While the missives will almost certainly make payment of the price a material condition, it is not as yet universal practice to make the giving of entry material although the one is the logical counterpart of the other. Such a condition is, however, becoming more common and condition C2 makes this obligation on the seller material. Such a provision would, in theory, permit the purchaser to resile in the event of the seller's failure to give possession and avoids any discussion concerning what is a reasonable time within which entry has to be given. Some offers provide that a deduction will be made from the price for every day that entry is delayed, but it is uncommon for sellers to accept such a provision.

4.53 The clause provides for payment of interest, notwithstanding consignation of the price and whether or not possession has been taken by the purchaser. It is unusual for the price to be consigned but even if consignation is permitted, interest at the rate specified by the seller is payable, and not the lower rate which a deposit account or deposit receipt would attract were the price consigned, provided, of course, the seller can implement his or her obligations. As will be seen in a succeeding chapter, there is still some doubt whether the purchaser is liable to pay interest if the seller vacates the property and offers possession to the purchaser which is declined, but the clause above puts the matter beyond doubt.

4.54 Before interest is payable or the seller can resile, the seller must be in a position to implement the bargain. In other words, he must have a signed deed and have exhibited a valid marketable title with clear searches or land registration reports. The seller must also have the keys available and be able to give entry, or entry and vacant possession as the case may be. In some missives, this provision is qualifed with a provision to the effect that the seller must be in this position, or would have been but for the fault of the purchaser or his agents. Such a provision makes it clear that the purchaser cannot avoid payment of interest or deprive the seller of the right to resile where he or his solicitor has been at fault by, for example, failing to examine the titles or draft the disposition within a reasonable time.

4.55 The rate of interest suggested in the clause should be sufficiently high to compensate the seller should he require to obtain bridging finance if the purchaser fails to pay on the due date. This will be discussed more fully in Chapter 6 but it is essential to specify a rate or provide a formula for calculating it. This should bring home to the purchaser the need to have the price on the agreed date. In most missives, the rate is linked to the rate charged by a specific bank, usually the selling solicitor's bank, but there must be a basis on which interest can be calculated. It is increasingly common for banks to charge an arrangement fee for a bridging facility and the clause makes it clear that that fee is also recoverable from the purchaser along, obviously, with the interest charges.

4.56 It is clearly desirable to have a date after which the seller need no longer wait for the purchaser to pay. Most missives provide that payment of the price is material, and as has been said, if the price is not paid, the seller could resile immediately. Most sellers will, however, hope that the sale to that particular purchaser will proceed, but will reserve the right to resile after the expiry of a specified 'long stop' period, usually either 14, 21 or, as in the standard missives, 28 days. Such a clause would not prevent the seller from resiling prior to the expiry of that period if it were agreed between the parties within the period that the purchaser could not implement the bargain at any time.

4.57 Should the seller resile and resell, it is desirable that the clause spells out the seller's right to claim damages from the original purchaser. Such damages would include, for example, any loss should the second sale produce a lower figure. Even if the second sale does not produce a lower figure, the seller will not wish to be out of pocket and should be able to claim for any additional expenses incurred in the resale such as legal fees, advertising and estate agency costs.

Clause C3 – Retention for repairs

4.58 'In the event that the subjects of sale are affected by a District or Regional Council Notice ordering repairs to the subjects of sale or the common parts of any building of which the subjects of sale form a part or a Common Repairs Scheme, there shall be retained at settlement a sum which represents the proportion of the estimated cost to be borne by the seller in respect thereof, augmented by 25%, and this sum shall be lodged on Deposit Receipt in the joint names of the seller's and the purchaser's solicitors against exhibition of the receipted final accounts for the works involved.'

This is a useful provision from the purchaser's point of view in cases where the subjects are affected by some notice which orders repairs, whether to the subjects themselves or any common parts or in relation to some common repairs scheme. Where properties have been renovated, it is not uncommon to find that the work is being carried out or has been carried out as the result of a local authority notice or as part of a scheme. Where the work has not been carried out and the purchaser still wishes to proceed, it is useful to have a formula whereby part of the price can be retained on joint deposit receipt to cover the cost. Similarly, even where work has been carried out, it is not uncommon to find that the final bill has yet to be paid to the contractors or to the local authority. In some cases, work may have been carried out during the ownership of a previous party and in these cases where there is doubt, it is useful to have a provision of this type where the money can be consigned and at least the purchaser is protected. Such a provision also provides necessary encouragement to the seller to have matters sorted out at an early date.

Clause C4 – Proposals by neighbours

4.59 'It is a condition of this offer that the seller is unaware of any proposals by neighbouring proprietors or other parties which would adversely affect the subjects of sale.'

This clause is designed to elicit from the seller information about everything and anything which other persons may be doing or thinking of doing to their properties which might adversely affect his own property. It would probably be difficult to establish any liability on the seller under this clause, unless it could be shown that the seller knew of something and did not disclose it. An example of something covered by the clause would be a proposal by a neighbour to put an extention on his property which would come very close to the subjects of sale and thus affect privacy, or obstruct a view. In most cases, the seller would have to have had some notice served on him but even if he had notice, the proposal must be such that it would adversely affect the subjects of sale. Clearly not every proposal would be in that category but the test is objective rather than subjective. The seller should think carefully before accepting this clause. The term 'neighbour' is not defined nor is the word 'proposal' restricted to proposals to build or develop. If a proprietor at the end of the street some three houses away proposes to build a public house on the corner would this be covered?

Clause C5 – Central heating

4.60 'The central heating system (if any) included in the price shall be in full working order as at the date of entry. Any material defects in the system as at that date notified to the seller or the seller's agent within 7 days of the date of entry will be remedied at the seller's expense. Any telephone apparatus in the subjects of sale which is not the property of British Telecom will be included in the price. The seller will not cause the telephone to be disconnected.'

This clause deals with two separate and unrelated matters, the central heating and the telephone. Clauses about the condition of central heating systems are common. It is obviously inconvenient for a purchaser to find on the date of entry that the central heating system does not work properly. A seller should think carefully about accepting such a clause, especially where the central heating system is not modern. Sellers may, for example, wish to qualify the clause by inserting words such as 'having regard to the age and design of the system' after the words 'in full working order' and sellers should never accept clauses which state that an existing system complies with modern regulations. Even if the seller is minded to accept, the inspection period after entry should be as short as possible. A prudent seller should ensure that the purchaser is given clear practical instructions on how to operate the system and, if possible, have it inspected himself prior to entry. While a purchaser might run the risk that the seller would have the repairs carried out in the least expensive way, the seller would not wish to be exposed to the risk that the purchaser might employ the dearest firm to do the work and, in the case of an unscrupulous purchaser, have other work done at the same time.

Where a claim is made under this clause the seller should ask to see a detailed statement of what work was done, to ensure that the liability is restricted to essential repairs. If the property is being sold by someone who has never been in occupation, for example a heritable creditor, the offer will be qualified, probably to the effect that no warranty is given about the central heating system at all, or the seller may give the purchaser an opportunity to inspect the system prior to the conclusion of missives in order to satisfy himself about the condition of the system, but offer no warranty in respect of the period after conclusion of missives.

4.61 The second part of the clause needs little explanation. It is designed to ensure that the seller does not have the telephone disconnected and thus involve the purchaser in a hefty reconnection charge. Where there is a sale by a heritable creditor or trustee in bankruptcy it may not come as a surprise to the purchaser to find that the telephone has been disconnected, possibly also along with the electricity and gas supplies.

Clause C6 – Guarantees

4.62 'The seller is not aware of the existence in the subjects of sale (or the building of which the subjects form part) of woodworm, dry rot, wet rot or rising damp and, in the event that a Guarantee has been issued in respect of any of these, said Guarantee is valid in all respects and the benefit thereof shall be transferred to the purchaser. Further the said Gurantee, with the specification and estimate to which it refers, shall be delivered at settlement.'

In modern practice, guarantees for specialist work such as the eradication of woodworm, dry rot, wet rot or rising damp are passed on to the purchaser. It is important to note, however, that guarantees do not tend to cover the whole property but merely a particular part of the property which has been treated. Accordingly, it is important to obtain the original specification of the work done for attachment to the guarantee. In some cases, specialist firms issue insurance policies against the risk of an outbreak and these policies can normally be assigned to succeeding purchasers. Selling solicitors should take careful note of the opening words of this clause. There will be many selling solicitors who will wish to delete them in their entirety. The clause states that the seller is not aware of the existence in the subjects of sale or in the building of which the subjects form part of any woodworm, dry rot, wet rot or rising damp. Those who favour such a warranty argue that this is a matter completely within the seller's knowledge. The definition of 'knowledge', however, in relation to fungal decay is obscure. A seller may have known about a damp patch on a ceiling or a musty smell in a cupboard for some time without necessarily connecting it with fungal decay or rising damp. A purchaser, however, may take the view that if the seller knew of the actual defect, he is covered by the condition. Moreover the clause covers not only the property purchased but 'the building of which the subjects form part'. If the purchasers have a dry rot problem a year after the date of entry and a top flat proprietor avers that he had mentioned a rot problem in the roof timbers to the seller some time ago will the purchaser have a claim against the seller? If clause C6 is accepted in its entirety the answer may well be in the affirmative. Many practitioners feel that the principle of '*caveat emptor*' in so far as the structure and state of repair of the premises is concerned is sensible especially given the range of surveys now available to a purchaser[1].

1 See para 1.02 ff above.

Clause C7 – Sales by limited company

4.63 'If a limited company has had an interest as heritable proprietor in the subjects of sale within the period of positive prescription:
(a) in the case of any such company other than the seller, there will be delivered or exhibited prior to the date of entry Searches in the Register of Charges and that company's file kept by the Registrar of Companies, both brought down to the first business day following on disposal of the subjects of sale by that company, to disclose no entry prejudicial to the granting of the deed effecting such disposal; and
(b) in the event of the seller being a limited company, there will be delivered to the purchaser at the date of entry (i) Searches in the Register of Charges and in the seller's file kept by the Registrar of Companies dated not earlier than seven days prior to the date of entry to disclose that no notices of liquidation, receivership, appointment of an administrator or striking off have been registered against the seller and (ii) a letter from the creditor under any floating charge created by the seller confirming that no steps have been taken or will within the ensuing twenty eight day period be taken or will within the ensuing twenty eight day period be taken to crystallize such floating charge and (iii) a Letter of Obligation by the seller's solicitor undertaking on behalf of the seller to deliver to the purchaser within two months of the date of entry continued Searches in the said Register of Charges and file kept with the Registrar of Companies brought down to a date twenty two days after the date of recording/registration of the Disposition in favour of the purchaser, which Searches will disclose no entries affecting the disposal of the subjects of sale by the seller.'

This clause is designed to deal with the two cases where a company is selling and where a company has been the heritable proprietor during the prescriptive period.

4.64 Where a company is selling, the purchaser will wish to ensure that there is nothing which will prevent the company from selling. An inhibition against the company is one possibility, but that is something which is not peculiar to transactions involving companies. Peculiar to companies are, firstly, liquidations, receiverships, administration orders, striking-offs and the like and, secondly, the existence of floating charges which upon crystallisation have the effect of a fixed security.

4.65 Where a company is in liquidation, the directors are divested of their powers and although the assets of the company remain vested in it, only the liquidator has the power to deal with them. Under the Insolvency Act 1986[1] in the case of a winding up by the court, the liquidator may apply to the court to have the assets of the company vested in him. This is, however, unusual. Where the liquidation is voluntary, that fact must be registered in the Companies Register within 15 days of the winding-up resolution[2]. Non-voluntary liquidations and the appointment of a provisional liquidator must be registered 'forthwith'[3]. As we shall see later, these matters impinge upon the period of the search in the register of charges which the purchaser should request.

1 Section 145.
2 Insolvency Act 1986, s 84.
3 Ibid, s 130; Insolvency (Scotland) Rules 1988 1986, SI 1986/1915, r 4.2.

4.66 If an administrator has been appointed, he is required to intimate his appointment to the Registrar of Companies within 14 days of the order for administration[1]. The company remains a going concern, its assets remain vested in it, but the directors are divested of their powers which are exercised by the administrator. The administrator, however, cannot disclaim any contracts entered into by the company prior to his appointment[2].

1 Insolvency Act 1986, s 21.
2 For the powers of an administrator see Insolvency Act 1986, Sch 1.

4.67 If the company has been struck off or otherwise has its name removed from the list of incorporated companies, its assets vest in the Crown as *bona vacantia* and are administered on behalf of the Crown by the Queen's and Lord Treasurer's Remembrancer[1]. The Q &

LTR will normally be prepared, on payment of expenses, to grant any conveyance to the person entitled to ownership[2].

1 Companies Act 1985, s 419.
2 *The Conveyancing Opinions of J M Halliday* (ed by D J Cusine) p 41.

4.68 Where there is a floating charge over the company's heritable property and that property is sold, the charge ceases to affect the property, but the purchaser's concern will be to ensure that the charge has not crystallised. Crystallisation will take place on the winding-up of the company[1] or on the appointment of a receiver[2]. Winding-up has already been dealt with, but if a receiver is appointed either by the creditor in terms of his floating charge or by the court, any contract entered into prior to the appointment remains in force, but the receiver does not incur any personal liability thereon[3].

The possible existence of a receiver, liquidator or administrator requires the purchaser to consider the length of the search in the Charges Register and Companies Register and the implications of purchasing from such a person[4]. The Charges Register will reveal floating and fixed charges, and in addition, any receivership. A search here will not, however, reveal whether the company has gone into liquidation, nor whether an administrator has been appointed. That information is revealed in the G fiche which is another part of the company file. Assuming that a search is instructed or is being continued in both the Charges Register and in the G fiche, it should commence with 27 October 1961, the date when the Companies (Floating Charges) (Scotland) Act 1961 came into force, or the date of incorporation of the company, whichever is the later. Current practice is to continue the search from that date down to a date 22 days after the close of the property search. The reason for this is that a floating charge must be registered within 21 days of its creation[5]. It is usual practice in any transaction to see an interim report on all searches including company searches prior to settlement and the standard missives clauses provide that the interim report in the Company and Charges Registers will be dated not earlier than seven days prior to the date of entry. If the date of settlement of the transaction is later than the date of entry, it is desirable to ensure that an interim report is received not earlier than seven days prior to that. However, the clause covers everything which the purchaser from a company would expect to see on inspection of the company's file. It should be noted that although the existence of a notice of sequestration will also be revealed in the Personal Registers, there will not be an entry there in respect of a compulsory liquidation.

1 Insolvency Act 1986, ss 53–54.

2 Companies Act 1985, s 463(1).
3 Insolvency Act 1986, s 57(4).
4 In so far as these matters are concerned see Gretton 'Purchasing from trustees in bankruptcy, liquidators and receivers' Law Society of Scotland General Conveyancing Course, October 1991.
5 Companies Act 1985, s 393.

4.69 As an addition to the clause C7, some missives will provide for warranties and indemnities to be given by directors of the company. It is interesting to observe that if one were purchasing from a well-known public limited company it is unlikely that such warranties would be asked for. They might, however, be sought where the seller is a private family-controlled company regarded as a less sound body. In some cases, however, such warranties are given in the following terms:

'There shall also be delivered at the date of settlement warranties from the directors of the company that (a) they are unaware and have no reason to believe that any steps have been taken or are likely to be taken to wind up the company, or appoint a liquidator, receiver, or an administrator or otherwise place the company in a position where it is or will be unable to implement its obligations hereunder, and (b) provided the disposition in favour of the purchaser is recorded within [   ] days of the date of settlement, they will be jointly and severally liable to indemnify the purchaser against any loss resulting from his title being adversely affected by the liquidation or winding-up of the company, or the appointment of a receiver or an administrator.'

Such a clause puts the directors in the position of personal guarantors for the company and is not always acceptable to directors, especially those who do not hold shares in the company.

4.70 Clause C7 provides for a letter of non-crystallisation to be granted by the creditor under any floating charge confirming that no steps have been or will be taken to crystallise the floating charge within a 28-day period. The date of this letter should be as close to settlement as possible. Some letters of non-crystallisation go further than this and it is not unusual for a purchaser's solicitor to incorporate a preferred style in an offer, especially where it is known that the seller is a company. A fuller letter might be in the following terms:

'We the .... Bank plc the holders of the undernoted Bond and Floating Charge granted by the above named Company hereby confirm that:
   (First) as at today's date we have taken no steps to crystallise the said Bond and Floating Charge, and (Second) we consent to the sale of the undernoted subjects by the said Company and to their release from the

ambit of the said Bond and Floating Charge provided the disposition thereof is recorded in the General Register of Sasines/registered in the Land Register within the undernoted period.

Yours faithfully'

Such a letter should note the details of the floating charge, the subjects of sale and the 28-day or other period required.

4.71 Clause C7 provides for a letter of obligation to be granted by the selling company's solicitors undertaking on behalf of the selling company to deliver completed searches in the Register of Charges and Company's file within two months of entry brought down to the end of the 22-day period. Obviously no solicitor is likely to grant a personal letter of obligation in respect of company searches.

Clause C8 – Letter of obligation

4.72 'In exchange for the purchase price on date of entry, there will be delivered a Letter of Obligation from the seller's solicitors, in terms to be adjusted, but incorporating said solicitors' obligation in respect of delivery or exhibition of the Searches in the Property and Personal Registers.
or
A Letter of Obligation from the seller's solicitors in the form recommended by the Registration of Title Practice Book.'

This clause is included as an optional clause and does not usually feature in offers for domestic property. As a matter of practice, where missives for a domestic transaction are silent, the purchaser's solicitor is entitled to assume that he will receive the selling solicitor's obligation at settlement. As a matter of law, however, the solicitor is not a party to the contract between the purchaser and seller and cannot be forced to grant an obligation. It is for this reason that clause C8 features as one of the standard clauses. It should, however, be noted that the obligation undertaken in clause C8 is undertaken by the seller. What the seller is really guaranteeing is that he will be able to persuade his solicitor to grant a personal obligation. It would be improper professional practice for a selling solicitor to accept the terms of clause C8 on behalf of his client and then subsequently indicate that he had no intention of providing his client with the necessary obligation. It is recommended that letters of obligation should be given only in respect of searches, discharges and other minor matters over which the solicitor has absolute control. Selling solicitors should not give obligations to deliver items which may not

be in existence or which may be difficult to obtain or to have carried
out specific works or repairs[1].

1 For a discussion on letters of obligation in general see *Halliday* vol II, para 23–09 ff.

Practice suggestions for framing clauses in missives

4.73 Despite the tendency to standardisation, the solicitor's obligation, whether acting for purchaser or seller, is still to frame the
missives in accordance with the requirements of the particular transaction and having regard to the respective interests of the parties.
Practitioners should always remember that the test for professional
negligence is essentially an evidential one. The standard of care owed
by a solicitor to his client is both contractual and delictual. A client is
entitled to that standard of care and skill to be expected of a reasonably competent and careful practitioner. A solicitor does not fall
below that standard if he makes an error of judgment in an individual matter. It must be shown that any error or omission was such
that an ordinary competent solicitor would not have made. Accordingly, in negligence cases opinion evidence is sought from experi-
enced and qualified conveyancing practitioners as to what a
reasonably competent solicitor would or would not have done at the
time of the alleged mistake. Practitioners should not assume that if
they adopt the Law Society approved standard clauses, they will be
totally protected from a claim for negligence. Similarly, practitioners
should not assume that if they use their own form of offer or acceptance or require to qualify the standard clauses, they are in some way
breaching a sacred code. Neither the standard clauses nor any other
standard form of missive will be appropriate to every transaction and
a solicitor's actings will be judged on the appropriateness or otherwise of the missives he has drafted to the particular circumstances of
the transaction. Practitioners are in the habit now of sending their
clients copies of all offers, qualified acceptances and other formal
correspondence. While this is a useful and commendable practice, it
does not absolve the solicitor from the need to communicate
effectively with his client, reporting where appropriate and ensuring
that his client understands the position when giving instruction[1].
Where the Law Society of Scotland's standard missives are used, the
client's guide which is designed to be read along with the missives
should be sent to the client with a copy of the actual offer. Subject to
the foregoing general observations, the authors offer the following
practical guidelines in relation to the framing of clauses in offers and
qualified acceptances.

1 See Ch 1 on the role of the solicitor; 'Keeping the client informed – an exercise in self-preservation' Dr Robert Rennie, Law Society PQLE course on General Conveyancing, November 1990; Code of Conduct for Scottish Solicitors, October 1989, clause 5(e).

Impose obligations and not understandings

4.74 The use of the words 'it is understood that' to proceed what should in effect be a warranty or obligation undertaken by one party or the other should be avoided. It is very common in missives to see these words used in relation to a vast array of matters. However, phraseology of this type does not always achieve the desired result of placing a binding obligation on one of the parties. A clause which states:

'It is understood that the roads, footpaths and sewers are public'

begs the question of whether this is simply an understanding on the part of the purchaser, the seller or the world at large. As a statement, it may be accurate or inaccurate. The problem with this type of clause is it does not convert the statement into a warranty or an obligation and ultimately the court might have difficulty in interpreting just what the clause means. The object of framing clauses in missives is of course to avoid vagueness and uncertainty of this type. A clause should simply be left either as a bare condition of the offer,

'The roads, footpaths and sewers are public'

or alternatively should be phrased as a positive obligation on one party to produce evidence of a particular state of affairs:

'The seller will provide at his expense a certificate prior to the date of entry from the appropriate local authority confirming that the roads, footpaths and sewers are public and taken over and maintained by the local authority'.

Delete and re-draft rather than modify

4.75 Various clauses in qualified acceptances make reference to clauses in the original offer and in some cases a further formal letter or letters will further qualify the qualified acceptance in relation to the same offer clause. If there is a dispute later on in the transaction in relation to the particular matter covered by the clause and subsequent modifications, it can be fiendishly difficult to actually work out what has been agreed. A typical example of a clause which is often modified to death is a condition in relation to woodworm and dry rot. The standard missives clause C6 is in the following terms:

'The seller is not aware of the existence in the subjects of sale (or the building of which the subjects form part) of woodworm, dry rot, wet rot or rising damp and, in the event that a Guarantee has been issued in respect of any of these, said Guarantee is valid in all respects and the benefit thereof shall be transferred to the purchaser. Further the said Guarantee, with the specification and estimate to which it refers, shall be delivered at settlement.'

This might be met with a qualified acceptance in the following terms:

'3. With reference to your clause C6, a Guarantee from Messrs Fungus Worm & Co Ltd, is enclosed herewith and your clients will be held to have satisfied themselves as to its terms.'

This might be further modified by the purchaser to the following effect:

'With reference to your modification 3, your clients will be bound to produce the survey report covering the work done.'

The sellers may think that the effect of these three clauses is that provided their clients can produce the original survey report on which the guarantee is based then there is no further obligation. The purchasers on the other hand may be of the view that the first line and a half of the clause, whereby the seller states he is not aware of any woodworm, dry rot or rising damp still applies. It would have been infinitely preferable from the seller's point of view if clause C6 had been deleted in its entirety and then re-cast in a form acceptable to the seller:

'Clause C6 of the Law Society of Scotland standard clauses incorporated in your offer is delete. There is enclosed herewith a survey report and Guarantee from Messrs Fungus Worm & Co Ltd. The seller undertakes to co-operate in having this Guarantee transferred to the purchaser should any consent be required.'

The effect of this is that the seller has granted no warranties but that the purchaser has had produced to him the guarantees which are available.

Avoid 'with reference to'

4.76 If it is intended to modify a particular provision then it should be deleted or modified with express words of deletion or modification. It is asking for trouble to simply use the words 'with reference to the clause. . .'. An example of this type of loose draftsmanship is often found when dealing with title deeds. Standard clause B2 is in the following terms:

'There will be no pecuniary burdens affecting the subjects of sale after settlement and the Titles do not contain any other burdens of an unusual or unduly onerous nature'.

Very often this type of clause is met with a qualification in the following terms:

'With reference to your clause B2, the titles are enclosed herewith'.

What the seller intends by this qualification is that the purchaser will accept whatever burdens and conditions are contained in the deeds. However, a qualification of the type illustrated above may not achieve this purpose. The qualification does not attempt in terms to delete or modify clause B2 nor does it even state that the seller will be bound to have satisfied himself. The qualification is really only a statement that the titles have been enclosed. At best it is an invitation to the seller to examine them in relation to matters covered by clause B2. An appropriate qualification would be in the following terms:

'Clause B2 is delete. The ground burdens affecting the subjects of sale have been redeemed. Our client's title deeds are enclosed herewith and your clients by acceptance hereof shall be bound to accept the burdens and conditions contained therein'.

Don't tell stories – impose or remove obligations

4.77 In some cases a party lodging an offer will wish a warranty covering a particular point from the seller. Similarly when submitting a qualified acceptance a seller may wish to pass on information to the purchaser which the purchaser must accept and thus negate any suggestion of warranty from the seller. In either of these two situations it is important to place the matter in a proper legal context whereby either the seller accepts an obligation or alternatively the purchaser accepts evidence of a situation and the fact that the seller grants no warranty and undertakes no obligation in that respect. Typical examples of loose drafting in this type of situation are to be found when dealing with the vexed questions of planning permissions, building warrants and completion certificates for alterations to the subjects. It is easy when acting for a seller to fall into the trap of simply telling a story in the hope that this will in some way modify or negate a clause in the offer, such as clause B8 of the standard conditions. Clause B8 states:

'If the subjects of sale have been converted or altered in the 10 year period prior to the date of conclusion of the bargain to follow hereon the seller will provide at his expense such evidence as may reasonably be required by the purchaser that (i) the relevant works were carried out and completed in conformity with all necessary local authority permissions and warrants, and, (ii) all other necessary consents and permissions, including that of the superior were obtained and any conditions attaching thereto were fully implemented.'

An example of a loosely drafted qualification in relation to that clause is as follows:

'Your clause B8 – the subjects were converted five years ago by the addition of an attic bedroom and internal stairway. The conversion was carried out by a previous owner to the seller and there is enclosed herewith the planning permission and building warrant being the only documents delivered by the said previous owner to the seller.'

What the seller intends by this qualification is to force the purchaser to accept the situation on the basis of the only available documentation. The seller does not have a completion certificate nor does he appear to have a superior's consent. However, the qualification as framed merely tells a story. It does not in terms bind the purchaser to accept the situation. It is also worthy of note that the qualification does not deal with any other alterations. When dealing with a comprehensive clause such as B8, it is worthwhile considering whether to delete the clause in its entirety and simply forward the available permissions with a new clause inserted into the missives to the effect that no other permissions or consents in respect of any alterations will be exhibited or delivered. That is undoubtedly the safest course. If it is decided simply to modify the clause without leaving a general cover in respect of other alterations then the suggested modification might be in the following terms:

'Clause B8 of the Law Society of Scotland standard clauses incorporated in your said offer shall be modified to the following effects:
a) The only conversion or alteration of which the seller is aware is the installation of an attic bedroom and internal stair which works were carried out by the owner previous to the seller. The seller does not warrant or guarantee that there have been no other conversions or alterations.
b) In so far as the seller is aware, the said installation of the attic bedroom and internal stair were works carried out and completed in conformity with all necessary local authority permissions and warrants but no warranty or guarantee is given by the seller to this effect.
c) There are annexed to this qualified acceptance and relative to this clause planning permission and building warrant from Eastwood District Council in respect of the aforementioned attic conversion and installation of internal stair. No other consents, permissions (including superior's consents), warrants, letters of comfort or completion certificates will be

exhibited or delivered by the seller in respect of the aforementioned alteration or any other alteration or conversion.'

It will be seen at a glance that this is a complicated modification of a comprehensive original clause and the benefit of deleting clause B8 in its entirety and simply inserting a clause suitable for the seller's purpose will be readily appreciated. The authors should make it clear that they are not suggesting that such a modification should be accepted by a purchaser in relation to alterations in each and every case[1].

1 See para 4.38 ff above.

Where items have to be produced, insert a time limit

4.78 Clause B10 of the standard clauses provides a time limit from the date of conclusion of missives for the production of documentary evidence required to implement other obligations of the seller in clauses B1 to B9 of the standard clauses. Where there is an obligation to produce a document it is often a good idea to specify a time limit within which the document must be produced and a sanction in the event that the time limit is not met. The difficulty here relates to the question of materiality. The authors have already noted that in the absence of a stipulation to the contrary the obligation on the seller to produce a valid and marketable title is not deemed to be material and the seller is entitled to a reasonable time after the date of entry to produce the same before the purchaser can resile[1]. When acting for a seller a solicitor should scrutinise materiality clauses carefully, especially where they impose a time limit. Before accepting such a clause a seller's solicitor should be reasonably sure that the time limit can be met and check carefully with the seller if there is doubt. It is very difficult to explain to a disappointed seller just why the purchaser was able to resile because a duplicate completion certificate relating to a ten-year-old extension could not be produced within fourteen days after conclusion of missives in circumstances where the seller is adamant that the completion certificate was granted. There are many cases where purchasers desperately look for excuses to resile and materiality clauses and time limits for the production of documentation very often afford them this opportunity. Having said that, from the purchaser's point of view, a materiality clause with a time limit does at least give the purchaser an option at the date of entry where matters of substance have not been produced by the seller. If no materiality provisions exist and there are outstanding matters at settlement the purchaser's solicitor can be placed in a very awkward position in advising his client whether or not he has the right to resile.

1 See para 4.22 above.

Set out the remedies in the missives

4.79 Even where the missives include all the rights and obligations which the parties wish to undertake and to be undertaken and these are properly expressed as obligations, difficulties can still be caused for the parties where the remedies which flow from a breach of these obligations are not set out. There are three basic remedies for breach of contract: specific implement, repudiation and damages. These remedies are discussed in more detail later[1]. Specific implement is always a difficult option especially in cases where one of the parties finds it impossible to implement. Generally speaking the choice between the parties is among repudiation without damages, repudiation with damages and simple damages. The *actio quanti minoris* may feature if the missives allow for its application[2].

Basically, a party can repudiate and claim damages where there has been a material breach of contract. Where the breach is not material then damages may be the only remedy. It is now universal practice when acting for a seller to insert a penalty clause providing for interest in the event of late settlement, usually at a penal or persuasive rate above the base lending rate of one of the major clearing banks coupled with a right to repudiate if payment is not made within a set time. With a clause of this type the parties know exactly where they stand and are not left wondering about 'reasonable time' or whether interest is due as a matter of damages where possession is not taken[3]. From the seller's point of view it can also be useful to stipulate what remedies the purchaser will have in the event that the seller cannot produce a particular item or satisfactorily implement one of the obligations in the missives. A good example of this type of stipulation is in relation to the production of planning certificates. Where the seller's solicitor has already obtained a planning certificate then this can simply be sent to the purchaser's solicitor with the qualified acceptance either deleting the planning clause or modifying it to the effect that the purchaser will accept the certificate as being in full implement of the seller's obligations. Where the seller's solicitor is not in possession of an up-to-date planning certificate at the date the offer is received it is now common practice to stipulate in the qualified acceptance that the planning certificate will be exhibited to the purchaser's solicitor and if it discloses anything materially adverse to the subjects the purchaser's only remedy will be to resile from the bargain without damages being due to or by either party. This type of qualification is usually coupled with a time limit within which the purchaser must intimate repudiation failing which he will be held to accept the planning certificate as being in full implement of the seller's obligations in terms of the missives. The unfortunate difficulty with this type of clause is that it introduces into the missives what is in effect a suspensive condition. Similar qualifications are sometimes inserted in relation to the production of titles and other matters.

1 See Ch 6.
2 See para 6.28 below.
3 See para 6.24 ff below

Tie qualifications into particular clauses in the offer

4.80 When issuing a qualified acceptance it is important to relate particular qualifications to particular clauses in the missives. General qualifications which bear to relate to the offer as a whole are to be avoided. A bad example of this type of practice arises in relation to the submission of title deeds by the seller so that the purchaser is deemed to have satisfied himself. In most offers there are various matters relating to the titles which are covered by different clauses. In the Law Society standard clauses matters of title are mentioned in clause A2 (minerals), A3 (ground burdens), A7 (validity and marketability in sasine titles), A8(a) and A8(b) (validity and marketability in sasine and first registration transactions), A8(c) (links required for dealings in registered titles), A8(d) (entries, deeds and diligences in land registration cases), B1 (overriding interests), B2 (ground burdens and onerous conditions), B3 (implementation of title conditions), B4 (reservations of minerals) and B5 (common rights). If it is intended to force the purchaser to satisfy himself in relation to all or any of these title matters by forwarding the title deeds of the property, including any writs referred to for burdens, with the qualified acceptance then the qualification or qualifications should refer to each clause in the offer which is intended to be modified in this matter. Despite this, there are cases where a seller seeks to qualify all these matters in a general way in the following manner: 'The title deeds for the subjects are enclosed herewith and your clients will be deemed to have satisfied themselves in relation thereto'. This clause is intended, presumably, to cover all title matters in the missives but it does not go anything like far enough to achieve that effect. A qualification of this type should refer to each and every clause in the offer which it is intended to modify and the precise nature of the modification intended for each clause should, where necessary, be spelled out. It is the authors' view that it is over-ambitious to attempt this in one qualifying clause. It is better to deal with the individual clauses in the offer by individual qualifications referring to the title deeds in each case. An obvious example of the proper framing of this clause would be in relation to a minerals reservation. Standard clauses A2 and B4 taken together may require to be qualified where the seller's property is in an old mining area such as Lanarkshire. An appropriate qualification would, it is suggested, be in the following terms:

'Clauses A2 and B4 of the Law Society of Scotland's standard clauses incorporated in your offer shall be modified to the effect that your clients will accept the terms of the mineral reservation clause as contained in our client's title which is sent herewith notwithstanding the fact that it provides that there shall be no compensation payable for surface damage caused by mineral operations.'

Alternatively, the original clauses in the offer may be deleted and redrawn in the acceptance.

Remember the common law obligations

4.81   Where the seller chooses to delete certain clauses from an offer it should be borne in mind that unless other provisions are substituted common law obligations will still apply. Accordingly a mere deletion of clause B2 in the standard conditions will mean that the common law obligation on the seller to deliver a valid and marketable title containing no onerous conditions will remain enforceable. If it is intended that the purchaser must accept the burdens and conditions contained in the title deeds then the common law obligation must be negated by an appropriate qualification. The same applies to the other common law obligations on the part of the seller to deliver a valid disposition, exhibit clear searches or other land register equivalents and give possession.

Be specific in relation to alterations or additions where appropriate

4.82   In some cases a purchaser will be aware that a property has been extended, converted or altered. It is good practice when taking instructions from a purchaser to ask for details of any such alterations, extensions or conversions[1]. Similarly, if the solicitor is in possession of details of the survey carried out on the property for the purchaser, he may be aware of alterations, additions or conversions noted by the surveyor. In these cases it is appropriate to specify in the offer the particular alteration, addition or conversion for which permissions are sought. The general clause dealing with such matters should still be left intact in case there have been other alterations which have gone unnoticed by the purchaser or the surveyor. To particularise in this area is helpful not only to the purchaser but also to the seller because it gives an early indication of the documentation which will be required.

1 See para 1.19 above.

Consider the timing for the production of titles, permissions and warrants

4.83 It is normal practice nowadays to produce titles, planning permissions, warrants, completion certificates, superior's consents and specialist guarantees with a qualified acceptance on the basis that the purchaser will have to accept the same. In the authors' view this is an unfortunate development which marks a significant change in the way in which solicitors operate the system of house purchase. Earlier practice dictated that missives be concluded simply and quickly and thereafter the parties were left to implement their obligations; the purchaser to pay the price, take entry and enter with the superior by registration and the seller to deliver a valid disposition, valid marketable title, clear searches and give entry. When missives were simple this system worked admirably. With the advent of extraneous matters such as building warrants, matrimonial consents and affidavits, planning certificates and the like, the practice has altered. The recent practice poses difficulties especially for the purchaser's solicitor who can sometimes be left with a ludicrously short period in which to carry out a substantial amount of work by way of examination of titles, warrants, permissions, guarantees, plans and other matters. At the same time as this important and detailed work is being carried out the purchaser is usually desperate to know that the bargain has been concluded. The combination of these two pressures on the solicitor can often lead to mistakes being made. Although this unfortunate development may be seen as something which works wholly for the seller's benefit there can be drawbacks even from that party's point of view. Where missives are concluded and deeds and documents in implementation of the seller's obligations are produced during the course of the transaction, the seller has at least the certainty of knowing that there is a contract. If the purchaser takes objection to anything which has been produced then there can at least be an argument between the two solicitors before the purchaser is asked to concentrate his mind on the question of repudiation. Where titles and other matters are sent with a qualified acceptance the purchaser obviously has the simple option to withdraw because there is no concluded bargain. At that point it is infinitely easier for the purchaser's solicitor to put pressure on the seller's solicitor to produce extra documentation such as letters of comfort, consents from superiors, up-to-date planning certificates and the like. As a bargaining matter the purchaser can threaten to resile. If the missives have been concluded before all the documentation has been produced the purchaser must weigh up seriously any question of repudiation against the likelihood of the seller being able to cure a defect or in some cases against the likelihood of a court accepting that the defect warrants repudiation. Even from the seller's point of view therefore there is sometimes an argument for concluding the bargain and producing documentation at a later date[1].

1 See Donald B Reid 'Superior's consents' Current Developments in Conveyancing Lecture for University of Strathclyde Centre for Professional Legal Studies, October 1992.

When buying from companies specify the warranties which will be required

4.84 Apart from new housing it is unusual in the context of domestic house purchase to find that the seller is a limited company, but it is not impossible to encounter this situation. Some companies do own domestic heritable property for use of their employees and most builders and developers are limited companies. It should be borne in mind that directors' warranties and indemnities in relation to liquidations, receiverships, administration orders and striking-off notice are not things which directors can be forced to grant. These things should be specifically contracted for if they are required. Very few directors of building companies will be prepared to grant any such warranties or indemnities.

Materiality clauses

4.85 Selling solicitors should be on the lookout for a materiality clause in the small print of any Schedule. Clause B10 of the Law Society standard clauses virtually makes the whole of section B a material matter in so far as it relates to items which have to be exhibited, by providing that a purchaser can resile if these items are not delivered. There are some schedules attached to offers which provide that each and every clause will be deemed to be material. A seller should be wary of accepting this type of clause. If everything is made material then the fact that a feuduty redemption receipt cannot be traced by a certain time may afford the purchaser an excuse to resile from the bargain. In a case like this the seller's solicitor will be in a difficult position unless he has meticulously explained to the seller the principles of materiality in relation to breach of contract and repudiation. In these circumstances the seller would be quite within his rights to question why his solicitor had accepted such a draconian concept of materiality in relation to a trivial matter like a feuduty redemption receipt.

What are the subjects of the offer?

4.86 Solicitors tend to think of the subjects as being the heritable property but in most offers certain moveable items are included. Selling solicitors should beware of clauses which apply to 'the whole subjects of this offer'. The Law Society's standard clause A4 states:

'The seller will maintain the subjects of sale in their present condition (fair wear and tear excepted) until the purchase price is paid or the purchaser takes possession, whichever date is the earlier. In the event of the subjects being destroyed or materially damaged prior to that date either party shall be entitled, but not obliged, to resile from the contract to follow hereon without penalty and without prejudice to any entitlement to claim damages from the other party.'

Ths clause refers to the 'subjects of sale'. It is submitted that this definition will include any moveable items. If a carpet is completely destroyed in a freak accident an argument might be mounted by a purchaser that he is entitled to resile from the bargain. The counter-argument presumably would be that the destruction of one carpet was not material in the context of the totality of the subjects of sale (ie heritage and all the moveables) but it is a point to consider.

Avoid matters which have to be agreed in the future

4.87 One of the main advantages of the Scottish system of house purchase is that it allows a contract to be concluded for the purchase and sale of heritable property speedily and affords the parties a certainty which other systems lack. If matters are left to be agreed between the parties after the conclusion of missives this certainty can disappear. There are perhaps two areas in the context of domestic heritable property where matters are sometimes left to be agreed. These are in relation to plans, and to inventories of moveable items. Where domestic heritable property is a new plot of ground or a split-off from an existing building involving exclusive areas of ground, common areas of ground, paths etc, it is preferable that the plan of what is to be conveyed ultimately in the disposition is annexed to the missives. A clause in an offer or a qualified acceptance to the effect that the area or extent of the subjects shall be agreed between the parties and set out on a plan prepared for the parties is not really satisfactory. If it is impossible to provide a plan for the missives then at the very least such a clause should indicate what is to happen if the parties ultimately cannot agree on the plan. The obvious solution would be that either party would then be entitled to resile without penalty. In relation to moveable items it is likely that a list will be available at the time the offer is submitted but in a case where a house is being bought with its whole contents from a body of trustees a list is not always to easy to compile. In these circumstances it is still preferable for a formal inventory to be attached either to the offer or to the qualified acceptance. To offer for a property 'together with the whole contents thereof' is unsatisfactory and likely to be productive of dispute and argument. In such cases it is better to have an inventory professionally prepared by a firm of auctioneers which can then be annexed to the missives before they are finally concluded.

Suspensive conditions

4.88 If an offer is to be made subject to a suspensive condition, care should be taken in the framing of the appropriate clause. A suspensive condition in relation to the purchase of domestic property tends to relate to initial matters such as surveys and loan finance but suspensive conditions can also appear in cases where a property, such as a plot of ground, is being purchased subject to the obtaining of planning permission and building warrants. In relation to suspensive conditions, as to finance and surveys, it is important when acting for a purchaser to make it clear that the clause is inserted solely for the purchaser's benefit and the purchaser will be the sole judge of the satisfactory nature or otherwise of any finance or survey which is obtained. When acting for a seller it is important that there is a time limit within which the purchaser must purify the suspensive condition as to finance or survey. Any time limit should however make it clear who is entitled to resile when the time limit has expired. A loosely worded clause in the following terms is to be avoided: 'With reference to your clause 7, the purchaser shall be bound to intimate purification of said clause within seven days of the date of this qualified acceptance'. A qualification of this type fails to state what is to happen on the expiry of the time limit. There are various possibilities. Either the seller can stipulate that if the purchaser has not intimated failure to purify the clause within a set time then the clause will be deemed to be purified and the purchaser will have to proceed, or the seller can stipulate that he can resile without penalty if the purchaser has not intimated purification within the time limit. A third alternative is simply to provide that the missives will fall automatically if no intimation is received. Normally a seller would wish the opportunity of deciding whether to resile or to allow the purchaser more time. Suspensive conditions in relation to planning permission or warrants to be obtained require careful consideration. Clearly there should be some time limit within which the permissions must be obtained and again it must be clear who is entitled to resile if the time limit is not met. In some cases where the party imposing the suspensive condition is the only party entitled to resile the condition can be construed as being wholly in favour of that party. In such a case that party can waive the condition and proceed with the contract without the consent of the other party[1]. If on the other hand the missives state that either party is entitled to resile in the event that the suspensive condition is not purified within the time limit or if the wording of the particular clause indicates in some other way that the clause is also for the benefit of the other party, then the purchaser cannot waive the suspensive condition without the seller's consent[2]. In all cases it is a question of interpreting the particular suspensive condition. In a recent case[3] a condition which was qualified to the effect that the bargain would be voidable at the instance of either party in the event that permissions and consents had not been obtained by a stated date was still held to be solely for the benefit of the purchasers. There have been a number of cases dealing with particular clauses in differing terms[4]. When acting for a purchaser the message of these conflicting cases is clear. If the purchaser wishes the right to waive the clause and proceed without the seller's consent, he should stipulate for this in the missives[5].

1 *Dewar & Finlay Ltd v Blackwood* 1968 SLT 196; *Gloag* pp 437 and 438.
2 *Ellis & Sons Second Amalgamated Properties Ltd v Pringle* 1975 SLT 10.
3 *Imry Property Holdings Ltd v Glasgow YMCA* 1979 SLT 261.
4 On this point see *Halliday* vol II, para 15–07; *Aberfoyle Plantations v Cheng* 1960 AC 115; *T Boland & Co Ltd v Dundas's Trustees* 1975 SLT (Notes) 80; *George Packman & Sons Ltd v Young* 1976 SLT (Notes) 52; *Gilchrist v Payton* 1979 SC 380; *Heron Garage Properties v Moss* [1975] 1 WLR 148; *Zebmoon Ltd v Akinbrook Investment Developments Ltd* 1988 SLT 146; *Tarditi v Drummond* 1988 GWD 37–1542 and 40–1652.
5 For a style of suspensive conditions in relation to planning permission and building warrants giving the purchaser a right to withdraw see *Halliday* vol II, para 15–106.

Builders' missives

4.89   As has already been noted it is normal for builders who are selling ground on which they are also building to frame their own offer to be signed by the purchasers as individuals[1]. There is no doubt that there is a feeling among the legal profession that such missives are generally framed with the builders' interests in mind. Having said that there is a wide variance among builders as to the conditions they seek to impose and some builders' missives are perfectly fair to both parties. A purchaser's solicitor should be sure that the purchaser understands the clauses in the missives before the purchaser signs and the solicitor should not be afraid to qualify such pro forma missives where it is appropriate to do so. Each missive will require to be looked at on its own merits but the following are points which may arise from time to time.

1 See para 2.02 above.

Deposits and stage payments

4.90 Most builders' missives provide for a deposit of some sort or another. If this is a small amount then there is no difficulty, but purchasers' solicitors should be wary of paying over large percentages of the price whether as a deposit or as instalments at various stages of building before a title is delivered[1]. In many cases builders accept that title has to be granted earlier than final settlement where stage payments are required. It is normal for builders' missives to provide that a deposit will not be refundable in the event that the purchaser does not complete the purchase, quite apart from any other claims the builder might have for breach of contract.

1 *Gibson and Hunter Home Design Ltd* 1976 SC 23.

Date of entry

4.91 Most builders' missives tie the date of entry to the completion of the dwellinghouse. Some builders' missives state that the purchaser must pay the price when the house has been certified as complete by the builder or within a set period thereafter. This is not generally acceptable unless it is tied to the house also being passed as fit for habitation by the local authority. Completion certificates are rarely available as soon as the house has been passed.

Payment of the price

4.92 Virtually all builders' missives make payment of the price a material condition of the contract and allow for repudiation by the builder after a set period. Normally the price is settled between the purchaser's solicitor and the builders' solicitor in exchange for a signed conveyance. In some builders' missives, however, there is a provision which stipulates that payment of the price must be made by telegraphic transfer either to the builders' solicitor or more unusually to the builders themselves. There are obvious dangers in accepting this type of clause. If telegraphic transfer is to be made the solicitor must ensure that he has cleared funds in his possession. Similarly, before the telegraphic transfer is instructed arrangements must be made with the builders' solicitor to ensure that the necessary disposition or other title is delivered. The difficulty with telegraphic transfer is that it cannot be instructed conditionally. Accordingly a covering letter should be sent to the builders' solicitors to arrive before or at the same time as the funds pointing out that payment is conditional on the settlement documentation being delivered by return, failing which the funds transferred must be repaid. The risks are increased where funds are to be paid directly by transfer to the builders and not to their solicitors. It is difficult to see how the builders themselves can come under anything like a professional obligation to refund money or hold pending the delivery of a signed deed. One wonders what would happen if a telegraphic transfer was made to the builders on the same day on which a receiver or liquidator was appointed and the disposition or other conveyance had not been despatched by the builders' solicitors to the purchaser's solicitors[1].

1 *Gibson and Hunter Home Design Ltd*, above.

Penalty clauses

4.93 Penalty clauses in builders' missives generally specify a higher rate of penalty interest than is normal in domestic conveyancing in general.

Plans

4.94 Seldom is a title plan attached to a builders' missive. In most cases the property will be described with reference to a plot number on a layout plan which may or may not have been seen by the purchasers at the site. The purchasers should be asked whether or not they have seen a site plan and are satisfied with the area of ground. During the title examination it is imperative that the purchasers see and approve the draft title plan.

Title conditions

4.95 Builders' missives often stipulate that the purchaser will accept the title conditions already laid down by the builders in a deed of conditions covering the whole development. After a purchaser has signed missives in these terms no objection can thereafter be taken to the burdens set out in the deed of conditions.

Title examination

4.96 Some builders' missives provide that the titles can only be examined in their own solicitors' offices although most builders are prepared to send out sets of titles or copies.

Searches

4.97 Most builders' missives provide that no searches of any kind including searches in the Register of Charges will be provided. This normally is extended to include forms 10, 11, 12, 13 or 16 for land registration cases. Clearly in these cases the purchaser's solicitor must obtain the appropriate searches or reports to protect the purchaser and any lender.

Specifications

4.98 It is unusual to find construction plans or specifications annexed to a builders' missive unless the house is being built specially for a particular plot. Most houses are purchased on the basis that they are a particular type of house and most builders' missives allow the builder to vary sizes, specifications and materials.

Permissions and warrants

4.99 Most builders' missives provide that the builder will not be bound to produce planning permissions or building warrants and that a completion certificate will not necessarily be available at settlement.

Actio quanti minoris *and non-supersession*

4.100 Few builders' missives provide that the *actio quanti minoris* will be available to the purchaser and some builders' missives contain no non-supersession provision except in relation to the issue of a land certificate in land registration cases. Both of these factors can be important. Builders' title plans are notoriously inaccurate and in some cases the purchaser will be faced with a fresh plan which offers less than was shown on the original layout. Similarly completion certificates and National House Builders Council documentation by their very nature are not usually available until after delivery of the deed. Such matters may be regarded as collateral and survive the delivery of the deed but the latest case law on supersession seems to doubt whether any obligations relating to the heritage can be regarded as collateral.

Variation of estate layouts and plans

4.101 Many builders' missives provide that the builder is entitled to vary estate layouts and plans. This type of clause can affect the purchaser in two ways. Firstly, it may allow the builder to alter the actual boundaries of the plot being purchased from those shown to the purchaser at the site office. Secondly, it may allow the builder to alter the whole character of the estate by altering house designs, roads and amenity areas. Thus the purchasers of an expensive ten-apartment bungalow may find themselves forced to accept a reduced plot surrounded by flats instead of other bungalows or double feus.

CHAPTER 5

The relationship of the missives to the disposition

5.01 This chapter will consider the following matters: (a) the nature of the right conferred by the missives; (b) conflict between the missives and the disposition; and (c) the effect of delivery of the disposition, particularly in relation to the missives.

(a) The nature of the right conferred by the missives

5.02 The missives constitute a contract between the parties and so that gives rise to personal obligations and rights. Under the missives, the purchaser has personal rights against the seller, the most important being to demand delivery of the disposition in exchange for the price. The seller likewise has a personal obligation to deliver the deed, again in exchange for the price. No real right is conferred on the purchaser under the concluded missives, and the mere execution of a deed without delivery is not sufficient to transfer ownership[1]. In *Gibson and Hunter Home Design Ltd (in liquidation)*[2], G entered into missives to purchase a house from a builder. Although the builder had executed the disposition in favour of G, a heritable creditor who was consenting failed to execute the deed before the company went into liquidation. The court held that in the absence of delivery of the disposition, G had only a personal right against the builder. As he had paid over the purchase price, he had no option but to rank with the ordinary creditors. That decision has been followed recently[3]. There are therefore considerable risks in paying over the purchaser price, or a significant part of it, without the disposition being delivered in exchange[4]. If the purchase price of heritable property is to be paid by instalments, which nowadays is uncommon, it is safer for the purchaser to obtain and record a disposition in his favour and for the seller to obtain from the purchaser a standard security for the balance of the purchase price.

1 See Kenneth Reid 'Ownership on registration' 1985 SLT (News) 280.
2 1976 SC 23.
3 *Margrie Holdings Ltd v Commissioners of Customs & Excise* 1991 SLT 38; *Watters v Motherwell District Council* 1991 SLT (Lands Tr) 2.
4 Halliday *Conveyancing Law and Practice in Scotland* (1985) vol II, para 15–82; RAE 'Script for two nightmares: letters of obligation' (1975) 20 JLSS 260.

(b) Conflict between the missives and the disposition

5.03 Insofar as questions of heritage are concerned, the only conflict between the missives and the disposition which is likely to arise is in relation to the description or extent of the subjects, since the disposition itself, generally speaking, only carries forward the missive contract insofar as the actual conveyance of the heritage is concerned. With the advent of land registration and a closer examination of physical boundaries and their relationship to existing title boundaries, conflicts of this nature more often arise. Basically a purchaser is only entitled to a conveyance of the subjects as described in the missives subject to such formal modifications in wording as are necessary to render the description appropriate for a deed which is to enter the Register of Sasines or the Land Register. The classic exposition of this principle comes in the leading case of *Houldsworth v Gordon Cumming*[1]:

'It is manifest, therefore, that if a question arises as to the description to be inserted in a Disposition, the first thing to be settled is what is the exact subjects sold; and that is to be determined, not by the existing titles, but by the Contract of Sale, interpreted, as every document whatsoever must, more or less, be interpreted, by reference to the surrounding circumstances.'

In that case there was a contract to sell 'the estate of Dallas' as shown outlined on a plan. When the titles to the estate were delivered for examination to the purchaser's solicitors, it was noticed that the actual estate as contained in the titles comprised a larger area. A dispute arose between the parties as to the subjects to be conveyed but neither party wished to resile. It was held that the purchaser was only entitled to a disposition of what he had contractually purchased in terms of the contract, namely those subjects outlined on the plan. If, however, the estate had been sold under missives or a contract of sale under a general name without any restriction then the inference would have been that the whole estate comprised in the title under the general name had been sold. As Lord Kinnear put it:

'I should be disposed to concede further that, if an estate is sold under a general name, without reservation or restriction expressed in the contract, or capable of being proved by competent evidence, the reasonable inference is that what is intended is the estate so named which the seller holds under a valid title.'

1 1910 SC (HL) 49 at 55 per Lord Kinnear.

5.04 Where a purchaser concludes missives for the acquisition of an ordinary dwellinghouse there is normally no plan attached to the missives. Generally speaking the offer is in respect of a dwellinghouse described by postal address and 'the ground pertaining thereto'. Questions arise where the title which is offered by the seller is either greater or smaller than that physically pertaining to the dwelling-house. In land registration cases a P16 report often discloses an inconsistency between the title boundaries shown in the existing sasine title and the physical boundaries as shown on the ordnance survey sheet. By and large the principles laid down by Lord Kinnear apply. Provided the missives do not indicate that any part of the ground physically pertaining to the house is reserved or excluded then the seller must give title to the whole of that ground. Furthermore, if the seller's title turns out to be insufficient to support the whole of that physical area, there will be a breach of contract and the seller will require either to obtain title to any omitted area or suffer the conse-quences of that breach. Conversely, if it turns out that a seller's title is greater than the ground physically pertaining to the subjects the seller cannot be forced to convey the whole title. This question was con-sidered by the late Professor Halliday in 1977 when he was asked to give an opinion in circumstances where a seller sought to hold back part of the garden ground of a dwellinghouse after missives had been concluded. The seller stated that there had been an oral agreement with the purchaser after conclusion of missives to exclude some ground. The purchaser denied the existence of such an agreement. Professor Halliday was clear in his view that the *dictum* of Lord Kinnear applied. He stated:

'That *dictum* was pronounced in relation to the sale of an extensive landed estate. It seems to me to apply with much greater force to the sale of a small country dwellinghouse with a garden and curtilage ground where it would not be anticipated that the seller would be retaining part of the ground pertaining to it.'

Professor Halliday pointed out that it was not competent to alter the written missives by parole evidence. He was clear in his view that the seller had to convey all that was in his title since all that ground physically pertained to the dwellinghouse[1].

1 *The Conveyancing Opinions of J M Halliday* (ed by D J Cusine) p 147.

5.05 Where there are discrepancies of a minor nature which are purely accidental then matters can often be resolved by use of a boundary agreement between adjoining proprietors to bring the title boundary into line with the physical boundary[1]. These agreements simply state that the boundary line is, for the future, to be a different line from that laid down in the titles to the properties with reference to an attached plan. The consent of heritable creditors to such agreements is not required although it may be advisable to inform the heritable creditor of the proposed alteration.

1 Land Registration (Scotland) Act 1979, s 19.

(c) The effect on the missives of delivery of the disposition-supersession

5.06 It is probably not inaccurate to say that, prior to 1981, few practitioners gave much thought to the relationship between the missives and the disposition. If pressed on the matter, they might have responded by saying that the disposition superseded the missives in their entirety, but might have added, after further reflection, that that was the case only in so far as the disposition and the missives dealt with the same matters, ie probably only the parties, the property, the price and the date of entry. They might have suggested that all other matters contained in the missives, eg planning, the status of roads etc and moveables, were irrelevant to the transfer of the heritage and hence could not be superseded by the disposition. The notion that the disposition supersedes the missives entirely is called the single contract theory, whereas the double contract theory is the term used to describe the view that the missives are superseded only in relation to the matters which appear also in the disposition. The origins of these theories and the circumstances in which the double contract theory came to be replaced by the single contract theory are well explained in an article by Kenneth Reid[1]. As he observes, although in the early part of the nineteenth century both theories received support from the judiciary, by the end of the century the single contract theory had been established by a number of House of Lords' decisions.

1 'Prior communings and conveyancing practice' (1981) 26 JLS 414.

5.07 The classic statement of the single contract theory was made by Lord Watson in *Lee v Alexander*[1] and repeated in *Orr v Mitchell*[2]. The statement is as follows:

'According to the law of Scotland, the execution of a formal conveyance, even when it expressly bears to be in implement of a previous contract, supersedes that contract *in toto*, and the conveyance thenceforth becomes the sole measure of the rights and liabilities of the contracting parties'[3].

It should be noted that it is the delivery and acceptance and not the execution of the conveyance which is significant. Although, as Kenneth Reid points out in his article, the reasons for espousing the single contract theory are not fully convincing, it is now established law until overturned by the House of Lords.

1 (1883) 10 R (HL) 91.
2 (1893) 20 R (HL) 27.
3 *Lee v Alexander* above, at 96; *Orr v Mitchell* above, at 29.

5.08 One of the things which would be immediately obvious to anyone looking at missives in 1883 is that they dealt only with matters which would also be dealt with in the disposition. However, by 1903, the missives which were in issue in *Jamieson v Welsh*[1] dealt also with moveables. In more recent years, missives have dealt with many more matters such as roads, footpaths and sewers, planning and building control, central heating, fair rents etc, none of which would expect to find a home in the ultimate conveyance. It is not therefore surprising that in 1966, in the sheriff court case of *Bradley v Scott*[2] the sheriff held that a clause dealing with a building control matter, ie whether an extension had been erected in accordance with the building regulations, was a collateral matter. In the same way, the court in *Jamieson v Welsh* held that a clause relating to moveables was collateral. Until 1981, conveyancing practice and judicial thinking had moved away from the single contract theory.

1 (1900) 3 F 176.
2 1966 SLT (Sh Ct) 25.

Winston v Patrick

5.09 In 1981, thinking on the relationship between missives and the disposition appeared to change, or at least began to develop. In *Winston v Patrick*[1] a clause not dissimilar to that in *Bradley v Scott* was under consideration, but perhaps somewhat surprisingly *Bradley* was not referred to in argument, nor by the court. It is possibly true to say that more has been written about the decision in *Winston* than on any other conveyancing topic in recent years[2]. It is not our purpose to examine *Winston* in any depth, but its main significance is that it redefines the scope of collateral obligations. It will be recalled that *Winston* was concerned with a clause in missives which provided that the statutory requirements in connection with the erection of an extension had been complied with. The clause was in the following terms: 'The seller warrants that all statutory requirements in connection with the erection of the subjects of sale and any additions, extensions and alterations thereto have been fulfilled'.

1 1980 SC 246.

2 Eg Kenneth Reid 'Prior communings and conveyancing practice' (1981) 26 LJSS 414; Anon 'The warranty lives on: *Winston v Patrick* again' (1982) 27 JLSS 37; Kenneth Reid 'Avoiding *Winston v Patrick*' (1983) 28 JLSS (Workshop) 330; D J Cusine '*Winston v Patrick* revisited briefly' (1986) 31 JLSS 16; Kenneth Reid 'Five years on-living with *Winston v Patrick*' (1986) 31 JLSS 316; Kenneth Reid '*Winston v Patrick*: the problems continue' (1988) 33 JLSS 7; 'Missives and the disposition' (1988) 33 JLSS 57; D J Cusine '*Winston v Patrick* and their heirs and assignees' (1988) 33 JLSS 102.

The scope of the decision

5.10 Although the Sheriff Principal attempted to define the scope of the term 'collateral', the Second Division decided the case on two narrow grounds without offering any general guidance on what is encompassed within the term 'collateral obligations'. The first ground was that the clause did not oblige the seller to do anything in the future and merely stated the position as at the date of entry. In that connection, Lord Wheatley said, 'Counsel for the defenders maintained that clause 9 did not incorporate any personal or collateral obligation to do anything in the future. . . We are of the opinion that the proper construction of the clause . . . is the one for which the defenders' counsel contended[1]'. It is possible to spend a considerable amount of time analysing that statement[2], but it is frankly not possible to know precisely what his Lordship meant. For example, for an obligation to be collateral, is it both necessary and sufficient to require the seller to do something after the date of entry, or is an obligation to do something in the future merely one example of a collateral obligation? We await a more helpful statement from the Inner House. The second ground was that in an earlier House of Lords case[3] the court had refused to allow evidence of what was contained in the missives. The earlier case however concerned a warrandice clause in a disposition and not the missives.

1 1980 SC 246 at 249.
2 See Kenneth Reid's article (1981) 26 JLS 414.
3 *Hughes v Hamilton* (1819) 1 Bligh 287.

Exceptions to the supersession rule

5.11 However, the decision in *Winston* has made it clear that although the single contract theory prevails, there are exceptions. At one point in his judgment, Lord Wheatley made the following comment. It is strictly speaking *obiter*, but it is an attempt to define the scope of the exceptions to the prior communings rule.

'It was also accepted [by counsel for the pursuers] that there were exceptions to that general rule [ie the prior communings rule]. Examples of these were (a) where the missives incorporated obligations in relation to moveables which would not be appropriate to be included in a disposition of heritage, (b) where in the missives there was a collateral obligation distinct from the obligation to convey the heritage, and (c) where there was an agreement in writing either in the missives or in a separate document or in the disposition itself that a personal obligation included in the missives would subsist and remain in force even if it was not included in terms in the disposition[1].'

In reality, there are only two exceptions, because an obligation to deliver moveables was an established exception prior to *Winston* on the ground that such an obligation was collateral[2]. Although the decision in *Winston* is considered by many to be unfortunate, either because it failed to set out any general principles, or because it flew in the face of existing practice, or both, nevertheless conveyancers had to deal with the consequences. This they did by inserting, at first in the missives alone, a clause to the effect that notwithstanding delivery of the disposition the missives would remain in force. These 'non-supersession' clauses have been refined in the light of further examination of the literature on the matter and the reported cases, which have followed upon *Winston*.

1 1980 SC 246 at 249.
2 See *Jamieson v Welsh* (1900) 3 F 176.

Non-supersession clauses

5.12   Although there has not yet been a case before the Inner House, there have been numerous sheriff court cases and a few Outer House ones. These cases have dealt with or at least raised a number of matters:
(a) What is the minimum period for which the missives should subsist after settlement?;
(b) what is the appropriate place for a non-supersession clause?;
(c) how effective are such clauses?; and
(d) how should collateral obligations be expressed in order to be effective?

5.13   *(a) The time limit.* Immediately after *Winston* non-supersession clauses were frequently encountered in which there was no period specified. In that event, such a clause subsists for 20 years[1]. However, the practice began in some cases of having fairly short periods, eg three months, or six months, but at least one case, *Pena v Ray*[2] demonstrated the problems which could be encountered if the period was too short. That case involved the sale of a castle which was being renovated by the seller. The missives provided that the necessary works would be carried out at the seller's expense 'on or before the . . . date of entry'. The missives were to remain in force for a period of three months after settlement. However, the necessary works were not completed by the date of entry, and the purchaser raised an action for specific implement some six months after settlement. Because of the time limit in the missives, the court had no option but to dismiss the action. Ironically, the time limit was inserted by the purchaser, as is usually the case, but had there not been any such limit, the missives might have endured for the prescriptive period. In the light of varying practice, a period of two years was suggested, on the ground that by that time the search in a sasine transaction should have been produced and in a land register transaction, the land certificate[3]. That suggestion was endorsed in a later article by Kenneth Reid[4] and it is now almost invariable practice. Nevertheless, it is essential in each case to consider whether that period is long enough in the light of any obligations which are known by the parties to be outstanding at the date of settlement. It is submitted that in a straightforward domestic transaction, two years should be sufficient. In framing such a clause, it is important to ensure that the time limit does not expire after an action has been raised, but before it is decided or settled, and in order to deal with both, the following wording appears in the Law Society of Scotland's standard missives clauses[5]:

'This offer and the missives following hereon will form a continuing and enforceable contract notwithstanding the delivery of the disposition except insofar as fully implemented thereby. The missives, however, will cease to be enforceable after a period of two years from the date of delivery of said disposition, except insofar as they are founded upon in any court proceedings which have been commenced within the said period.'

1 Prescription and Limitation (Scotland) Act 1973, s 6; *Barratt Scotland Ltd v Keith* 1992 GWD 4–208.
2 1987 SLT 609.
3 D J Cusine '*Winston v Patrick* revisited briefly' (1986) 31 JLSS 16.
4 'Five years on – living with *Winston v Patrick*' (1986) 31 JLSS 316.
5 Clause B11, April 1992 (ie the second version).

5.14   *(b) The appropriate place for the clause.* It has to be accepted that the established practice, certainly in domestic transactions, is to have a clause in both the missives and the disposition. That practice is largely the result of two sheriff court decisions emanating from Aberdeen[1] where the sheriffs held that it is not sufficient to have a clause in the missives on the ground that if the disposition supersedes the missives it does so *in toto*. That may be logical, but it has been argued that if it is possible, as it is, to contract out of a rule of the law of evidence, it should be possible to do this in the missives alone[2]. Another possible argument is that a clause keeping the missives alive is collateral. It is worth observing also that in *Winston* counsel conceded that it would have been sufficient to have had a clause in the missives alone. Even although that was a concession, there is a view that had the then Lord Justice-Clerk thought that such a concession was unwise or an incorrect understanding of the law, he would have made an observation to that effect. The matter awaits a ruling from the Inner House, but *ob majorem cautelam*, the clause usually appears in both documents. There have been a number of cases which have supported each position[3]. As an alternative to having a clause in the disposition, the conveyancing committee of the Law Society expressed the opinion that an exchange of letters at settlement after delivery of the disposition would suffice to circumvent the 'supersession' argument[4]. This is not commonly done in domestic transactions, but is more common in commercial and agricultural transactions.

1 *Finlayson v McRobb* 1987 SLT (Sh Ct) 150; *Wood v Edwards* 1988 SLT (Sh Ct) 17.
2 D J Cusine '*Winston v Patrick* and their heirs and assignees' (1988) 33 JLSS 102.
3 The following cases have decided that the clause should be in both the missives and the disposition: *Finlayson* above; *Wood* above; *Greaves v Abercromby* 1989 SCLR 11. The opposite view was taken in *Fetherston v McDonald (no 2)* 1988 SLT (Sh Ct) 39; *Jamieson v Steward* 1989 SLT (Sh Ct) 13; *Jones v Heenan* 1988 SLT (Sh Ct) 53.
4 March 1988.

5.15 (*c*) *How effective are such clauses?* Immediately after *Winston* it was assumed that the effect of the decision could be circumvented by a non-supersession clause in the missives. This practice was refined to include a time limit, after which the missives would cease to be effective. Thereafter, non-supersession clauses were inserted also in dispositions. Some doubt has been cast on the effectiveness of such clauses by the decision of Sheriff Gerald Gordon in *Greaves v Abercromby*[1]. In order to understand the decision in *Greaves* it is necessary to hark back to a comment by Lord Wheatley in *Winston* where he mentioned three situations in which clauses in the missives would remain alive after delivery of the disposition. The third of these was 'where there was an agreement in writing either in the missives or in a separate document or in the disposition itself that a personal obligation included in the missives would subsist and remain in force even if it was not included in terms in the disposition[2]'. Sheriff Gordon put particular store on the term 'personal obligation' and he observed that that term and 'collateral obligation' were used together by Lord Wheatley and that one of the issues which remains unresolved is whether he regarded the two as synonymous. In *Greaves*

Sheriff Gordon held, in his view following *Winston*, that non-supersession clauses can deal only with personal obligations, and personal obligations by definition are unrelated to the transfer of the property. In other words, they must be collateral. However, since it was established long before *Winston* that collateral obligations survive delivery of the disposition anyway, it follows that non-supersession clauses are unnecessary and of no effect, unless they deal with collateral matters. It is submitted, with respect, that this decision is incorrect in that, if only by implication, it makes nonsense of the notion of non-supersession clauses which the court in *Winston* recognised. It has to be said, however, that Sheriff Gordon's careful judgment is based on a close analysis of what was actually said in *Winston* and the passage from *Winston* cited may be self-contradictory. Further doubt has been cast by the more recent Outer House case *Porch v Macleod*[3] in which a house had been erected without either planning permission or a building warrant. The clause was similar to that in *Winston*, but in *Porch* there was a non-supersession clause in standard form, and so it was argued by the purchasers that the missives could be looked at after settlement of the transaction. Lord Milligan rejected that argument by looking at the exact terms used by Lord Wheatley in *Winston* and he came to exactly the same conclusion as Sheriff Gordon.

1 1989 SCLR 11.
2 1980 SC 246 at 249.
3 1992 SLT 661.

5.16 (*d*) *What are collateral obligations?* Since the decision in *Winston*, the law has been and still is in a state of confusion. Prior to *Winston* the thinking among practitioners (which was supported by the few reported cases) was that anything which appeared in the disposition and also the missives would be superseded on delivery of the disposition, but anything else was collateral. At that time, the two most important cases were *Jamieson v Welsh*[1] and *McKillop v Mutual Securities*[2]. In *Jamieson* it was held that an obligation to deliver moveables which were included in the price and specified in the missives was collateral and hence survived the delivery of the disposition. A similar decision was reached in *McKillop*, where there was a contract for the sale of a shop which was being reconstructed. After settlement of the transaction, it was found that there was a structural defect which rendered the shop unsafe. It was held that there were, in reality, two contracts; one for the sale of the heritable subjects and a separate contract for services, the latter being collateral. It was therefore held that the pursuer could sue for damages for breach of the latter after delivery of the disposition. In a third case, *Bradley v Scott*[3], the sheriff held that a clause warranting that there were no outstanding local authority notices affecting the subjects of sale was collateral.

1 (1900) 3 F 176.
2 1945 SC 166.
3 1966 SLT (Sh Ct) 25.

5.17 Although both *Jamieson* and *McKillop* remain unaffected by the decision in *Winston*, the exact definition and ambit of collateral obligations has been altered radically by *Winston*. In that case, it was held that the following obligation was not collateral: 'The seller warrants that all statutory and local authority requirements in connection with the erection of the subjects of sale and any additions, extensions and alterations have been fulfilled'. The Second Division indicated that this was no more than a statement about the state of affairs at the time of transaction and did not relate to any time after the date of entry. However, the court did recognise that there were exceptions to the single contract theory, which have recently been stated in the Outer House to be the only exceptions[1]. The exceptions which have already been noted are: (a) the obligation to deliver moveables; (b) a collateral obligation; and (c) where there is an agreement in writing to the effect that a personal obligation will subsist after delivery of the disposition. In a subsequent case, Lord Milligan observed that before exception (c) could add materially to exception (b) 'what must be envisaged is a non-collateral but personal obligation in the missives coupled with the agreement in writing referred to. The circumstances in which a condition will fall within the third exception but not within the second appear unexplored[2]'.

1 *Taylor v McLeod* 1990 SLT 194 at 199 per Lord Milligan; *Porch v Macleod* 1992 SLT 661 per Lord Milligan.
2 *Taylor v McLeod*, above at 199.

5.18 As has been said, in *Winston* and later cases it has been recognised that the decisions in *Jamieson*[1], to the effect that delivery of moveables, and in *McKillop*[2], to the effect that an obligation to carry out work on a shop which was being constructed, were collateral are still sound law[3]. The decision in *McKillop* has been followed in two very recent cases. One was *Hardwick v Gebbie*[4], in which a builder was employed to erect a house in accordance with certain plans and specifications. After entry, the purchasers discovered several discrepancies between the finished product and the specifications. They raised an action for breach of contract and Lord McCluskey held, following *McKillop*, that the obligation was collateral primarily on the basis that the parties clearly contemplated that 'the obligation should

be a future and continuing one[5]'. The other was *King v Gebbie*[6] where
the facts were very similar and Lord Caplan reached the same conclusion as Lord McCluskey. In *Black v Gibson*[7], Lord MacLean held that
an obligation to deliver a completion certificate could not be fulfilled
until after entry and so a clause obliging the seller to produce such a
certificate survived the delivery of the disposition.

1 (1900) 3 F 176.
2 1945 SC 166.
3 Eg *Taylor v McLeod*, above; *Hardwick v Gebbie* 1991 SLT 258; *King v Gebbie* 1992
  GWD 24–1379.
4 1991 SLT 258.
5 1991 SLT 258 at 263.
6 1992 GWD 24–1379.
7 1991 GWD 15–938.

5.19   Since *Winston*, there have been numerous other cases all raising
the same point, ie whether a particular obligation is or is not collateral.
In *Jones v Heenan*[1], it was held that a clause not dissimilar to the clause
in *Winston* was collateral. '[The seller] warrants . . . that these items
[*inter alia* a swimming pool] are and will be in proper working order
and condition at entry.' It could have been held that this was simply a
statement rather than a future and continuing warranty, but it was
deemed to be collateral. It is respectfully submitted that the approach
in *Jones* is preferable to that in *Winston* in that there should not be any
need to couch a warranty in terms which appear to oblige the seller to
do something after the date of entry. Other warranties such as the
statutory warranties in the Sale of Goods Act 1979 are not construed in
that way[2]. However, although there are cases in which the missives
have required the seller to do something after the date of entry, eg
repair defective items, and these have been clearly held to be collateral[3], there are also cases such as *Jamieson v Stewart*[4], *Greaves v
Abercromby*[5] and *Porch v Macleod*[6] where despite such words, the
clause has been held not to be collateral. More recently, it has been
held that a clause which says 'The seller will warrant. . . .' fell to be
construed as a warranty to be given at a later date and not a present
warranty[7].

1 1988 SLT (Sh Ct) 53.
2 Section 11; *Gloag* pp 609–613.
3 *Wood v Edwards* above; *Jones v Heenan* above; *Central Govan Housing Association v R
  Maguire Cook & Co* 1988 SLT 386; *Taylor v McLeod*, above; *Bourton v Claydon* 1990
  SLT (Sh Ct) 7.
4 1989 SLT (Sh Ct) 13.
5 1989 SCLR 11.
6 1992 SLT 661.
7 *Parker v O'Brien* 1992 SLT (Sh Ct) 31.

Conclusion

5.20 Prior to *Winston*, it is submitted that the law was clear; since *Winston*, it is muddled and unclear and clarification is needed urgently. Although the single contract theory largely prevailed, the words of two of the judges in *Jamieson v Welsh* are instructive. Lord President Balfour said[1]:

'It is quite in accordance with principle that where a disposition bears to be in implement of a contract mentioned in it, or where the kind of property to which a contract related has been made the subject of a disposition, this should conclude all question as to the meaning of the contract in so far as it relates to that property, as, for example, the extent or incidents of it, but I am unable to see any ground upon which it could be held to conclude all question in regard to property which it does not purport to convey, eg corporeal moveables, merely because the two kinds of property were dealt with in one contract . . . [T]he disposition does bear to be granted or accepted as in implement of any contract, so that its terms do not import that the contract is discharged in so far as it related to anything not conveyed by the disposition.'

Lord Kinnear said: 'Nor will it do to say that this contract [the missives] cannot be looked at because of the subsequent disposition, because it is only by looking at it that the argument arises at all[2]'. These sentiments are echoed by Lord Moncrieff in *McKillop v Mutual Securities*[3]:

'No doubt when parties are at issue as to the purport of certain matters regulated *ad interim* by the missives, as for example as regards the subject of sale, a formal document which also purports to deal with the same matter will displace the less formal writings which had preceded it. But if in the missives there be not only an agreement for purchase and sale but be also . . . a second independent though collateral agreement . . . such an independent agreement will not be discharged by the taking of a formal disposition, seeing that the formal disposition does not enter into the area of that particular agreement.'

1 (1900) 3 F 176 at 180.
2 At 182.
3 1945 SC 166 at 172–173.

5.21 It is submitted that these statements, especially that of the Lord President, are wide enough to encompass the principle that the missives and the disposition have to be looked at to determine which matters are common to both, and to endorse the principle that the disposition will supersede the missives only in relation to such matters. This view does of course favour the double contract theory which had in earlier cases been disavowed by the House of Lords. At one point it was announced that the Scottish Law Commission was looking at the *Winston* saga[1] but to date no proposal, or discussion paper has appeared. Pending a definitive statement from the Inner House, or perhaps even Parliament, solicitors who frame missives need practical guidance and so the question: is what does the framer of missives do in the present climate? If mass emigration of the legal profession is not an option, the following comments may be of some assistance.

1 Twenty Third Annual Report 1987–88 (Scot Law Com no 114, para 2–2).

Suggestions for practice

5.22   The first option is to do nothing, in the hope that the problem will be resolved by a higher court, or retirement will come. This is not tenable. The problem is with us and, in the interests of the client, it must be addressed. Failure to do so is probably professional negligence. With that sobering thought, we pass to consider other options.

5.23   The second option is to deal with the matter in the missives. This involves both (a) keeping the missives alive after delivery of the diposition and (b) ensuring that clauses dealing with other matters not germane to the disposition are themselves not superseded. It is submitted that until the cases of *Wood v Edwards*[1] and *Finlayson v McRobb*[2] are declared to be unsound, it is not enough to have a clause in the missives alone. Moreover, ensuring that clauses dealing with collateral matters referred to survive the disposition appears to be less easy. Given the decisions in *Greaves v Abercromby* and *Porch v MacLeod*, which held that non-supersession clauses are effective only for collateral obligations, there is no point in having a non-supersession clause. That is not the practice and it is submitted that the present practice of having such clauses ought to continue until the law is clarified. If one takes the commonest example of the central heating system, the warranty should be in the present tense. 'The seller warrants. . .' If the phrase is 'The seller will warrant. . .' that may be inadequate on the basis of *Parker v O'Brien*[3]. However, it is also essential to require the seller to do something after settlement, should that prove necessary, because 'The seller warrants. . .' was held in *Winston* to be a statement about the position at the date of the missives and did not provide a remedy to deal with the position thereafter. The warranties should therefore be stated to be referable to the date of entry, for example, 'At the date of entry, all conditions of title will have been implemented, except those of a continuing nature'. In this connection, it is important to bear in mind that if a warranty is non-collateral, it will *not* survive the disposition even if it is coupled with an ancillary positive obligation. That is demonstrated by

Porch where the clause was as follows: 'All necessary consents and warrants . . . have been obtained and complied with . . . and satisfactory evidence to substantiate this will be exhibited . . . before and delivered at settlement.' The fatal words were 'have been obtained'. That was held to be a non-collateral warranty and hence could not survive, despite the positive obligation.

1 1988 SLT (Sh Ct) 17.
2 1987 SLT (Sh Ct) 150.
3 1992 SLT (Sh Ct) 31.

5.24   The third option is to ensure that the non-supersession clause is inserted not only in the missives, but also in the disposition, and that the missives provide for this. However, this may not get over the problem of the definition of collateral obligations thrown up by the decisions in *Greaves* and *Porch*.

5.25   The fourth option which is an alternative to the non-supersession clause is to enter into a post-settlement agreement. In order to avoid any argument that this agreement might itself be superseded by delivery of the disposition, it is desirable that the agreement should be entered into after delivery of the disposition and it would be prudent to narrate that delivery of the disposition has taken place. The post-settlement contract should incorporate the terms of the missives, or even repeat them in full. It should then go on to state which clauses are to remain in force and provide for the period during which the post-settlement contract is to remain in force. This will usually be two years, following the established practice in non-supersession clauses.

5.26   In the present uncertainty it would be rash and arrogant of us to suggest that any of the options which we have mentioned above is guaranteed to succeed. Any warranty which may appear to have been given by the authors is non-collateral and will not survive the date of publication of these presents! It seems, however, that the safest course is to enter into a post-settlement contract along the lines suggested by the Law Society. The missives should of course bind the parties to enter such an agreement.

5.27   We are of the opinion that *Winston v Patrick* is wrongly decided, either because a clause dealing with planning matters ought to be regarded as collateral, or taking a more narrow view of the decision that a warranty does not depend for its efficacy on a statement requiring the granter to do something in the future. As we have already pointed out, this is not so in the law on sale of goods and, more obviously, in the context of the sale of heritage, it has never been suggested that the phrase 'I grant warrandice' which appears in a disposition cannot be founded upon after settlement. Our suggestion would be to revive the double contract theory, or to adopt the single contract theory, but recognise that it applies only to those clauses that are common to both the missives and the disposition.

CHAPTER 6

Breach of missives

Introduction

6.01 This chapter is concerned with the remedies which are available to the parties to the missives, in the event of a breach. Some years ago, the most common breach of the terms of missives was a delay in settlement, usually because the purchaser was unable to pay the price, or the full price, on the agreed date. However, there can be other breaches, such as a delay or failure on the part of the seller to deliver a valid marketable title to the subjects, or to give vacant possession on the date of entry. This chapter will consider the respective obligations of the parties and then the consequences of breach, including delays in settlement.

In theory, there can be numerous breaches of the terms of the missives and when there is a breach, it is clearly important to read the missives carefully. It may be, for example, that a clause is declared to be material, in which event a breach of such a clause will entitle the innocent party to resile[1]. In some missives all the clauses are declared to be material. Although such a provision will have been inserted by the purchaser for his benefit, it has to be borne in mind that the seller may also seek to take advantage of the provision.

1 Gloag *The Law of Contract* (2nd edn, 1929) p 592; McBryde *The Law of Contract of Scotland* (1987) para 14–69 ff.

The obligations of the parties

6.02 These obligations are usually spelt out in the missives, but even if they are not there are certain obligations imposed on either party by operation of law. The obligations imposed on the seller are:
(1) to deliver or exhibit a valid marketable title to the subjects within a reasonable time and containing no conditions contrary to the provisions of the missives;
(2) to give entry to the subjects, usually with vacant possession;
(3) to deliver a valid disposition of the subjects;

155

(4) to deliver, or exhibit searches in the Property and Personal Registers, or the equivalent reports from the Land Register[1] which show nothing prejudicial to the seller's title or his ability to grant a valid disposition. (In a sasine transaction, this is usually referred to as a 'clear search' but the two are not synonymous); and

(5) to implement the other obligations in the missives.

The obligations of the purchaser are:

(1) to pay the purchase price on the agreed date;

(2) to become infeft within a reasonable time in order to relieve the seller of his liability for performance of the obligations in the title; and

(3) to implement any other obligations in the missives.

These obligations are in many ways counterbalancing and it is important to consider each obligation separately, beginning with the seller's obligations.

1 For Land Register transactions, see paras 4.24 to 4.29 above.

(1) *To deliver or exhibit a valid marketable title*

6.03 The first issue which arises is whether there is a distinction between a title which is valid and one which is marketable. In other words, is it possible to have a title which is valid but not marketable? Although as has been pointed out earlier, there is such a distinction[1], it is submitted that, in practice, the obligations in relation to the title and those in relation to the searches are complementary and therefore it is unlikely that anyone would accept a title which is valid but unmarketable, as where the seller was inhibited. What is comprehended within the term 'valid marketable title' has been covered in Chapter 4[2].

In any consideration of the validity of the title, a distinction has to be drawn between defects in the title and the absence of a title at all. If there is a defect in title, unless the missives oblige the seller to produce a title within a particular period, he must be given a reasonable opportunity to remedy the defect[3]. If, however, the seller has no title to the subjects or part of the subjects which he has contracted to sell, the purchaser is entitled to resile immediately and without affording the seller any opportunity to put matters right, eg by acquiring a title to minerals, or the other part of the subjects of sale[4]. The leading case is *Campbell v McCutcheon*[5], where the seller agreed to sell subjects without excluding the minerals which were reserved to the superior. The purchaser resiled and his entitlement to do so was upheld by the court. In the course of his judgment the Lord President (Clyde) said, 'If he chose, the defender, when he discovered that the seller had in fact no right to a part of what was purported to be sold, was entitled to withdraw the offer and the contract then came to an end[6]. It is clear from the opinion of the Lord President with whom Lord Carmont concurred that the purchaser need not wait until the date of entry before resiling[7]. It was argued that because the purchaser resiled prior to the date of entry, he had deprived the seller of an opportunity to acquire the minerals where the seller had indicated a willingness to do this, and to proceed with the sale. Both of these points were rejected by the court, the distinction being drawn between a defect in the title itself and no title at all to the subjects or part thereof. It is now almost invariable practice to state in the missives that the minerals are included in the sale, in so far as the seller has right thereto[8]. There are various kinds of mineral reservation clauses in titles and these are dealt with in Chapter 4. Even if the minerals are excluded in terms of the missives, the severity of a particular reservation may give rise to questions of marketability, although in such a case the seller would be entitled to be given a reasonable period within which to cure any defect.

Another example of a lack of title arises where the contract is for the purchase of a house and garage and it is discovered that the garage is built on someone else's ground. In such a situation, in practice a purchaser will usually allow the seller time to acquire a title, but he need not do so, and may resile immediately on the basis of *Campbell*. As we shall see later, the *actio quanti minoris* is not available and the purchaser is therefore left with the only option – to resile at settlement, unless a reduction in the price can be agreed between the parties. The view has been expressed that damages may be claimed for the loss of the bargain[9].

1 See para 4.22 above.
2 See para 4.22 ff above.
3 Three years has been held to be unreasonable – *Fleming v Harley's Trs* (1823) 2 S 373, but not six months – *Raeburn v Baird* (1832) 10 S 761.
4 *Campbell v McCutcheon* 1963 SC 505; *Whyte v Lee* (1879) 6 R 699; *Moray v Pearson* (1842) 4 D 1411.
5 Above.
6 1963 SC 505 at 511.
7 Lord President Clyde at 510; see also *Morris v Ritchie* 1992 GWD 35–1950.
8 See the clause referred to at para 4.14 above.
9 Walker *The Law of Civil Remedies in Scotland* (1974) p 748.

(2) *To give possession*

6.04 It should be noted that a contractual provision specifying 'possession' does not mean vacant possession. In *Lothian & Border Farmers v McCutcheon*[1] it was held that the existence of a lease was not a contravention of missives which specified only for entry. In order to ensure that the purchaser is given vacant possession, if that is what is wanted, the purchaser should provide for 'entry and vacant possession'.

Although this may come as a surprise to many clients, 'entry', or 'entry with vacant possession' does not mean immediate entry[2], and, on the analogy of *Rodger (Builders) Ltd*[3], the seller must be given a reasonable time to give entry[4]. Most missives provide that payment of the price on the date of entry is a material condition, but not all make the giving of entry also material. Occasionally, missives provide for a deduction from the purchase price in the event that the seller fails to give entry on the due date, but such provisions are not common, if only because the prudent seller will seek to have them deleted.

If the purchaser is also selling, or the seller is also purchasing another property, the solicitor will try to ensure that the dates of entry in both contracts coincide, but some purchasers may wish to take entry to their new house at an earlier date than the date of entry to the one which they are selling, in order to settle in. It is therefore sensible to advise the client that although the dates of entry do coincide, there is no guarantee that it will be possible to move into the new house at any particular time or on the date specified. Even if the giving of entry on the due date is made material, in practice, a purchaser will not normally wish to resile from the bargain if entry on that date proves impossible.

If the contract provides for entry with vacant possession, the purchaser will also be entitled to resile if the seller is unable to give vacant possession to the whole subjects. In *Stuart v Lort-Phillips*[5] the missives were for the purchase of subjects extending to 21 acres, but at the agreed date of entry, the seller was unable to give actual possession, as per the missives, to 7 of these acres. It was held that the purchaser was entitled to resile on the ground that the seller's failure amounted to a material breach of contract. The purchaser, in such a situation, would be entitled to damages in the normal way.

---

1 1952 SLT 450.
2 *Heys v Kimball & Morton Ltd* (1890) 17 R 381.
3 1950 SC 483.
4 See Halliday *Conveyancing Law and Practice in Scotland* (1987) vol II, para 15–72; D J Cusine & P N Love 'Delays in settlement of conveyancing transactions' in *A Scots Conveyancing Miscellany: Essays in Honour of Professor J M Halliday* reprinted in (1992) 60 SLG 41.
5 1976 SLT (Notes) 39.

(3) *To deliver a valid disposition of the subjects*

6.05 This means that the disposition must be of the whole subjects which the purchaser contracted to buy and not just the subjects held as per the seller's title. In *Houldsworth v Gordon Cumming*[1] Lord Kinnear said, '. . . if a question arises as to the description to be inserted in a disposition, the first thing to be settled is what is the exact subject sold; and that is to be determined not by the existing titles, but by the contract of sale . . .'[2]. Thus, in *Equitable Loan Co of Scotland Ltd v Storie*[3] missives were concluded for subjects in Edinburgh, but the disposition purported to convey less than was contracted for and so the purchasers were entitled to have the disposition reduced.

It need hardly be said that the disposition must be properly executed and attested and be otherwise valid, eg where appropriate it must contain a clause of deduction of title[4]. Unless otherwise agreed, the seller must grant absolute warrandice[5], but this will be implied if a full price was being paid for the subjects[6]. As well as a disposition, the purchaser is entitled to delivery of any writs which it has been agreed to deliver, but, as a disposition need no longer contain a clause assigning writs (and because of this inventories of writs are rare) the purchaser's entitlement is to those writs which form part of the prescriptive progress of title to the particular subjects of purchase, together with such others as may be necessary to support his title, such as confirmation of executors and discharged security writs within the prescriptive period[7]. Where the writs necessary to support the purchaser's title are common to other subjects, as in a tenement, anyone who has custody of these writs is under an obligation to exhibit them to the other proprietors if required.

1 1910 SC (HL) 49.
2 At 55; see also Lord Chancellor Loreburn at 49; *Johnston's Trs v Kinloch* 1925 SLT 124; para 5.03 above.
3 1972 SLT (Notes) 20.
4 See *Halliday* vol II, Ch 22.
5 *Mackenzie v Neill* (1889) 37 SLR 666.
6 Titles to Land Consolidation (Scotland) Act 1868, s 5.
7 *Porteous v Henderson* (1898) 25 R 563.

(4) *To deliver or exhibit clear searches, or the equivalent land register reports*

6.06 This obligation is usually contained in the missives and repeated in a letter of obligation granted at settlement. If the purchase is being funded by a lender, the lender will require clear searches against not only the seller, but also the purchaser, to be delivered or exhibited. If the missives do not provide otherwise, then, as a matter of professional practice at least, a purchasing solicitor is entitled to assume that the selling solicitor will grant a personal letter of obligation at settlement, and not one on behalf of the client. If the selling solicitor does not intend to do so, the purchasing solicitor should be made aware of this as soon as is practicable. It is, however, usual for the selling solicitor to grant such a letter of obligation, but only in respect of the searches in the Property and Personal Registers, and not in respect of the Register of Charges, or the Companies Register. There is no difference in principle between the two, but as there may be a great difference between the values of the relative transactions where the seller is a limited company, the custom is to obtain any letter of obligation from the client company and to have that backed up, if possible, by guarantees of various kinds by the directors. The granter of a letter of obligation relating to the Property Registers will undertake to deliver a search where the search relates exclusively to the property being purchased, but in other circumstances, for example where the subjects being purchased form part of larger subjects, he may undertake only to exhibit it. In land registration cases where the property is to enter the Land Register for the first time, (a 'first registration') the obligation is to exhibit a clear form 10 report followed by a clear form 11 continuation report closer to settlement. In cases where the property is already registered the equivalent reports are 12 and 13.

Prior to settlement, the selling solicitor will usually exhibit an interim report on the search, or a form 11 or 13, and the purchaser is entitled to assume such reports will be exhibited, unless the missives provide otherwise. It is usual in builder's missives to find that the builder will not obtain such reports. The interim report or form 11 or 13 should be obtained as close to settlement as possible, because, at present, there is a gap of approximately two years after settlement before the final search appears. This period will reduce dramatically in sasine transactions with the computerisation of the Presentment Book, and so will the risk covered by a letter of obligation. In land register cases, land and charge certificates are taking years to appear in first registration cases, and first split-off from registered titles are taking even longer. However, dealings in existing land certificates can be turned round in a matter of months.

As a general rule, a search in the Property Register, the Land Register, the Personal Registers, the Register of Charges or the Companies Register is not a clear one if it discloses a deed or diligence, or the appointment of a liquidator, receiver, or administrator which renders the title unmarketable. Such incumbrances or deeds may have previously been pointed out to the purchaser, and he may have agreed to accept the title so encumbered or have agreed in the missives to accept the position as disclosed. If a deed appears in the Property Register, or the Land Register, it will be obvious whether the deed renders the title unmarketable. If it is a discharge of a standard security by the seller, it will not; if, on the other hand, it is an undischarged second security by the seller, it will and the seller's solicitors will be forced to secure the discharge or the security, or its restriction at their expense in terms of their letter of obligation. The solicitor would then have a right of relief against the seller, for what that may be worth.

However, the issue of what is a clear search usually arises in relation to the Personal Registers. Frequently, when an interim report is exhibited, the purchasing solicitor finds that there are a number of inhibitions against the seller. The two primary rules are that an inhibition is effective only against voluntary acts of the person inhibited, and that it does not affect acquirenda. If the seller was inhibited prior to entering into the missives, the missives are struck at by the inhibition, but if the inhibition post-dates the conclusion of the missives, the seller has an obligation to complete the contract by granting the disposition etc, and the inhibition does not strike at the sale[1]. Similarly, inhibitions affect only subjects owned by the party inhibited as at the date of registration of the inhibition, unless the subjects are destined to the debtor by some indefeasible title, such as an entail[2]. In this connection, an inhibition will affect property acquired where the title has still to be recorded[3]. Nevertheless, the issue is frequently not whether the inhibition is legally effective, but whether the search is clear, because although it appears after completion of the missives, the inhibition may still be there, and, of course, whether it struck at the missives is not clear from the face of the search. The general view[4], which is supported by the decision in *Dryburgh v Gordon*[5], is that the search is not clear. The same issue arises in connection with standard securities. In *Newcastle Building Society v White*[6] the debtor in a standard security was inhibited after the granting and recording of the security. The building society subsequently exercised its power of sale, but the purchaser argued that the search was not clear. The sheriff held that ex facie of the search, it was evident that the inhibition was not effective against the standard security and hence that the search was clear. However, in land registration transactions, the Keeper will issue a land certificate, without an exclusion of indemnity, where it can be shown that missives were concluded prior to the inhibition.

We have indicated a sufficient number of problems which may arise from searches to make it clear that a selling solicitor should think carefully before granting a letter of obligation, and equally, the purchasing solicitor should consider whether it is appropriate to accept the obligation being offered, particularly where the obligation is not being given by the solicitor, but the client. The letter binds the granter personally[7] and if the granter is a solicitor, letters of obligation granted for the usual purposes in a conveyancing transaction will be covered by the master policy. It is, however, thought to be unwise for a solicitor to undertake to have a disposition signed, or to produce local authority letters which are 'clear', but it is clearly normal to undertake to provide a search, or a feuduty redemption receipt, or a recorded discharge.

1 *Halliday* vol II, para 21–79.
2 Titles to Land Consolidation (Scotland) Act 1868, s 157.
3 *Dryburgh v Gordon* (1896) 24 R 1.
4 See *Halliday* vol II, para 24–86; Gretton *The Law of Inhibition and Adjudication* (1987) p 143 ff.
5 (1896) 24 R 1.
6 1987 SLT (Sh Ct) 81.
7 *Johnston v Little* 1960 SLT 129.

(5) *To implement the other obligations in the missives*

6.07 These include such things as delivering the moveables which are included in the purchase price, and exhibiting or delivering planning permissions, building warrants, completion certificates, superiors' consents, minutes of waiver, feuduty redemption receipts, consents, affidavits or renunciations under the Matrimonial Homes (Family Protection) (Scotland) Act 1981. It is outwith the scope of this book to deal in detail with breach of any of these obligations individually. However, our view is that a failure to perform any of the above obligations, with the exception of exhibiting a feuduty redemption receipt and delivery of the moveables, are material breaches of contract entitling the purchaser to resile. As McBryde points out[1], whether or not a breach of contract is material is a question of fact and is not to be decided by looking solely at the missives. In order to decide the matter Gloag says:

'the question is whether a particular stipulation goes to the root of the matter, so that a failure to perform it would make the performance of the rest of the contract a different thing from what the other party had stipulated for, or whether it merely partially affects it, so that compensation may be adequately given in damages[2].'

However, the matters mentioned in our view are of such significance that we regard them as material. Whether the purchaser does in fact resile will depend on the circumstances and probably only in extreme cases is it likely that he will. In any event, it would be wise to intimate to the seller a time limit for implementation, failing which the

purchaser will resile[3]. Some of the matters which remain outstanding
at the date of settlement may be incorporated into a letter of obligation, eg the delivery or exhibition of a feuduty redemption receipt.

1 *McBryde* para 14–61; see also *Walker* p 750.
2 *Gloag* p 603.
3 *Halliday* vol II, para 23–55.

Moveables

6.08   There is no doubt that a failure to deliver the moveables entitles
the purchaser to raise an action for implement against the seller, and
failing implement, damages. In many instances, because the seller has
moved from the house and possibly out of the area, it is frequently
unlikely that the purchaser will obtain delivery and an action for
implement or damages may be too costly, or inconvenient to contem-
plate. The purchaser then has to lick his wounds and put the episode
down to experience. Assuming there is some prospect of recovering
damages, or reaching some settlement, or the purchaser raises court
proceedings, despite advice to the contrary, the issue which arises is
whether the purchaser is entitled to recover the cost of new items in
place of those which have been removed, or whether he is entitled only
to the second-hand value of the goods. The general rule is that the
purpose of the law of damages is to put the innocent party, the
purchaser, in the position that he would have been in had the contract
not been breached[1]. If that rule were absolute, the purchaser might be
entitled only to the second-hand value of the goods removed. However, that rule is not absolute. As was said in one case involving a
motor car, 'Different considerations may apply where the article is
not one which can readily be bought and sold or which is adapted and
used for a special purpose[2]'. Where moveable items are not delivered,
the seller has failed to implement one aspect of a composite contract
which relates to both heritage and moveables. It should be within the
contemplation of the seller that the purchaser will be purchasing the
house and the moveables for use as a home and that if the moveables
are not delivered, the the purchaser would have to replace them to
make the home complete. Where there is no immediate or ready
market for goods of the type, quality and condition of those removed,
the purchaser will be entitled to recover the replacement cost of the
items. It may be that in any negotiations the purchaser may concede
some discount on the basis that the items removed might have had a
limited life on the grounds of age, or perhaps that they would not have
been the first choice of the purchaser, had he been buying new items,

but in law there is no requirement on him to accept any such discounting. Where there is a ready second-hand market for the goods, the purchaser would be expected, as part of the obligation to take reasonable steps to minimise his loss, to explore that market, but it is submitted that that obligation requires him to test only the local market, if there is one and for only a reasonable period, in order to see whether it is possible to acquire second-hand goods to replace those removed.

1 *Duke of Portland v Wood's Trs* 1925 SC 640 at 651 and 652 per Lord President Clyde.
2 *Pomphrey v James A Cuthbertson Ltd* 1951 SC 147 at 135 per Lord Jamieson.

The purchaser's options and remedies

6.09 Should the seller be unable at the agreed date to implement any of his or her obligations, the purchaser is not required to pay the price, as the obligations undertaken by one party to a bilateral agreement, if they are the counterparts of each other, are prestable only if the other party is in a position to implement his obligations[1]. The purchaser is therefore entitled to delay settlement until the seller is able to implement his obligations. However, a purchaser who is anxious to obtain entry may consider these courses of action: (i) making a payment to account of the purchase price; or (ii) consigning the purchase price.

1 *Turnbull v McLean & Co* (1874) 1 R 730 at 734 per Lord Justice-Clerk Moncreiff; *Bowie v Semple's Exrs* 1978 SLT (Sh Ct) 9; *Halliday* vol II, para 15–64.

(i) *Payments to account*

6.10 It used to be common for payments to account to be made. The seller was usually willing to accept a payment of that part of the purchase price which the purchaser was providing and to allow interest to run on the balance (ie the loan amount) at the 'overdraft' rate until settlement. The practice is now uncommon, because sellers are no longer prepared to wait, but also because of the decision in *Gibson and Hunter Home Designs Ltd (in liquidation)*[1]. Standing *Gibson*, a payment to account is not a wise step to take, because if the seller is made bankrupt or goes into liquidation prior to delivery of the conveyance, the purchaser firstly will rank as an ordinary creditor for any part of the purchase price which has been paid and secondly, will not be able to insist upon a conveyance being granted by the trustee or liquidator. The purchaser who nevertheless insists upon making a payment to account should be persuaded to pay over as little as possible. That would probably not be attractive to the seller who would presumably want a sufficiently large payment to cover any expenses likely to be incurred in a resale, should the purchaser fail to pay the remainder of the price. A payment to account is not therefore attractive to either party[2].

1 1976 SC 23.
2 *Halliday* vol II, para 15–82.

(ii) *Consignation*

6.11 Most missives provide either that consignation will not be permitted, (as in builders' missives) or that, notwithstanding consignation, interest will run on the price at the same rate as if the price had not been consigned. Assuming that consignation is permitted and the missives are silent about interest, interest will run at the lower rate which deposit receipts attract on the basis that the seller is in a more secure position than he would have been had the price not been consigned[1]. It should be noted that if the purchaser is borrowing to finance the purchase, the lender's instructions will prohibit consignation, because it will be a condition of the loan that the loan cheque can be encashed only if a signed deed is to be delivered to the purchaser in exchange for the purchase price. Even if there is no loan, the purchaser should be wary of consigning the price, because, in some instances, consignation has had the same effect on the transaction as Mogadon would have on most readers.

1 *Prestwick Cinema Co Ltd v Gardiner* 1951 SC 98.

The purchaser's obligations

6.12 The obligations on the purchaser at common law are: (i) to pay the price on the agreed date; and (ii) to become infeft as soon as reasonably practicable. We shall deal with the first obligation when discussing delays in settlement in general. In relation to the second obligation it is submitted that although there is little authority on the point[1], there is an obligation on the purchaser to become infeft as soon as is practicable. The reason for this obligation is to ensure that the seller is relieved of any liability for performance of the title conditions. To our knowledge there are few problems in practice because, firstly, the purchaser is usually also a borrower, in which event the heritable creditor will insist on the disposition and the standard security being recorded or registered as quickly as possible to ensure a proper security and, in the usual case, a first ranking on the security subjects;

and, secondly, the selling solicitor's letter of obligation will usually contain a condition that the disposition in favour of the purchaser be recorded within a specified period, frequently either 14 or 28 days. If the usual wording is adopted, the obligation to deliver a search may not fall completely if this condition is not complied with but the condition does mean that the granter of the obligation will not be responsible for entries in the search or exclusion of the indemnity which arise in the 14 or 28-day period.

1 See McDonald *Conveyancing Manual* (4th edn) para 28–91; *Walker* p 738; see also *McDonald v City of Glasgow Bank* (1879) 6 R 621; *Stevenson v Wilson* 1907 SC 1445.

Implementing the other obligations in the missives

6.13 If there are other obligations undertaken by the purchaser in terms of the missives, apart from the obligation to pay the price, the purchaser is clearly obliged to implement these. An obvious one would be to apply for planning and other permissions within any stated time limit, where the missives are conditional upon these being obtained. The purchaser will almost certainly have provided in the missives for the entitlement to resile without penalty in the event that such permissions are not granted within the stated periods, but the purchaser would be in breach of the contract and possibly material breach if he had obliged himself but failed to obtain the permissions timeously. In these cases, it is important from both the seller's and the purchaser's point of view that the time limits and rights to resile are set out clearly in the missives and not left to argument, or interpretation by the purchaser. If the purchaser is entitled to waive any suspensive condition, this should be dealt with expressly in the missives[1].

1 *Halliday* vol II, paras 15–07 and 15–106; *Dewar & Finlay Ltd v Blackwood* 1968 SLT 196; *Ellis & Sons Second Amalgamated Properties v Pringle* 1975 SLT 10; *T Boland & Co Ltd v Dundas' Trs* 1975 SLT (Notes) 80; *George Packman & Sons Ltd v Young* 1976 SLT (Notes) 52; *Imry Property Holdings Ltd v Glasgow YMCA* 1979 SLT 261.

Breach and delays in settlement

6.14 In this connection, we shall deal firstly with settlement procedures and then breaches of the various obligations including delays in settlement.

(i) *Settlement procedures*

6.15 The purchase price is usually paid by a cheque drawn on the purchasing solicitor's client account. That has the advantage that the selling solicitor may, as a matter of professional practice, treat that cheque as being the equivalent of cash. The purchasing solicitor is entitled to stop the cheque only in exceptional circumstances where the seller is in clear breach of his or her obligations under the missives; for example, where the disposition is not executed properly, or the house has burned down on the date of entry. The purchasing solicitor cannot stop his cheque because of a financial difficulty of the purchaser, as where his loan arrangements fall through, or his client's cheque in favour of the solicitor 'bounces'. Likewise, it is not open to the purchasing solicitor, at the time of dispatch of the cheque, to require the cheque to be held as undelivered except where the seller's obligations under the contract are unimplemented unless, of course, that has been agreed with the seller's solicitor. It is permissible to require the purchasing solicitor's cheque to be held as undelivered, pending receipt of the signed deed, but not (except with the express consent of the seller) until the purchaser's loan cheque has been cleared, or the purchaser's solicitor has been put in funds.

(ii) *Delays*

6.16 Although, as has been said, delays in settlement on the part of purchasers used to be the most common form of breach and indeed many articles were written about it[1], more recently, missives have almost invariably contained a clause dealing with such a delay and making provision for the payment of interest and a right to resile and claim damages for any losses incurred on the resale. For example, clause C2 in the Law Society's standard form offer is as follows:

'It is a material condition of the bargain to follow hereon that (a) the purchase price will be paid on the date of entry and (b) the seller will give entry with vacant possession to the subjects of sale. Without prejudice to the foregoing if (but only if) at the date of entry the seller has (a) implemented all obligations incumbent on him in terms of the bargain to follow hereon and (b) is in a position to give possession of the subjects of sale to the purchaser, the purchaser will pay to the seller interest on any part of the purchase price outstanding at said date at a rate of 4% per annum above the lowest base rate for lending charged by any of the Scottish clearing banks during the period of non-payment (together with any arrangement fee or other charges incurred by the seller on any borrowing by him necessitated by the purchaser's failure to pay the purchase price timeously); and that notwithstanding consignation and whether or not the purchaser shall have taken occupation of the subjects of sale; and in the event of any part of the purchase price remaining unpaid on the expiry of a period of four weeks from the date of entry, the seller will be entitled but not obliged, forthwith to resile from said bargain to follow hereon and to resell the subjects of sale, under reservation of all claims which may be competent to the seller to recover from the purchaser all loss and damage sustained by the seller on any such resale and interest as aforesaid.'

Given this practice, it may seem unnecessary to spend much time explaining the law on the matter. However, the justification for doing so is that missives may, *per incuriam*, not contain such a clause, or there may be an omission in the clause itself, or there may be a doubt about what the clause means. There are some issues which have not yet been resolved by the courts and the purpose of this part of the chapter is to help to identify these, as well as setting out the law as we understand it, which may provide a starting point in the event of a problem arising. We fully appreciate that a compromise is usually reached, but it is desirable when one is attempting to reach an accommodation to know what the relevant law is.

It is sometimes the case that the fault lies with one party only, but in some cases there may be fault on both sides which means that neither is in a position to settle on the due date. What happens thereafter is a matter for negotiation, but one thing which is well established is that if the purchaser takes entry without paying the full price, he will be liable to pay interest.

1 AGM Duncan 'Delays in settlement' (1963) 3 Con Rev 189; J M Halliday 'Delays in settlement' (1980) 48 SLG 68; A J McDonald 'A question of interest' JLSS (Workshop) 103; I W Noble 'Liability to pay interest' JLSS (Workshop) vii; I W Noble 'A question of interest' JLSS (Workshop) 272; D J Cusine 'Delays in settlement yet again' (1983) 28 JLSS 273; I W Noble 'Delays in settlement' (1983) 28 JLSS 116; D J Cusine & P N Love 'Delays in settlement of conveyancing transactions' in *A Scots Conveyancing Miscellany: Essays in Honour of Professor J M Halliday* reprinted in (1992) 60 SLG 41.

6.17 *Purchaser unable to settle.* It is commonly the case that the transaction does not settle because the purchaser does not have the funds on the date of entry. In that case, the purchaser should be advised to obtain overdraft facilities, rather than delay settlement and incur interest, possibly at a fairly high rate.

Although this is the practical advice, and the fair and proper thing to do, the law is to the effect that if the missives do not provide otherwise (and they usually do), time is not of the essence of a contract for the purchase and sale of heritable property[1] and so, the purchaser must be given a reasonable time within which to make payment. What is a reasonable time will depend on the circumstances. In the leading case of *Rodger (Builders) Ltd v Fawdry*[2] the purchaser had not paid on the agreed date – 11 November 1947. On 25 November, the seller's solicitors gave the purchaser three days within which to pay, intimating that if he failed to do so, they would regard the sale as void and be free to resell. On the expiry of the three-day period, the seller resold and the original purchaser brought an action of reduction of the disposition granted to the second purchaser and the relevant missives. The Lord Ordinary (Sorn) whose decision was upheld on appeal, held that unless time has been made of the essence, a failure to pay on the agreed date does not entitle the seller to rescind the contract. He went on to say:

'payment of the price by a fixed date may be made an essential condition of such contract. If there is an unnecessary or unjustifiable delay on the part of the purchaser in paying the price, the seller may limit a time within which payment must be made and, provided the time limited is a reasonable one in the circumstances, failure to pay within that time will be treated as breach of an essential condition entitling the seller to rescind[3].'

While that is a correct statement of the law, it is difficult to advise a client about 'reasonableness' and the safe course of action is to err on the side of caution by giving a sufficiently long period in the circumstances, in the hope that a court would not regard it as unreasonable. Lord Sorn recognised the difficulty and pointed out that there are two types of case, one in which the seller knows that the purchase price will eventually be paid and the other where there may be doubt about it. In the first type of case, his Lordship said that while pressure could legitimately be applied, patience had also to be shown. In the other case, the setting of a time limit was something which could more readily be resorted to. The problem for the seller's advisers is knowing into which category the defaulting purchaser falls. It would therefore be prudent to assume in all cases that the defaulting purchaser intends to pay eventually and on that basis, a combination of pressure and patience is required. The decision in *Rodger (Builders) Ltd* followed earlier cases[4] and has itself been followed[5]. Because the seller may be in doubt about what is a reasonable time, one course may be to raise court proceedings and leave it to the court to fix a time within which payment has to be made. In *Johnstone v Harris*[6] the purchase price was due to be paid on 28 May 1974, but it was not. Early in June, the sellers raised an action in the sheriff court craving implement of the missives by payment of the price and failing payment for declarator that the purchaser was in breach of contract, thus entitling the sellers to resell. In December 1974, the sheriff granted decree in terms of the crave for implement and allowed the purchaser six weeks in which to pay. The sellers were unsuccessful in finding another purchaser and they raised an action in the Court of Session for damages.

The approach taken by the sheriff was not criticised and the only issue was the duty of the sellers to mitigate their loss. The Lord Ordinary (Ross) held that while there was an obligation on the sellers to take reasonable steps to mitigate their loss, that obligation did not arise until it was clear that the purchaser was not going to perform his obligations under the missives, ie on the expiry of the six-week period, and not, as counsel for the purchasers had contended, on 28 May, the original date of entry. In such a case, the other issue which will arise is the question of damages. We shall deal with this issue in the context of the seller's entitlement to interest.

It might be thought that the raising of an action would be met with the defence that it is premature on the basis that the purchaser must be given notice of a reasonable time within which to pay and only after that may an action be raised. However, in *Lloyds Bank Ltd v Bauld*[7] the raising of the action itself was held to be notice, which had the effect of making time of the essence. There was a suggestion by the Lord Ordinary (Stott) in *George Packman & Sons v Dunbar's Trs*[8] that where there has been inordinate delay it may not be necessary to give an ultimatum. That may be sound law, but it would be prudent to give an ultimatum in all cases *ob majorem cautelam*.

In *Bosco Design Services Ltd v Plastic Sealant Ltd*[9] there was an appeal from the decision of the Lord Ordinary (Stott) to the effect that in such a case, the pursuer was seeking two decrees – one for declarator that the contract was at an end and the other for damages – and, in his opinion, that was incompetent. As the First Division pointed out, however, the pursuer is seeking alternative remedies and would be personally barred from attempting to implement both.

As has already been said, the prudent course of action is to make provision in the missives for a possible delay in settlement by the purchaser and a resale of the subjects as a result, and that is invariably done in practice. The clause in the Law Society's standard form of missives has already been quoted and is illustrative of the type of provision commonly encountered.

1 *Rodger (Builders) Ltd v Fawdry* 1950 SC 483.
2 Above.
3 1950 SC 483 at 492.
4 *Black v Dick* (1814) Hume 809; *Burns v Garscadden* (1901) 8 SLT 321.
5 *Inveresk Paper Co v Pembry Machinery Co Ltd* 1972 SLT (Notes) 63.
6 1977 SC 365.
7 1976 SLT (Notes) 53.
8 1977 SLT 140.
9 1979 SLT (Notes) 33.

6.18 *The seller unable to settle.* This usually comes about either because the seller is unable to move out on the agreed date, or because he is unable to deliver a marketable title, or the requisite searches. As has already been said, if the giving of entry on the agreed date is made material by the missives, the purchaser may be able to resile, but in practical terms is unlikely to wish to do so. Where the giving of entry is not made material, the purchaser's safest course is to adopt the procedure suggested in *Rodger (Builders) Ltd* by first giving the seller a reasonable time and then by giving an ultimatum.

Where the problem lies with the title, a distinction has to be drawn between the situation in which the seller is able to give a title and where he is not. Where the seller can give a good title, an action of implement can be raised against him. In *Plato v Newman*[1] there was a sale of a first floor flat and a dispute arose about maintenance obligations. The seller argued that it was impossible to implement his obligations and that it would be inequitable to require him to do so, because he had granted dispositions of other flats in the building which were inconsistent with the terms of the disposition which the purchaser sought. The court nevertheless granted decree of specific implement because the seller had bound himself to grant a disposition in terms of the missives. Where the seller cannot give a good title, as where he does not have a title, or there is an incurable defect in the title, the purchaser's remedy is to resile from the bargain and claim damages. What we are considering here is a situation in which there is a fundamental defect or lack of title as in *Campbell v McCutcheon*[2]. As has already been noted, a purchaser can resile at once if the seller cannot give a title to the whole subjects contracted for[3], but where there is a defect in the title, the purchaser must be given a reasonable time in which to put this right.

It may be that the purchaser discovers the defect in title only after settlement. This should not normally happen unless the defect is latent. Where *restitutio in integrum* is possible, then the appropriate course is an action of reduction and damages, if any loss has been sustained. Where *restitutio* is not possible, the claim appears to be for damages[4].

1 1950 SLT (Notes) 30.
2 1963 SC 505.
3 See para 6.03 above.
4 See *Loutitt's Trs v Highland Railway Co* (1892) 19 R 791; *Gloag* p 614.

6.19 *Both parties unable to settle.* In a case where neither the seller nor the purchaser is in a position to settle on the agreed date, the only course of action which is appropriate is to negotiate a settlement. The parties may find themselves in this position because, despite advice to the contrary, the date of entry is too close to the date of the offer to allow for the necessary conveyancing, including the loan element, to be completed. If, despite the risks, the purchaser takes entry, he will be liable for interest on any part of the purchase price which is unpaid. As has been noted, the seller cannot force the purchaser to pay any part of the price and take entry in circumstances where he or she cannot implement the bargain[1].

1 *Bowie v Semple's Exrs* 1978 SLT (Sh Ct) 9.

Interest and damages

6.20   Until it became standard practice to insert interest and rescission clauses in missives to deal with delays, there were a number of articles on the subject[1]. There have also been a number of recent cases on the point[2], but some issues remain unresolved. Given the almost universal practice, they may remain unresolved.

The general rule is that a breach of contract which consists only of a failure to pay money gives rise to a claim for interest and not damages[3]. There are exceptions to this which we will look at later, but first we shall attempt to set out the rules (for there are apparently no principles)[4] governing the payment of interest. What is clearly settled is that interest is due in three situations: (a) *ex contractu*; (b) *ex lege*; (c) *ex mora*. Why a distinction is drawn between interest being due *ex lege* and *ex mora* is not clear, and no such distinction is drawn by Erskine[5] or Bankton[6] but these three categories have been used for some time[7].

1 See para 6.16, note 1, above.
2 *Thomson v Vernon* 1983 SLT (Sh Ct) 17; *Tiffney v Bachurzewski* 1985 SLT 165; *Inverness Golf Club v James Parr & Partners* 1987 GWD 6–169; *Caledonian Property Group Ltd v Queensferry Property Group Ltd* 1992 SLT 738.
3 Erskine *An Institute of the Law of Scotland* (8th edn, 1871) III, 3, 86; Bell *Principles of the Law of Scotland* (10th edn, 1899) § 32; *Stephen v Swayne* (1861) 24 D 158 at 163 per Lord President McNeill.
4 John Murray 'Interest on debt' 1991 SLT (News) 305.
5 *Erskine* III, 3, 79.
6 *An Institute of the Laws of Scotland* (1751–53) I, 456,1.
7 *Blair's Trs v Payne* (1884) 12 R 104 at 108 per Lord Craighill.

Interest due ex contractu

6.21   It is uncommon in practice not to encounter a clause in the missives which deals with delays in settlement and hence with the payment of interest. Frequently, the offer is silent about the consequences of a delay by the purchaser, and it is the seller who inserts the clause in the qualified acceptance. It is sensible, however, for the purchaser's solicitor to consider inserting a clause, because he will then be in command of the situation and may be able to obtain an acceptance of his own clause which has the advantage that he knows what his clause entails. It is important to specify a rate at which interest is payable, or a precise formula such as X% above the rate charged by the Y Bank on particular accounts, eg the unsecured overdraft rate, if only because there is no 'legal rate'[1]. From the seller's point of view, the rate specified should be sufficiently high to cover the cost of any bridging facility which the seller might need to obtain, in the event that the purchaser is unable to pay on the due date. At one time it was common for both solicitors to accept that if the seller had to go on overdraft, the purchaser would pay that rate until settlement. It has, however, been held that the fact that the seller might have to go on overdraft is not something which a purchaser should foresee[2]. It is respectfully submitted that the decision is incorrect. Most house purchase transactions are financed by a loan and most sellers are going to be purchasing other properties with the proceeds of the sale. Accordingly, it ought to be within the contemplation of the parties at the outset that the seller may require a bridging facility and hence will be involved in extra expense in addition to the loss of interest on his money[3]. In *Caledonian Property Group Ltd v Queensferry Property Group Ltd*[4] Lord MacLean held that it was foreseeable, in a commercial property transaction, that if the purchaser delayed the sellers might have to incur overdraft interest. It is respectfully submitted that that is the correct approach and that his Lordship's observation is equally applicable to the purchaser of domestic properties. 'It must therefore have been in their [the purchasers'] reasonable contemplation that the pursuers, like themselves, required funding to provide the purchase price or at least part of it, given its magnitude[5].' That can be contrasted with the statement of Lord Hunter in *Tiffney*:[6]

'Counsel for the pursuer . . . attempted an argument that the necessity of the seller obtaining a bridging loan for the purchase of an alternative residence when an existing residence was being sold was something which should be within the contemplation of any purchaser. This, in my opinion, is a somewhat extravagant proposition.'

Until such time as that statement is declared to be inaccurate in relation to the purchase and sale of domestic property, it is essential to have a precise formula for calculating interest at a sufficiently high rate. The inclusion of a high rate of interest in the missives may also have the effect of concentrating the purchaser's mind.

1 *Greenock Harbour Trs v Glasgow & SW Railway* 1909 SC (HL) 49; *Prestwick Cinema Co v Gardiner* 1951 SC 98.

2 *Tiffney v Bachurzewski* 1985 SC 108.
3 *Halliday* vol II, para 23–60.
4 1992 SLT 738.
5 1992 SLT 738 at 740.
6 1985 SC 108 at 113.

Interest due ex lege

6.22 It is in this area that the law is unclear and principles almost impossible to discern. It is thought that the following propositions are, however, settled:

(a) Where the purchaser consigns the full purchase price, the seller is entitled to interest at the rate applied to the consigned sum, for example, the deposit receipt, or building society rate. The reason for this has already been mentioned.

(b) Where the purchaser pays only part (or even none!) of the purchase price, and is given entry, he is liable to pay interest on the balance of the purchase price. The liability arises because the purchaser has possession and can enjoy the 'fruits' of the property[1]. The matter is put thus by Erskine:

'Thus, . . . in a sale of lands, the purchaser is, by an act of the law itself, bound to pay interest for the price of the subject bought, from the term at which he enters into possession, as long as he retains the price; for the price becomes a *surrogatum* or thing substituted in place of the subject sold; and therefore the interest of the price must be given in consideration of the fruits of that subject[2]'.

A similar statement is to be found in Bell's *Commentaries*[3]. These comments make it clear that interest is due, even although the seller is not in a position to settle on the due date[4], but it would be wrong to conclude that the actions of the parties are irrelevant. They may be reflected in the rate of interest awarded to the seller. In *Traill v Connon*[5] interest was awarded at the rate of 4 per cent, which was one per cent below the usual rate at the time. In the words of Lord Justice-Clerk Moncrieff, the reason for this was that 'the seller had not a complete or undoubted title to give[6]'. This raises the issue of the appropriate rate of interest. The previous 'legal' rate of 5 per cent is no longer applicable[7], but standing *Tiffney*, interest at the bridging-loan rate would not be recoverable unless the seller had made it known to the purchaser at the time of the missives that he might have to bridge if the purchaser did not settle timeously. If that is not done, the seller would be entitled to a reasonable rate which might be the average of the rates payable to banks and building societies on secured loans. It is submitted that such a rate would not be unreasonable, but at a time when there is a myriad of rates, both tied and fluctuating, it is difficult to ascertain.

(c) Where the seller continues in possession the purchaser is not bound to pay interest, since he is not enjoying the fruits of the subjects. That proposition follows from the statement in *Erskine* referred to above.

What is unfortunately not settled is whether the seller is entitled to interest if he vacates the subjects, offers possession to the purchaser, but the purchaser declines to take entry. The assumption is that the seller is able to settle the transaction, should the purchaser proffer the price. One view is that, because the seller has not been paid on the due date, he is entitled at least to interest, because there has been a breach of contract. That is the view of academic writers[8], but in two sheriff court cases it was held that no interest is due[9]. In *Thomson v Vernon* the sheriff referred to the passage in *Erskine* and continued, 'It follows from this reasoning that only actual entry will do. A right to entry is not enough because it infers only a right to enjoy the fruits[10]'. It has been argued that the passage in *Erskine* is dealing only with the situation in which the purchaser actually takes entry and is silent on the situation in which entry is offered, but declined[11]. If these sheriff court decisions are good law, the seller is in a difficult position. If he vacates the subjects, no interest is payable unless the purchaser takes entry. The purchaser has not paid the price and for all the seller knows may never pay; on the contrary, the purchaser may turn up at any time with full payment (but without offering interest) and obtain entry. The theoretical course open to the seller would ultimately be to resile, but that could only be done after he had given the purchaser a reasonable time within which to pay the money, or immediately, if the missives made payment on the due date material. These sheriff court cases do, however, have the merit of pointing out the desirability of making matters clear in the missives. However, when the case of *Tiffney*[12] reappeared in the sheriff court, it was held that interest was due even although the purchaser had not taken entry. The sheriff's reasoning with which we respectfully agree was that interest was due simply because there had been a breach of contract in that the purchaser had not paid on the due date.

(d) The seller is not entitled to interest unless he is able to perform his obligations, or would have been but for some fault on the part of the purchaser. In *Bowie v Semple's Exrs*[13] the sellers were not able, at the date of entry, to implement the bargain, because they did not have confirmation in their favour. They offered the purchaser entry on a payment to account and they asked for interest on the balance of the purchase price. The purchasers declined this offer and refused to take entry and only after some five months were the sellers in a position to settle. Their claim for the interest was refused on the ground that the purchaser's obligation to pay the price was a counterpart of the sellers' obligation to give a good title. The purchaser was not obliged to take entry, unless a title was being offered. Similarly, in *Davidson v Tilburg Ltd*[14] it was held that a purchaser was not bound to pay within a 28-day period where the sellers still had obligations to implement and the sellers were not able to resile because of the non-payment.

1 *Erskine* III, 3, 79; *Stewart v Earl of Cassilis* 21 Dec 1811 FC.
2 *Erskine* III, 3, 79.
3 I, 693.
4 *Grandison's Trs v Jardine* (1895) 22 R 925.
5 (1877) 5 R 25.
6 (1877) 5 R 25 at 27.
7 *Halliday* vol II, para 23–58; *Kearon v Thomson's Trs* 1949 SC 287 at 295, 296 per Lord President Cooper.
8 AGM Duncan 'Delays in settlement' (1963) Con Rev 189 at 196; J M Halliday 'Delays in settlement' (1983) 48 SLG 68 at 73; I W Noble 'Liability to pay interest' JLSS (Workshop) vii at vii; D J Cusine & P N Love 'Delays in settlement of conveyancing transactions' in *A Scots Conveyancing Miscellany* reprinted in 1992 (60) SLG 41.
9 *Thomson v Venson* 1983 SLT (Sh Ct) 17; *Tiffney v Bachurzewski* 1983 SLT (Sh Ct) 45.
10 1983 SLT (Sh Ct) 17 at 18.
11 See D J Cusine & P N Love, above.
12 1988 GWD 37–1530.
13 1978 SLT (Sh Ct) 9.
14 1991 GWD 18–1109.

Interest due ex mora

6.23 It has frequently been said that interest is due if the principal sum has been 'wrongfully withheld' and thus not paid on the due date[1]. It is not entirely clear what is meant by 'wrongfully withheld'. In *Blair's Trs v Payne*[2] Lord Fraser said, quoting Lord Westbury, '. . . the mere non-payment of the money was not sufficient. It must be "wrongfully withheld".' However the actual words of Lord Westbury do not give a clear indication that he regarded non-payment and wrongful withholding as different. His Lordship said, 'interest can be demanded . . . by virtue of the principal sum of money having been wrongfully withheld and not paid on the day when it ought to have been paid[3].' However, Lord Fraser did use the term *ex mora* which is something different from merely failing to pay on the agreed date, but even if wrongful withholding is different from mere delay in paying, the problem for the seller is that he will probably not be able to tell the one situation from the other and, for that reason, it would be unsafe to rely on 'wrongful withholding' as a ground for a claim for interest unless the delay had been inordinate. In such a situation, however, the seller will probably have adopted the 'ultimatum' procedure outlined in *Rodger (Builders) Ltd*[4].

1 *Carmichael v Caledonian Railway Co* (1879) 8 M (HL) 119 at 131 per Lord Westbury; *Kolbin v Kinnear* 1931 SC (HL) 128 at 131 per Lord Atkin.
2 (1884) 12 R 104 at 110.
3 *Carmichael v Caledonian Railway Co* (1879) 8 M (HL) 119 at 131.
4 1950 SC 483; see also *McBryde* para 20–109.

Damages

6.24   In this connection, we shall consider what may be claimed as damages by the seller and by the purchaser, where there has been a breach of the missives by one of the parties. It is appropriate to consider this from both the seller's and the purchaser's point of view.

6.25   (i) *The seller*. The seller may be seeking payment of interest which he has had to pay for his bridging finance. In addition, on the assumption that the sale does not proceed, and the seller resells, one has to examine the various heads of claim open to the seller in that situation.

As has been said, the basic rule is that a failure to pay money gives rise only to a claim for interest and not one for damages[1]. This is, however, only a general rule and even when Gloag was writing, there was a recognised exception. 'In the case where it was proved that the debtor was aware, at the time on entering into the contract . . ., that his failure to pay at the appointed term would cause exceptional loss[2]'. That statement refers to *actual* knowledge rather than what was reasonably foreseeable, but it is the authors' view that the test which should now be applied is whether the loss was reasonably foreseeable[3] and so it would not be essential to demonstrate that there was actual knowledge. It has already been suggested that *Tiffney*[4] is wrongly decided in so far as it suggests that it is not foreseeable that a seller might incur interest at overdraft rates if the purchaser fails to pay timeously[5]. Given that 90 per cent of all purchases are financed by loans and most people who are selling are doing so with a view to purchasing something else, we consider that a loss involving interest on a bridging facility is foreseeable in domestic property transactions. However, such a loss would not be foreseeable in every case[6]. For example, in a sale by executors, there would not be any loss to the executry except interest, unless the subjects were liferented and that was known to the purchaser. The same would presumably apply to sales by heritable creditors, trustees in bankruptcy, judicial factors, curators and other persons who are clearly acting in a representative capacity. Thus, our submission is that while it is foreseeable at the outset of every domestic transaction that the seller may suffer some additional loss if the purchaser fails to pay on the due date, in the special instances just mentioned, it is less likely there would be any such loss.

In the event that the purchaser cannot ultimately pay the price and the seller has to resell, there will commonly be a clause in the missives which covers this eventuality. Such a clause will give the seller the option to treat the contract as being at an end in the event that the purchaser has failed to pay after the expiry of a specified period from the date of entry. A period of either 14 or 28 days is usual. Some clauses go on to provide that the seller shall then be entitled to resell, while at the same time holding the purchaser liable for all losses which might be sustained including interest at a specified rate, and the expenses of the resale. The seller is of course obliged to take reasonable steps to mitigate his loss and this may require that the property be resold immediately. It is probably the seller's duty to do so if the market is favourable, but a house may take months to sell, even if it is put on the market immediately after the rescission of the first contract. The seller may, however, be fortunate and sell the house at a higher figure than the original, but much depends on when the sale takes place.

'If the seller, following normal procedure, eventually resells the house at a higher price than the original contract price, that must be taken into account in assessing the damages claimable from the buyer. If, however, the seller keeps the property for some time, without trying to resell, and eventually, years later, sells at a high price, the profit is not . . . taken into account[7].'

In most instances the seller will make a loss on resale. That was the position in *Grant v Ullah*[8] where U had agreed to purchase G's house for £31,457, with entry on 13 May 1983. On 20 May, U's agents resiled from the contract and G resold in December 1983 for £28,500. The court held that G was entitled to recover the following: (i) interest, as per the missives, for the seven days from 13 to 20 May 1983; (ii) the difference between the two prices; (iii) the rates and insurance premiums payable by G from May until December 1983; (iv) the interest on G's building society loan from May until December 1983 where U was aware of the loan prior to the conclusion of missives; (v) the difference between what G actually paid to his estate agent and what would have been paid had U proceeded with the purchase. Although G's solicitor had charged a reduced fee for the abortive purchase, the same principle would have applied to his fees.

Although it is not necessary to spell out in the missives the exact heads of damages which will be claimed, some things such as interest are frequently mentioned, and *Grant* is a useful case giving guidance on the other heads which may be claimed. In framing a clause to cover damages, care should be taken in relation to the period during which interest due *ex contractu* is to run. If the seller is likely to be on a bridging loan, interest should run from the original date of entry until the date on which the second purchaser makes payment of the purchase price. It should not run only until the date of the second sale, because that is likely to be interpreted as the date when the second missives are concluded, rather than the date of payment of the new price.

1 *Gloag* p 680; Walker *The Law of Damages in Scotland* (1955) p 182.
2 *Gloag* p 680.
3 *Gloag* p 696; *McBryde* para 20–53 ff; Halliday 'Delays in settlement' (1983) 48 SLG 68; D J Cusine & P N Love – see para 6.22, note 8, above.
4 1985 SC 108.
5 See also *Halliday* vol II, para 23–60, note 21.
6 See *Caledonian Property Group* 1992 SLT 738.
7 *McBryde* para 20–42; *Jarnal v Moola Dawood Sons & Co* [1916] AC 175.
8 1987 SLT 639.

6.26 (ii) *The purchaser.* The purchaser may sustain a loss if the seller fails to proceed with the transaction. The purchaser's loss is governed by the same principles relating to breach of contract as that of the seller. It is submitted that the purchaser would be entitled to recover: (i) additional legal fees in respect of a new purchase; (ii) additional surveyors' fees in the same connection; (iii) any fee for cancellation of the removal, if the breach took place very close to the date of entry where the seller should have anticipated that the purchaser might have made such arrangements. It has been held recently that a purchaser should be allowed proof of averments relating to loss of rental income, where there was a delay in giving entry. In *Brown v Gamsu* the agreed date was 2 March 1990, but entry was not given until 19 January 1991[1].

The purchaser's losses are not restricted to those incurred after the conclusion of missives. In *Fielding v Newell*[2] the purchaser was allowed a proof in respect of the following items of abortive expenditure: (i) her legal fees; (ii) her surveyor's fees; (iii) travelling and accommodation expenses incurred in connection with inspection of the subjects; (iv) travelling expenses incurred by her design consultants; and (v) telephone charges for contacting her solicitors and her surveyors. Apart from the items just mentioned, other claims may arise for the purchaser. If the purchaser has sold a house or surrendered a tenancy, and so has to arrange temporary accommodation until he secures a new property, a claim for the cost of that temporary accommodation will arise. In England, this has been held to be a foreseeable consequence of a failure on the part of the vendor to give entry. In *Beard v Porter*[3] the purchaser was unable to gain vacant possession because a tenant of the seller refused to remove. The purchaser was held entitled to the following heads of damages: (i) the difference in value between the contract price and the value of the property subject to the tenancy; (ii) legal expenses and stamp duty incurred in connection with the purchase of another house; and (iii) the cost of temporary lodgings until entry could be had to the new house. It is submitted that there is no reason in principle why a claim for the cost of temporary accommodation should be incompetent, where the need for it is reasonably foreseeable.

In the event that a disappointed purchaser has to acquire another property, the question which arises is whether he has any claim for a difference between the original price and the price of the new property. It is thought unlikely that such a claim would be sustained, given the difficulties over valuations and what is foreseeable[4]. It is certainly doubtful whether any *pretium affectionis* could be claimed in respect of a domestic property. In relation to commercial property, different claims may arise because different things may be regarded as reasonably foreseeable[5].

1 1992 GWD 40–2429.
2 1987 SLT 530.
3 [1948] 1 KB 321.
4 *Engell v Fitch* (1869) LR 4, QB 659.
5 *Caledonian Property Group Ltd* 1992 SLT 738.

6.27 *Deposits.* In some transactions the purchaser may have paid a deposit. Although this is uncommon in domestic transactions, it is not unknown when purchasers are buying a new house from a builder, and it is also common where the subjects have been sold by auction. In such cases, it is usual to provide that a deposit will be paid on conclusion of missives. There is authority for the view that if the contract provides for forfeiture of the deposit, then the rules on penalty clauses are inapplicable[1]. More recently, in *Zemhunt Holdings Ltd v Control Securities plc*[2] subjects were purchased at an auction and a 10 per cent deposit was paid on conclusion of the contract. The Second Division held that on a proper reading of the contract, the 'deposit' was not only to be regarded as a payment to account, but also to provide the defenders with a guarantee that the pursuers would perform their part of the bargain. As the pursuers had been in breach of contract, the defenders were entitled to retain the deposit. The moral is to provide that the deposit is returnable, if the seller is in

breach, but the deposit may be forfeit, if the purchaser himself is in
breach[3]. However, in *Singh v Cross Entertainments Ltd*[4] money was
lodged on deposit receipt 'to await settlement'. When the transaction did not go ahead, the sellers argued that the entitlement to
the money depended on the outcome of the transaction, but this
view was rejected by the Lord Ordinary (Coulsfield). In his
opinion, the money was returnable to the purchasers on the basis
causa data causa non secuta. It is obvious that for a purchaser to pay
over a substantial sum by way of a deposit is risky and hence not
recommended[5].

1 *Commercial Bank v Beal* (1890) 18 R 80.
2 1991 SLT 653.
3 See *Inverkip Building Co Ltd v Cityploy Ltd* 1992 GWD 8–436.
4 1990 SLT 77.
5 *Gibson & Hunter Home Designs Ltd* 1976 SC 23.

Actio quanti minoris

6.28 In some instances where there is a breach by the seller, the
most obvious thing for the purchaser to do would be to settle for a
reduction in the price. If, for example, the seller has contracted to
sell a house and a garage, but is unable to give a title to the garage,
the purchaser may nevertheless wish to proceed, in the hope that
he might get the use of the garage in any event. However, it is
settled law that where a disposition has been delivered, the purchaser must either resile or claim under warrandice if that is possible. In other words, Scots law rejects an *actio quanti minoris*. It has
been pointed out that this is a misunderstanding of the position in
Roman law, where there were two meanings of the *actio*[1]. One was
where the seller was claiming damages for selling too cheaply, and
the other was where the purchaser wished to claim damages for a
defect[2]. In properly rejecting the first type of action, the second
'baby' unfortunately went out with the bath water. It might be
argued that the *actio* can apply where the defect or discrepancy in
the title or other matter is discovered prior to the delivery of the
disposition, but there is no real authority[3], and there is a well-
established line of authority which does not countenance the *actio*
in the sale of heritage[4]. Because of this, most missives now provide
for the remedy. Thus the Law Society standard missives clauses
provide 'Notwithstanding any rule to the contrary the *actio quanti
minoris* will be available to the purchaser[5]'. Thus, if there is such a
provision, the purchaser may retain the heritage and claim a reduction in the price. The reduction should, of course, be an amount
which equates to the difference between the value of the subjects

sold and the value of the subjects actually conveyed, with whatever defect they may have.

1 For a recent example, see *Fortune v Fraser* 1992 GWD 40–2300.
2 R Evans Jones 'The *actio quanti minoris* debunked?' (1992) 37 JLSS 275; 'The History of the *actio quanti minoris* in Scotland' 1991 JR 190.
3 See *Wilson v Campbell's Creditors* (1764) M 13330; *Gordon v Hughes* 15 June, 1815 FC.
4 *Loutitt's Trs v Highland Railway Co* (1892) 19 R 791; *Brownlie v Miller* (1880) 7 R (HL) 66 at 71 per Lord Chancellor Cairns; *Wood v Mags of Edinburgh* (1886) 13 R 1006; *Hoey v Butler* 1975 SC 87; *Hayes v Robinson* 1984 SLT 300; *Widdowson v Hunter* 1989 SLT 478.
5 Clause B12.

CHAPTER 7

Commercial and agricultural missives

Introduction

7.01 This chapter is intended as a basic introduction to the preparation of missives involving non-domestic properties. The aim of the chapter is to set out some fundamental points concerning commercial and agricultural missives in a general sense and then to deal in some depth with certain aspects of this type of work.

7.02 It is generally accepted that the legal profession has been drastically affected by changes in the last ten to twenty years. When the authors commenced practice in 1967 domestic conveyancing was the mainstay of many firms. There was no price competition between firms because scale fees were laid down by the Law Society. There was not even a hint that there might be competition from banks, building societies or any other 'authorised' practitioner. Clients were generally happy with their solicitor, even perhaps a little in awe of him. Since those balmy and protected days the chill winds of competition have blown through the chambers of the profession. Scale fees have gone and average charges for domestic conveyancing have plummeted, whereas overheads have increased relentlessly and the profession has had to cast around for alternative sources of income. Many firms regard commercial conveyancing as a profitable type of work but there is a fear among some smaller firms about tackling commercial work. The purpose of this chapter is to give a general introduction to commercial missives for those who perhaps do not specialise quite so strongly in this field on a daily basis. There are certain factors which ought to be considered by the practitioner when he embarks on a commercial transaction. In some ways it is easier to say what you cannot or should not do in a commercial transaction. Most importantly a solicitor must not simply take the schedule of conditions which he uses for domestic property, delete certain conditions about the NHBC certificate, the Matrimonial Homes Act, the central heating system and the shrubs in the garden and hope that what is left, with a few additional clauses about the stock in the shop, will be suitable as an offer to buy a petrol filling station, an off-licence or a factory or nursing home. There are some general and important points of difference between commercial missives and domestic missives.

The individuality of commercial missives

7.03 Every offer for residential property follows much the same pattern. There will be some differences when dealing with, say, a flatted conversion but the schedule attached to the offer will usually fit any offer for a normal type of house. The differences between one set of domestic missives and another for such houses are usually limited to the address, the price, the date of entry and the extras. Commercial properties, however, and offers for them, have to be treated on an individual basis and on their own merits. The missives for commercial property are in their very nature bound to be more complicated than those for domestic properties. Even the following basic matters already mentioned such as price, entry, extras and planning reports have to be looked at in the light of the individual transaction and the clauses drafted accordingly.

(a) The price quite often falls to be apportioned between such matters as heritage, goodwill, fixtures and fittings, because of tax and stamp duty implications.

(b) There may be a question of VAT being charged on the price.

(c) The date of entry is sometimes not fixed but tied to the grant or transfer of an existing licence or permission or the occurrence of an event such as a landlord's consent to a change of tenant and change of use.

(d) Heritable fittings and fixtures acquired with a business are very often on lease or subject to hire purchase. If this is the case the solicitor must be sure, firstly, that the purchaser is aware of any liabilities to be taken on and, secondly, that the agreements can be transferred.

(e) The solicitor may require to check such things as the Food and Hygiene Regulations, Fire Regulations and Health and Safety at Work Regulations as well as the normal planning matters.

These individual matters are likely to require different treatment in each commercial transaction. Care must be taken in commercial missives to draft the appropriate clauses on an individual basis.

The character and use of the property-title conditions

7.04 The character of commercial property is completely different from the character of residential property and obviously the use for which commercial property is acquired is different. Commercial properties by their nature are often sited within commercial developments or part commercial/domestic tenemental property. For this reason there are more likely to be common rights and obligations, factors, service charges, service roads and other individual matters to be considered. When purchasing residential property in a tenement solicitors tend simply to ask a routine question in relation to factors, common insurance, common charges, outstanding local authority notices etc. With commercial property it is often much more important to know in detail the rights of access, the rights of parking and off-loading, the right to use bin stores and sometimes most importantly what rights customers of the purchaser may have to park vehicles. In so far as common repairs are concerned, these are likely to be a matter of significant importance to the commercial purchaser. Management charges and common charges are expensive items in commercial properties and care must be taken in ensuring that the purchaser understands fully what the obligations are likely to be. Moreover, although domestic tenemental property very often qualifies for grants for renovation work, commercial properties generally do not.

7.05 When residential property is purchased the burdens in the title, especially in modern estates, will follow a reasonably uniform pattern. Very often there will be a prohibition of trade, business and profession, a prohibition of keeping more than one animal, a prohibition of altering or extending, an obligation to fence, a prohibition perhaps of parking trailers, boats or caravans, and various other and fairly routine restrictions. While it is the duty of the solicitor to advise the purchaser in a domestic transaction of the title conditions likely to affect the purchaser, the chance of a purchaser breaching these general conditions is usually remote. After all, the purchaser knows he or she is purchasing the property for use as a dwellinghouse and the other title conditions are conditions which tend simply to back up that general use. It may be that on an odd occasion a purchaser will have some particular foible such as breeding dogs or keeping pigeons about which the solicitor is ignorant, which may bring the client into conflict with a title condition, but it is unlikely to be a catastrophic conflict which cannot be resolved. Even if it means that the purchaser has to park his boat or van elsewhere he or she will still be able to use the property as a dwellinghouse. The question of prohibited uses in title conditions is, however, of crucial importance when dealing with commercial properties because there is an infinite variety of commercial usage. It is important, therefore, to ascertain from the commercial purchaser the precise use which is intended and to ensure that this use will not in any way contravene any of the existing title conditions. Titles to older commercial properties very often contain prohibitions on the sale of spirituous liquor but it is not uncommon to encounter a situation where a shop which has been a grocers since the turn of the century has obtained a licence with no thought given to whether permission is required from the superiors or indeed neighbouring proprietors holding a *ius quaesitum tertio*. A title prohibition of this type can drastically reduce the value of the commercial asset. In some cases, of course, it will be argued for the seller of the property that the superior has acquiesced over a long number of years in the breach of such a condition. This is very often argued in the case of the sale of public houses where no one can state with certainty when the licence was obtained. It may well be an argument which can be supported but the practitioner must take care to assess the evidence which there actually is for acquiescence. If there is doubt then it is very important not to leave the purchaser with the risk but to explore the possibilities of obtaining a waiver or a discharge, bearing in mind any *ius quaesitum*.

Permissions, licences, consents

7.06 When an established domestic property is purchased the missives usually stipulate for production of a routine planning certificate and roads certificate but may not otherwise require the production of the appropriate permission for residential use unless the property is of recent construction or conversion. A great many commercial properties are, however, affected by the requirement to have licences and permissions under a great many different Acts of Parliament and regulations, quite apart from the ordinary requirement to have planning permission. It is well known that public houses, hotels and off-licences require to be licensed but even within that category there are a great many different types of licence. Similarly, it is well known that betting offices require to be licensed but there are a great many other types of permissions and licences which are now required. Nursing homes, for example, require to be registered under the local health board and retirement homes under the social work authority. A sub-post office appointment cannot be transferred without the consent of the postal authorities who interview all prospective purchasers of the business. Scrap metal dealers, secondhand car dealers and fast food takeaway operators require licences under the Civic Government Act 1982. More specialised properties or commercial complexes require a variety of different licences or permissions. An offer for a greyhound stadium for example may require the grant or transfer of a track betting licence, a public house or restaurant licence for catering facilities and gaming machine licences. Confirmation of compliance with fire safety and sports ground regulations would also be required in such a case. It is important to know what permissions are required for the continuance of any business carried on in the commercial premises, how easily these permissions can be transferred, and at what point in time they can be transferred. Clearly, there is no point in fixing a date of entry prior to the transfer or the granting of any of these permissions. What must be borne in mind in dealing with a commercial transaction is that the conveyancing, though important, is only one facet of the transaction and the obligation on the solicitor is not just to get a good title but to ensure that the purchaser can carry on whatever business is tied to the property.

Visiting the site

7.07   There is a school of thought which tends to the view that a solicitor should, where possible, visit any property which he is purchasing for a client, whether it be a residential property or a commercial property. The authors, personally, do not take the view that it is essential to visit all residential run-of-the-mill properties unless something appears in the course of the transaction which indicates that there is a difficulty with the boundaries or some other matter. In so far as commercial properties are concerned, however, it is very often a good idea to make a site visit. Much can be gleaned in this way and the solicitor can also get a feel for the type of business which the purchaser is acquiring. Clients (especially if it is their first business venture) tend to be very shorthand with their instructions and while a solicitor can generally get by in a domestic conveyancing transaction with an instruction to buy 'the semi-detached dwellinghouse at 25 Adele Street, Motherwell together with the garage and garden ground pertaining thereto' such an instruction can be less than adequate in the case of a commercial property. A visit to the site will clarify ancillary questions such as rights of access, parking spaces, common passages etc.

The danger of the pro forma offer in commercial transactions

7.08   It is wrong and dangerous to attempt to adapt a pro forma offer or schedule of conditions for domestic property into an offer for commercial property. It is possible, however, to have pro forma styles of offer which cover things like hotels, public houses and other run-of-the-mill commercial premises. Even in these cases it is not easy to dash off a pro forma offer, because each commercial property and business will have different characteristics. If a pro forma commercial offer is being used it should be carefully scrutinised clause by clause to make sure that all the clauses are applicable, and amendments should be added to cater for the individual transaction where necessary. Very different considerations apply where the purchaser is intending to move into the premises and run the business himself, and where the purchaser (eg a pension fund) is buying an investment; that is a property which is being acquired with a commercial tenant or tenants already in occupation under full repairing leases. The message here is clear. The pro forma is there to help as a guide but it is not there to be the master.

Transferring employees and stock

7.09 It is very often a feature of the purchase of commercial properties that other items such as stock are involved but, more importantly, there is the question of employees of the existing business. If you buy a business as a going concern then in terms of the Transfer of Undertakings (Protection of Employment) Regulations 1981, SI 1981/1794 employees normally go with the business. This is a very important point which must be raised with the client at the time of taking the initial instruction. The client must be aware of the obligations for continuing payment such as redundancy etc which he or she takes on and a suitable clutch of warranties and undertakings must be inserted in the offer to protect the purchaser from pending claims, tribunals etc. So far as stock is concerned it may be important to ascertain whether your client wishes this kept at a certain level. The missives should provide for a valuation of the stock and a time limit within which the stock should be paid.

Inventories

7.10 When purchasing domestic property it is usual to list moveable items included in the price by general wording, such as 'the carpets and floor coverings throughout the house, the fitted wardrobes in bedroom one and generally all items stated to be included in the estate agents schedule of particulars a copy of which is annexed and signed as relative hereto'. When dealing with a commercial transaction a clause of this type can be dangerous, as can wording in the form of 'all items of a moveable nature at present situated in the property and used in the running of the business'. In a hotel or a small factory the plant and equipment are likely to be more valuable than a set of secondhand curtains or carpets in the house and it is always a good idea to have an inventory agreed with the seller so that there is no doubt what is included.

VAT regulations

7.11 Whenever dealing with heritable property consideration will have to be given as to whether or not Value Added Tax is payable, and this is particularly relevant in commercial missives. Greater details on the rules can be found in the customs and excise booklet notice 742A (the rules on transitional relief can be found in notice 742). Whether the dealing is standard rated, zero rated or exempt depends on what is being dealt with. The basic rules are as follows:

(a) *New buildings*

7.12 Every dealing in a new building (any building less than three years old) must be taxed at the standard rate on the occasion of every dealing with that building. The building must be new rather than a conversion, reconstruction, alteration, enlargement or extension of an existing building. Customs and excise take a specific view that where missives do not deal with the question of VAT then the price is treated as being inclusive of VAT and an assessement for the appropriate amount of tax will be issued to the seller. It is obviously very important that you question the seller or purchaser on the question of VAT and ensure that the subjects are treated in the correct way both in the missives and by way of the issue of a tax invoice at the date of settlement.

(b) *Other grants that are standard rated*

7.13 The grant of any right to take game or fish must be taxed and there are special rules where land is sold along with valuable sporting rights as opposed to the sporting rights being sold separately[1]. Also taxable are granting vehicle parking facilities and the granting of any right to fell and remove standing timber.

1 See VAT News Release 58/91.

(c) *Exempt grants*

7.14   Most other grants of interests or rights over land or any licences to occupy land can be exempted. However, just to make matters more complicated the seller has the right to waive this exemption, or put another way he or she has the option to charge VAT. From 1 August 1989 the seller can opt to tax the otherwise exempt sale, and once the seller has opted to tax, any supply (every subsequent sale) must be taxed. In other words, once the option is exercised it is irrevocable. Again, therefore, it is very important to check with the client (if the seller) before concluding missives to ensure that this option has not been waived either by the seller or by a previous proprietor. If not the solicitor should ask the seller whether he wishes to tax the sale. The seller may have VAT he or she wishes to contra, or simply increase his own cash flow for a period. A similar option to charge VAT on rents of commercial properties is available to landlords granting new leases or when already leased commercial property changes hands. It is therefore standard practice in offers to purchase or take on lease commercial property, for the purchaser's or tenant's solicitor to provide that the price or rent is exclusive of VAT and that the seller/landlord has not elected and will not prior to the date of entry or throughout the term of the lease as the case may be, elect to waive exemption from VAT.

7.15   It must be emphasised that these are the very bare bones of the rules which apply. There are obvious problems and these must be taken to ensure that the rules are not misapplied. VAT is treated as a self-policing tax. If the solicitor or the client gets it wrong it is very difficult to change the tax treatment afterwards[1].

1 For a more detailed treatment of VAT on commercial properties see Goy and Walters *VAT and Property*.

Restrictive covenants

7.16   Where the business has an intrinsic value quite apart from the value of any property, it is important to consider the question of goodwill and how much of that value is tied up with the personality of the previous owner. In some cases a restrictive covenant may be appropriate. These covenants take various forms depending on the nature of the business concerned, but the following are normal types of covenant:

(a) a prohibition on enticing existing staff of the business;
(b) a prohibition on approaching existing customers of the business
     with a view to persuading them to transact elsewhere;
(c) a prohibition on using information obtained while owner of the
     business; and
(d) a prohibition on setting up in business in competition.

7.17 All restrictive covenants are subject to the existing law
(including EEC law) which deals with practices in restraint of trade.
For this reason, restrictive covenants must generally be limited in
point of time and area of operation. Different considerations are
applied by the courts in differing situations. It must be borne in mind
that if the covenant is made too restrictive, the court will not enforce it
and the covenant will be unenforceable completely[1]. It is common
practice nowadays to add a rider to a restrictive covenant to the effect
that the parties accept that the clause is reasonable. Even in such
cases, courts have refused to enforce what they regard as unreasonable
restrictions no matter what the parties may have contracted or
thought to be reasonable[2]. Some restrictive covenants go further than
this and contain a provision to the effect that if a court finds the
restriction to be unreasonable[3], the restriction will be deemed to be
watered down to what a court would have thought was reasonable.
This type of clause might conceivably be difficult to enforce unless the
court were prepared to declare what they would have regarded as
reasonable in the circumstances. Given the reluctance of any court to
rewrite contracts for the parties, this type of clause may be written
more in hope than anything else. If such a clause is used then it might
be preferable to link it to a specific arbitration clause whereby the
parties agree that, if the court or indeed an arbiter, decides that the
original clause is too restrictive, the arbiter will fix a reasonable
restriction.

1 See *Nordenfelt v Maxim, Nordenfelt Guns & Ammunition Co* [1894] AC 535; *Meikle v
   Meikle* (1895) 3 SLT 204; *Dumbarton Steamboat Co Ltd v MacFarlane* (1899) 1 F 993;
   Mason v Provident Clothing and Supply Co Ltd [1913] AC 724; *Herbert Morris Ltd v
   Saxelby* [1916] 1 AC 688; *Fitch v Dewes* [1921] 2 AC 158; *British Motor Trade
   Association v Gray* 1951 SC 586; *Esso Petroleum Co Ltd v Harper's Garage (Stourport)
   Ltd* [1968] AC 269.
2 *Dallas McMillan & Sinclair v Simpson* 1989 SLT 454.
3 For a general discussion of covenants in restraint of trade see McBryde *The Law of
   Contract in Scotland* (1987) para 25–55 ff.

7.18 Parties should also bear in mind that certain restrictive covenants require to be registered with the Director of Fair Trading under
the Restrictive Trade Practices Act 1976[1] and under EEC competition
law[2].

1 Restrictive Trade Practices Act 1976, as amended by the Restrictive Trade Practices Act 1977 and the Competition Act 1980.
2 Article 85 of the EEC Treaty.

Licensed premises

7.19 In a purchase of licensed premises as with many other commercial entities there is a purchase of heritable property or a lease, the purchase of a business, the acquisition of stock, fittings and fixtures and the acquisition by transfer or grant of a licence. It should be borne in mind that there are now different types of licence which can affect a public house or a hotel. There are also ancillary licences for entertainment and for gaming machines which are often involved with this type of property. It is important for the purchaser's solicitor to be aware of all the licences which benefit the property so that any offer can be made conditional on the grant or the transfer of these licences. It should be noted that regular extensions of permitted hours are not always transferable with the main licence, depending on which licensing board is involved. The safest course of action therefore is to apply for the transfer of the licence and the grant of the previous regular extensions at the same time. Some boards will, however, transfer the licence and all the existing regular extensions at the one time as a transfer. It is normal to gear the date of entry to the permanent transfer of the licence at the quarterly meeting of the licensing board or an adjourned meeting but there is provision for a temporary transfer of a licence to be granted between meetings of the board. If a transfer is to be effected on a temporary basis, there may be difficulties over payment of the price and repayment of secured loans since the bargain will still be theoretically subject to the suspensive condition that the temporary transfer is ratified when the licensing board next meets. Normally it is not advisable for a purchaser to take entry to a licensed business prior to the licence being transferred to him, whether temporarily or permanently. Before temporary transfers were available, it was common practice in some areas to allow the purchaser to trade under the seller's licence. Strictly speaking, however, the purchaser could be guilty of the criminal offence of trafficking in these circumstances.

7.20 The stock may be a significant factor in the purchase of any licensed business and normally an independent valuer is called upon to value the stock as at the date of entry with payment being due by the purchaser within a period of 14 days thereafter. It is normal to provide that the only stock to be paid for shall be such stock as is 'usable and saleable'.

7.21 The Transfer of Undertakings (Protection of Employment) Regulations 1981, SI 1981/1794 apply to licensed businesses sold as a going concern and the purchaser may be bound to take on full time employees as part of the business.

7.22 It is common in licensed premises for a number of the fittings to be leased, or in some cases simply lent, by the supplier of the stock. From the seller's point of view it is important to ascertain which items are in this category and whether any agreements can be transferred. From the point of view of the purchaser, it is important to realise that ownership of these items will not be transferred and also to know the amount of any continuing liability for leasing charges. Where the purchaser intends to change the supplier of liquor, he may well find that some of the aforementioned fittings and fixtures will be removed by the previous supplier.

7.23 In the case of a hotel, there should be a provision dealing with bookings and deposits which would normally also provide that the seller will pay all debts of the business and collect sums due to the business, up to the date of entry.

7.24 It should be borne in mind that the Matrimonial Homes legislation applies to any flats or dwellinghouses forming part of or attached to the licensed premises. Accordingly consents or affidavits may be required in appropriate cases.

Farms and agricultural subjects

7.25 Agricultural property is very much a business involved with the land. For this reason the land, its area, boundaries and the servitudes pertaining thereto or applying thereto are of fundamental importance. The authors offer the following checklist of other matters which should be looked at.

The subjects

7.26 The subjects will normally be described in any offer by the name of the farm. It is suggested, however, that this is not sufficient to avoid disputes at a later date. The acreage of the farm should be stated and a plan should be attached to the offer wherever possible. Any areas which are excluded from the sale should be clearly identified and where it is important that minerals including sand and gravel are included, these should be specifically mentioned. A typical list of items actually included in the subjects to be purchased, apart from the actual land itself, is as follows:

(a) The whole farm buildings as presently on the farm.
(b) The whole heritable fittings and fixtures in and about the farm and the said buildings, including all fireplaces, mantel and chimney pieces whether ornamental or not, sheds and garages, all as listed within the particulars of sale.
(c) The whole woods, trees and plantations if any on the farm and generally all timber standing cut and felled on the farm at the date of this offer.
(d) The teinds so far as belonging to the seller.
(e) The whole mines, quarries, metals and minerals under and within the farm except coal and mines of coal vested in British Coal Corporation so far as belonging to the seller.
(f) All growing shrubs, plants and bushes growing on the farm.
(g) The whole streams, water courses and lochs if any within or *ex adverso* the farm.
(h) The whole shooting and sporting rights over and on the farm and woods.
(i) The solum of all roads intersecting the subjects of the sale.
(j) The whole farmyard midden if any situated within the subjects.
(k) Formally constituted heritable servitude rights to use the water, drainage and sewage systems presently serving all parts of the farm including all springs, wells, catchment, tanks, connections, storage tanks, pipes, drains, sewers, septic tanks, soakaways and the like with rights of access to those parts of the said system if any lying outwith the boundaries of the farm on all necessary occasions for the purposes of inspection, cleaning, maintaining, repairing and renewing the same.
(l) Formally constituted heritable rights to use the accesses to all parts of the farm presently used by the seller.
(m) All other pertinents, rights and privileges pertaining to the farm and generally the seller's whole right, title and interest therein.
(n) All unexhausted manurial values and residual manurial values.

Price

7.27   The price may well require to be apportioned between heritage and stock, crops and implements and if these are to be taken over, hay, straw or silage. It may be that some of these items are to be taken over at separate valuation. In this case provision should be made in the offer for that valuation to be carried out, and the party who is to act as valuer.

Matrimonial homes

7.28 It should always be borne in mind that the Matrimonial Homes legislation does apply to farmhouses which are used as matrimonial homes. Accordingly it is not safe just to think of a farm as a commercial asset. Where the title is not in joint names, matrimonial consents or renunciations will be required and where the subjects are held in single name, an affidavit will be necessary.

Water and sewage

7.29 Very often in agricultural property the water supply is private. Where it serves residential buildings and agricultural operations, it may be necessary to ensure that it is adequate for human consumption[1]. If the water supply comes from a spring outwith the subjects purchased, then there must be appropriate servitude rights contracted for in the missives. The same applies in the case of septic tank outfall or soakaway which is not wholly within the farm boundaries.

1 The Water (Scotland) Act 1980; Water Supply (Water Quality) (Scotland) Regulations 1990, SI 1990/119; The Water Supply (Water Quality) (Scotland) Amendment Regulations 1991, SI 1991/1333; The Private Water Supplies (Scotland) Regulations 1992, SI 1992/575; The Scottish Office Environment Department Circular no 20/1992; The Scottish Office Pamphlet HMSO 6/92.

Woodlands

7.30 Where woodlands are included, it is important to specify that there are no forestry dedication agreements[1], forestry grant schemes or other matters which affect that part of the subjects and in terms of which the purchaser would succeed to outstanding obligations; and that the seller has not entered into any timber harvesting contracts. It is also useful at this stage to make enquiry as to whether the woodlands are insured along with the farm buildings.

1 In relation to dedication agreements see Forestry Acts 1947 and 1967.

Set aside

7.31 It is important to specify whether or not any part of the subjects has been registered for set aside purposes. Any part of the farm thus registered should be shown on the plan attached to the missives and provision should be made for supplying to the purchaser the cropping pattern for the ensuing years so that the purchaser can qualify for the set aside programme relating to any unregistered subjects.

Ploughing and sowing

7.32 The date of entry is of vital significance in agricultural subjects. Special arrangements are sometimes made in offers purchasing farms to allow the purchaser early access to carry out ploughing and sowing. If this is not done, the missives may provide that the purchaser may pay the seller for the cost of carrying out this work.

Quotas and grants

7.33 Details of any quotas or grants applicable to the subjects should be obtained and the missives should provide that the purchaser will obtain the benefit of any such quotas or grants in respect of a period after the date of entry. Obviously milk quotas are particularly important in relation to dairy farming[1]. The offer should provide that no grants in respect of buildings are repayable on the sale.

1 See Dairy Produce Regulations 1984, SI 1984/1047.

Special buildings and sites

7.34 Farms are more liable to be affected by certain special regulations which do not apply to residential properties or even commercial properties. It is advisable to expand the normal planning certificate clause by including provisions to the effect that the subjects do not comprise or include a site of special scientific interest[1]. Older farmhouses may also be buildings of architectural or historical interest and the farm may be located in a conservation area, both of which features would render development more difficult in the future. Similarly, some farms are the sites of ancient monuments or archaeological areas where there are special statutory rights of access[2].

1 Countryside Act 1968, s 15.
2 Ancient Monuments and Archaeological Areas Act 1979.

Tenancies and rights of occupation

7.35 If the property is being purchased with vacant possession it is essential to stipulate for vacant possession and that the subjects will not be affected by any leases or rights of occupation and, in particular, any agricultural holding[1]. Where the farm is being purchased after the termination of a tenancy, it is important to ensure that the appropriate notice has been given under the agricultural holdings legislation[1] and that the tenant has not served a counter notice or has at least failed to object to the notice. Where a tenant has agreed to vacate and there is no difficulty, the offer should provide that the seller/landlord will free and relieve the purchasers of any claims competent to former tenants under any of the agricultural statutes in respect of improvements, waygoing, disturbance or any other claims whatsoever. The right of the outgoing agricultural tenant to remove fixtures and fittings will also require to be dealt with.

1 Agricultural Holdings (Scotland) Act 1991.

Fences, walls etc

7.36 Fencing and the maintenance of boundaries is an important matter in agricultural property. It is normal to provide that all boundary fences will be mutual and maintained at joint equal expense by adjoining farmers, and similarly that all ditches on the boundaries shall be kept clear and free running at the joint expense of the two proprietors.

Roads and accesses

7.37 It is important to ascertain the status of the roads which either bound or intersect the farm. If the roads are public, then there is no problem, but where there are private roads it is important to know whether the solum of the road is included in the title. If it is not, then there must be an appropriate servitude right to use the road and the question of the maintenance arrangements for the road must be looked into. Where it is suggested that a servitude right of access has been constituted by prescriptive usage, the evidence of this usage must be examined, if only to ascertain the scope of the servitude. With the development of modern farming methods pedestrian accesses may have come to be used for vehicular purposes but the vehicular use may not extend to the full prescriptive period.

Farms purchased as investments subject to tenancies

7.38 In some cases farms are purchased in the knowledge that they are subject to an agricultural tenancy. In these cases any agricultural leases which have been granted must be examined as well as the title to the farm. The question of the apportionment of rent should be dealt with and the purchaser should be made aware of the amount which he may have to pay the tenant in compensation on the ultimate termination of the tenancy. All records of improvements must be passed on.

7.39 The purchase of agricultural property is as specialised as the purchase of commercial property and although styles of offer to purchase are available[1], it is always important to ensure that whatever offer is lodged is tailored to the particular circumstances of the farm.

1 Halliday *Conveyancing Law and Practice in Scotland* (1985) vol II, para 15–140; Stoddart 'An introduction to agricultural law' Law Society Update General Conveyancing Course, October 1991.

Index

Index